HANGING BY A THREAD

Paisley female power loom weavers in the late 19th century. Note the presence of the tenter, repairing the looms and supervising the women (photograph courtesy of Renfrew District Council, Paisley Museum).

Hanging By A Thread

*The Scottish Cotton Industry,
c.1850–1914*

W. W. KNOX

with the assistance of
M. S. Thompson

Carnegie Publishing, 1995

HANGING BY A THREAD
THE SCOTTISH COTTON INDUSTRY, c.1850–1914

First Edition
Published by Carnegie Publishing Ltd, 1995

Copyright © W. W. Knox, 1995

Photographs copyright © see captions

Typeset in 11/14 Monotype Bembo by
Carnegie Publishing Ltd, 18 Maynard St, Preston, Lancashire PR2 2AL
Printed and bound in the UK Cambridge University Press

British Library Cataloguing in Publication Data
A CIP record for this book is available from the British Library

ISBN 1-85936-011-4

All rights reserved
No part of this publication may be reproduced, stored in a retrieval system, or transmitted in any form or by any means mechanical, electronic, photocopying or otherwise, without the prior permission of the publisher.

*In memory of
Margaret Agnes Knox
(1951–1994)*

Contents

	Acknowledgements	ix
	Preface	xi
	List of Tables	xiii
	Abbreviations	xv
	Introduction	1
1.	The Economic Development of the Scottish Cotton Industry, c.1850–1914	17
	1. Employment	17
	2. Investment and Output	27
2.	Technological Change and the Labour Process	39
	1. Cotton Spinning	40
	2. Weaving	62
	3. Thread	77
3.	Wages and Working Conditions	87
	1. Spinning	93
	2. Weaving	99
	3. Thread	105
4.	Employers, Strategy and Organisation	115
	Employers and Organisation	140
5.	Worker Organisation and Industrial Conflict	145
	1. Trade Unionism in Spinning	146
	2. Trade Unionism in Weaving	152
	3. Trade Unionism in Thread	158
	4. Industrial Conflict	164
	Conclusion	173
	Bibliography	183
	Index	199

Acknowledgements

IN the research and writing of this book on the Scottish cotton industry a considerable number of people and institutions provided much welcome assistance of a financial and intellectual nature. Therefore, my first vote of thanks goes to the Economic and Social Research Council for having backed the initial project, and for providing additional funding to cover the period of absence of my research assistant. The Council staff were a joy to work with and their understanding in times of difficulty was especially appreciated by me. I must also thank the Research Committee of the Arts Faculty of my own university, and especially Dave Roberts, for providing financial assistance to cover the cost of carrying out some necessary statistical work once my ESRC funding had run out.

Of course, any researcher needs the support of efficient and helpful archivists and librarians. Thankfully, in Scotland there are a number of institutions in which these qualities are to be found in large measure. The staff of the Scottish Record Office, the National Library, the Mitchell Library, the University of Glasgow Business Archives and the Paisley Museum, and Art Gallery all made life as pleasurable as they could for myself and my research assistant. This could also be said of the firm of Coats Vyella, who allowed me access to their archival holdings. One or two individuals stand out however. Joe Fisher, of the Mitchell Library, Maureen Lochrie in Paisley, and Alison Horsburgh of the SRO, found and made available sources which only the most experienced and knowledgeable of staff would be aware of. The book would have impoverished without their help. In this light, I must also thank Julian Crowe, computing officer of the arts faculty of St Andrews, for his help in the presentation of data, and for spending his valuable time dealing with my ignorance.

I also benefited from discussions with colleagues about the Scottish cotton industry, in particular with Eleanor Gordon, Jock Hunter and Alan MacKinlay, all of the University of Glasgow. However, most of my appreciation goes to those directly involved in the project. Therefore, I must heartily thank Jill Hampton and Tracey White for carrying out some important, although at times, boring, work on the occupational census and property valuation rolls. Special thanks obviously goes to my research assistant, Mary Thompson, whose name appears on the book. Although I am responsible for all the writing and most of the interpretation, the book could not have been written without the footslogging and endless hours in archives that Mary put in. She was an exemplary researcher as well as an incredible sympathetic and understanding person to work with. I hope the book in some way justifies the work she put in to the initial project. This can also be said of my publishers who have placed their faith in the book and have been a delight to work with.

To end on a personal note I would like to thank a number of friends who saw me through a particularly tough period during which this book was being written. Many thanks to Catriona Burness, Helen and Pat Canning, Ewen Cameron, Bill Guthrie, Pat Hutchinson, Alan MacKinlay, Alan Redden, Dave Simpson, but especially to my son, David, and to Helen and Patty, who, in their different ways, were a great source of empathy and support. I cannot thank them too much.

Preface

MY INTEREST in the development of the Scottish cotton industry during the period 1850–1914 was stimulated by current concerns regarding the decline of Britain's manufacturing base. For a number of reasons I felt that the experience of Scottish cotton had important and interesting implications for the wider debate on de-industrialisation in Britain. Firstly, the cotton industry more than any other Scottish industry had encouraged moves towards industrialisation, particularly in the west of Scotland. However, the impact was ephemeral and industrial leadership was ceded to the integrated coal, iron and shipbuilding industries. The fast growth of the cotton industry was followed by gradual, but terminal, decline. By the end of the nineteenth century the spinning and weaving sectors of the industry had almost disappeared. The engine of the transformation of Scotland's economic base in the early nineteenth century had become its first industrial casualty. Thus, in many ways, the experience of the Scottish cotton industry anticipated the more general, and later, decline of British manufacturing industry. What factors were important in the decline of the industry? Did it suffer from what recent commentators have called the 'British disease', that is, poor management and internecine industrial relations? Secondly, the industry exhibited an economic dualism which saw spinning and weaving collapse at the end of the century and the thread making trade succeed. This development created scope for a more insightful comparative examination into the question of industrial decline, particularly since the main sectors were in fairly close geographical proximity to each other.

Why should the spinning and weaving trades of Glasgow fail, and the thread trade of neighbouring Paisley succeed? To answer this and other questions a thorough examination was made of factors which economists have thought important in determining industrial success, that is, the quality of entrepreneurship, the nature of the product and labour markets, the industrial structure, and the relationship between capital and labour in each of the three sectors. From detailed work in these areas of inquiry conclusions emerged which not only provided a convincing explanation of the decline of the Scottish cotton industry, but also made it possible to question the validity of overarching theories of industrial decline.

Therefore, although the book seems to be simply a study of the cotton industry in Scotland, the truth is that its proper scope and purpose are far wider than the title suggests, and its findings are potentially significant for those engaged in the great debate regarding industrial decline. This assessment is further strengthened by the inclusion of a great deal of comparative detail derived from the experiences of English, American and Japanese cotton industries in the period *c.*1850–1914. The more we can isolate the factors which are general in the process of past industrial success and decline, the greater will be the ability to avoid collapse in the future. While this book does not offer a blueprint for the maintenance of industrial success, its conclusions will offer some interesting and useful suggestions concerning the alchemy of winning and, alternatively, losing the economic war in a free market economy.

List of Tables

Table 1	The number of cotton workers in Scotland by sex, 1835–1911	19
Table 2	The sexual distribution of workers in cotton spinning in Scotland, 1850–1895	20
Table 3	The ages of female cotton workers in Lanarkshire, 1851–1901	22
Table 4	The distribution of female employment in Lanarkshire, 1851–1901	23
Table 5	The distribution of female employment in Renfrewshire, 1851–1901	24
Table 6	An index of employment in the Scottish cotton industry, 1835–1911	25
Table 7	The share of employment in the Scottish cotton industry, 1835–1911	26
Table 8	The ratio of steam to water power in Scottish cotton mills, 1835–1871	29
Table 9	The amount of moving power per Scottish mill, 1834–1871	29
Table 10	The ratio of looms and workers to factories in the Scottish cotton weaving trade at selected dates	33
Table 11	The ratio of looms to workers at selected dates	33
Table 12	Exports of Scottish spun yarn, 1861–1867	37
Table 13	The distribution of employment by age groups in the Scottish cotton industry in 1847	47
Table 14	Occupations and weekly wage rates at Ferguslie mill in 1878	84
Table 15	Estimates of average weekly earnings in the British cotton industry at selected dates	88
Table 16	Output, workers and wages in England and Scotland (spinning) in 1867 and 1907	91

Table 17	Output, wages and workers in England and Scotland (weaving) in 1867 and 1907	92
Table 18	Average weekly wages in the Scottish cotton industry and power loom weaving at selected dates	101
Table 19	Average weekly wage rates for selected occupations in the Scottish thread trade	107
Table 20	Average weekly wages for selected female occupations	112
Table 21	Place of birth of heads of households employed by Bridgeton textile firms at selected dates	124
Table 22	Place of birth of heads of households employed by Paisley textile firms at selected dates	124
Table 23	Main occupations of heads of households in tenancies of J. & P. Coats, 1871–1891	126
Table 24	Birthplaces of foremen thread workers in 1871 and 1891	127
Table 25	Place of birth of thread mill worker heads of households in 1871 and 1891	159
Table 26	Labour turnover in specific age cohorts at the Ferguslie mill in 1902	160
Table 27	Industrial disputes in the Scottish cotton industry, 1840–1914	166
Table 28	Statistics relating to industrial stoppages in the Scottish cotton industry, 1840–1914	168
Table 29	Workers and strikes in the thread and weaving sectors, 1840–1914	169
Table 30	Duration of strikes in the weaving and thread sectors, 1840–1914	170
Table 31	Days lost in strikes in the weaving and thread sectors, 1889–1914	172

Abbreviations

BLPES	British Library of Political and Economic Science
ESCC	English Sewing Cotton Company
GPLBS	Glasgow Power Loom Beamers' Society
GHHWS	Glasgow Handmill and Horizontal Warpers' Society
GWSPLTS	Glasgow and West of Scotland Power Loom Tenters' Society
GTC	Glasgow Trades Council
ILP	Independent Labour Party
NFWW	National Federation of Women Workers
PMAG	Paisley Museum and Art Gallery
PRO	Public Records Office
SBWBBS	Scottish Ball Warp Brush Beamers' Society
SCA	Sewing Central Agency
STTA	Scottish Textile Trades Association
SRO	Scottish Record Office
TTA	Thread Trade Association
UFC	United Free Church
UPC	United Presbyterian Church
WPPL	Women's Protective and Provident League
WSWFFWIU	West of Scotland Weaving Factories Female Workers Industrial Union

An artist's impression of the Paisley thread mill complex, c. 1888 (photograph courtesy of Renfrew District Council, Paisley Museum).

Introduction

THE eminent Marxist historian, Eric Hobsbawm, in a sweeping generalisation regarding the origins of British industrialisation, once claimed that when 'one says the Industrial Revolution one says cotton'.[1] For Hobsbawm, and others of his generation, the rapid growth of the cotton industry, and the knock-on effects its development had on other industries, transformed the British economy in a short space of time from a pre-industrial system based on agriculture and domestic industry to a dynamic and expanding industrial one.

Since then a newer school of economic historians has reassessed the impact of cotton on the British economy as a whole.[2] Their findings have led to a more conservative assessment of the role of 'king cotton'. Cotton is now seen as only one of a number of leading sectors in promoting the economy-wide changes which constitute industrialisation. But while cotton's importance is no longer considered paramount, and the scenario of economic growth is evolutionary rather than revolutionary, its significance for regional economies, such as Scotland and Lancashire, is still seen as very great.

Indeed, it was cotton which more than any other Scottish industry stimulated moves towards industrialisation, especially in the west of Scotland. Nine out of ten manufacturing workers in Scotland in 1826 were in textiles, with a ratio of six workers in cotton to three in linen, to one in woollens. But it was cotton with its novel methods of organising work, its rapidly changing technologies and its dynamic growth which acted as the leading sector. Between

---

[1] E. J. Hobsbawm, *Industry and Empire* (1968), p. 56.
[2] See, for instance, S. D. Chapman, *The Cotton Industry in the Industrial Revolution* (1972); G. N. von Tunzelmann, 'Technical progress during the industrial revolution', in *The Economic History of Britain, vol. 1: 1700–1860*, ed. R. Floud and D. McCloskey (1981), pp. 143–63.

1790 and 1820 Scotland's cotton industry was more advanced than England's as it took the lead in the use of the power-driven mule and, later, the self-acting mule. The productiveness of the new technology was so high that even during the French wars, when labour and raw material costs rose, prices fell.[3] The technological lead was sustained through the entrepreneurial flair of Scottish businessmen. By drawing on the surplus capital of landowners and others, and assisted by a large reservoir of cheap labour, the cotton masters were able to maintain a flow of investment upon which the technical efficiency of the industry depended. However, rapid growth created its own problems. Low wages, overwork and factory discipline, as well as the effects of the downside of the trade cycle, embittered employee/employer relations and the cotton industry became synonymous with exploitation, inhumanity, tyranny and class struggle. Industrial disputes were violent and occurred frequently, culminating in the 1837 cotton spinners strike. This dispute seriously weakened the spinners' union and paved the way for the reorganisation of the Scottish cotton industry.

The pivotal role performed by cotton in transforming the economic base of Scotland and the intense struggles between capital and labour it created have naturally attracted a great deal of interest from economic and social historians. After 1840, however, interest becomes less focused as attention is almost exclusively drawn towards the rise of the integrated industrial structure of coal, iron and steel, and shipbuilding which dominated the later nineteenth-century Scottish economy. Thus, while acknowledgement is made of the significance of the cotton industry in promoting industrial development in Scotland, the impact is seen as ephemeral. The fast growth of the industry was followed by an equally rapid decline as Scotland lost out to more efficient cotton producers in Lancashire and abroad.

Decline, however, was not inevitable. Scotland had a wealth of natural and physical assets as plentiful as any other cotton producing country or region. In addition to its entrepreneurial talent and an early technological lead, the Scottish cotton industry was able to

---

[3] R. H. Campbell, *Scotland Since 1707* (1985 edn), pp. 86–7.

rely upon the damp and wet climate of the west of Scotland which provided excellent conditions for the storing and production of cotton yarn and cloth. Furthermore, there was no shortage of either water or coal to supply the growing industry with its large appetite for fuel and energy. Water transportation, if not road and rail at this time, was the equal of other parts of Britain, and the port facilities of Glasgow, built up during the boom in the tobacco trade, laid the infrastructure of an expanding trading network with the USA and India. The quality of the labour supply was also in many ways superior to that of Lancashire. Andrew Ure's study of the early nineteenth-century cotton industry not only showed that literacy rates were higher in Scotland than in England, but that female cotton workers in Scotland were superior in 'physical condition, hardihood and strength' to the English.[4]

Given the strong economic and natural foundations upon which the development of the Scottish cotton industry was based continuous expansion seemed assured, and yet by the first decade of the twentieth century the industry, with the exception of thread manufacture, had all but disappeared. After accounting for the rise of the cotton industry and the impact its development had on the wider Scottish economy, the issue for historians is, therefore, one of the causality and chronology of its decline.

There are, however, a number of problems connected with historical sources which makes the task of delineating these issues problematic to say the least. Apart from the voluminous and multifaceted record collection of the thread firm J. & P. Coats of Paisley, business records relating to the activities of Scottish cotton firms are sparse. Extant records also have their drawbacks. In regard to wages most surviving company records list them only as an item in total expenditure; thus one cannot draw firm conclusions as to actual rather than nominal earnings, or the way the wage structure reflected the division of labour. Even the more detailed records of J. & P. Coats have only the barest information regarding these issues until the first decade of the twentieth century. The use of parliamentary reports on textile wages can help compensate for these

---

[4] A. Ure, *The Cotton Manufactures of Great Britain* (1836), pp. 277, 271.

discontinuities in our knowledge, but in all cases average rather than actual earnings are reported: a problem compounded by the degree to which piece working was common in the Scottish cotton industry. Another problem is estimating the level of investment and the growth and renewal of fixed capital. Although Cairncross and Hunter have been able to provide investment statistics for the firm of J. & P. Coats for the period 1833–83,[5] the absence of this type of data in the records of other cotton firms makes it impossible to construct other investment series. Moreover, as company purchase records rarely itemised the type of incoming machinery or replacements, it proved a major handicap when assessing the relative technological backwardness of the Scottish industry *vis-à-vis* its competitors.

The question of technology inevitably raises issues regarding consumption and output. Unfortunately there is a great deal of obscurity surrounding these matters. Although there exist data covering imports of raw cotton into Glasgow for the period 1840–67, after this there are only guess estimates, and after 1880 no statistics at all for Scotland. Similarly, when dealing with the output of Scottish cotton such evidence as does exists only relates to the periods 1861–7 and the first decade of the twentieth century. All other data concerning consumption and output in the Scottish cotton industry are subsumed under the aggregated national reports on the textile trades. Finally, on the question of industrial relations, the absence of employers' association and trade union records is a major handicap in writing the history of social relations in the cotton industry. In spite of the valuable material contained in the Webb Collection on Trade Unions, as well as reports on disputes in the local and national press, no records of trade unions operating in the Scottish cotton industry after 1850 exist. Likewise, outside the thread employers' cartel organised by Coats of Paisley, no records have been found relating to a cotton employers' association, in spite of references alluding to the existence of one in various parliamentary inquiries.

---

[5] A. K. Cairncross and J. B. K. Hunter, 'The early growth of Messrs J. & P. Coats, 1830–1883', *Business History*, 29 (1987), pp. 157–77.

The problems surrounding data and documentary sources should caution us against making definitive statements regarding the decline of the Scottish cotton industry. However, it should not deter us either, as other sources do survive. Occupational censuses and other official reports, as well as contemporary books and journals, are rich in detail and insight. Indeed, several historians have taken up the challenge posed above and their work has sparked a lively debate into the nature and timing of the industry's decline. Highly influential in the debate has been the view expressed by R. H. Campbell in his study of Scotland's economic development. Campbell, in a classic restatement of the early start thesis, pinpointed the 1820s as the turning point in the fortunes of the industry. These years saw an increase in both home and foreign competition, particularly in the coarse cloth market. This challenge was met by Scottish producers by increasing production and lowering costs. The response only compounded the difficulties of the industry since the outcome was lower profit margins, which led to a decline in investment and an inevitable loss of technical leadership. From the 1820s onwards the Scottish industry relied on the low wages of its workforce to remain competitive rather than the continuous upgrading of the machinery of production. As a result the textile machinery industry collapsed and Scottish producers succumbed to the more efficient firms of Lancashire and elsewhere.[6]

Campbell has been criticised by A. J. Robertson, in a seminal article,[7] for prematurely writing off Scottish cotton. Decline may have occurred in the 1860s, but, argues Robertson, it was not terminal, and not unique to Scotland. As a result of the American Civil War all cotton producing countries experienced a fall in production. Indeed, as far as Robertson is concerned, the 1860s may simply have accelerated the shake out of inefficient firms as it seems as though output in terms of higher exports was increasing in spite of fewer producers. Robertson dates the decline of the spinning branch of the industry from the early 1870s, accelerating,

---

[6] Campbell, *Scotland*, p. 89.
[7] A. J. Robertson, 'The Decline of the Scottish Cotton Industry, 1860–1914', *Business History*, 12 (1970), pp. 116–28.

along with power loom weaving, after 1890, with expansion taking place in the manufacture of sewing thread. By adopting a long-term perspective, which recognises sectoral discontinuities in experience and performance, Robertson provides a more convincing chronology of decline than Campbell's pessimistic early start thesis. But while Robertson's approach offers a more fruitful way of viewing the decline of the Scottish cotton industry, it has to be set in a more dynamic cyclical framework. As Chapter 1 makes clear, the economic development of the industry after 1850 is characterised by violent cycles of boom and slump, rather than the gradual process of decline put forward by Robertson. This phenomenon is best seen when important economic factors such as sectoral employment, output and labour productivity are subjected to detailed scrutiny. A sectoral analysis shows, for example, that decline was most marked in the combined sector of spinning and weaving rather than in separate areas of weaving and spinning production. This highlights the discontinuities of experience and performance within the industry as a whole. Such an approach also brings out some of the inadequacies and weaknesses in Robertson's explanation of Scottish cotton's declining fortunes.

Drawing on contemporary opinion, which emphasised the 'want of enterprise and energy on the part of millowners, carelessness on the part of the workers, and a lack of friendly common interest among all concerned',[8] Robertson puts forward two major reasons to explain the fall of the industry: the low productivity of the workforce and the low level of entrepreneurial talent in the Scottish cotton trade. Since low productivity was the outcome of entrepreneurial failings, Robertson places the blame for the collapse of the spinning and weaving sectors on the shoulders of the employers, claiming that the latter's failings 'may have been more serious in their effects on their industry's competitive position than those of the operatives'.[9] The cheap wage policy of the employers, he argues, only attracted poor quality workers which restricted output and led to the production of a high-cost, inferior product. The employers

---

[8] T. Ellison, *The Cotton Trade of Great Britain* (1886), p. 76.
[9] Robertson, 'Decline', p. 124.

were also ignorant of developments in cotton technology, particularly in the spinning department, which meant that machinery in Scotland was archaic compared to that of Lancashire.

The strong emphasis on entrepreneurial failure obviously is a product of theories regarding Britain's relative economic decline which flourished in academic circles in the 1970s.[10] However, while convincing on the surface, it remains essentially problematic as an approach to the question of economic decline. Empirically, it is impossible to verify what remains essentially a value judgement. Much of the weight of the thesis relies on circumstantial and subjective evidence divorced from the realities of the specific economic and institutional contexts which industries found themselves in at particular moments. All the available biographical evidence regarding the social and educational backgrounds of Scottish cotton masters points to the existence of a highly professional group of employers with a diverse range of educational and technical skills.[11] This point can best be illustrated by comparing the management stata in cotton with the quality of entrepreneurship displayed in other large manufacturing industries.

If we take shipbuilding, the leading industrial sector in Scotland for most of the nineteenth and twentieth centuries, it would appear that its expansion was founded upon a thin veneer of management expertise. In his study of shipbuilding managers, Slaven points to 'their narrow range of management skills', particularly in the areas of "financial control and marketing". He also criticises them for evolving an industrial strategy in which 'Survival replaced growth as the aim . . . of management'.[12] In spite of the shortcomings of the managers, Clyde yards dominated world production from the late nineteenth century to the early 1950s. From a different perspective Lorenz and Wilkinson state, in an essay dealing with the decline of British shipbuilding, that evidence for management's failings is based simply on its unwillingness to adopt more up-to-date

---

[10] P. L. Payne, *British Entrepreneurship in the Nineteenth Century* (1974).
[11] See, for instance, the entries in *The Dictionary of Business Biography, 1860–1960. vol. 1: the staple industries*, ed. A. Slaven and S. Checkland (Aberdeen, 1986).
[12] A. Slaven, 'Management and Shipbuilding on the Clyde, 1919–1976: a study of industrial decline', SSRC Report (1981), pp. 20–1.

technologies and forms of work organisation.[13] However, this approach, they argue, ignores the vital question of timing in an industry's competitive failure. British shipbuilding continued to lead the world long after cotton and steel had declined despite its continuing reliance on labour-intensive methods of production. Thus, as far as shipbuilding is concerned, management's reponse to the problems facing the industry 'can only be understood by considering the particular technical and market conditions in which firms operated, and the ways these conditions interact with the system of industrial relations'.[14] If we take the English cotton industry a similar argument can be advanced. In an important article regarding the industry's decline, Lazonick criticises the employers for their 'continued reliance on outdated technologies', and for their failure to adopt more modern forms of management.[15] From this it might appear that the quality of entrepreneurship is perhaps a more permissive factor in industrial expansion than one might assume.

The entrepreneurial thesis is part of a wider cultural explanation of industrial decline which is too general and because of this unable satisfactorily to answer questions regarding the timing of decline. The anti-industrial spirit invoked by Weiner in a recent study of Britain's relative economic decline suffers from this weakness.[16] At a time when world economic leadership was held by Britain the prevailing ethos of society was dominated by values traditionally held by the landed elite. Classics were preferred and esteemed more highly than science or engineering; a gentlemanly life preferred to a productive one, and so on. What Weiner seems to miss is that even although the second generation of industrialists may have preferred to live off their dividends rather than take an active part

---

[13] E. Lorenz and F. Wilkinson, 'The Shipbuilding Industry', in *The Decline of the British Economy*, ed. B. Elbaum and W. Lazonick (Oxford, 1986), p. 128.
[14] Lorenz and Wilkinson, 'Shipbuilding', p. 128.
[15] W. Lazonick, 'The Cotton Industry', in *The Decline of the British Economy*, pp. 40, 44.
[16] M.J. Weiner, 'The Decline of the Industrial Spirit: an overview and assessment', in *The Economic Decline of Modern Britain: the debate between the left and right*, ed. D. Coates and J. Hillard (1986), pp. 98–105.

in running their enterprises, their lack of interest created opportunities for the emergence of a managerial stratum, ambitious for wealth and status. Thus, even if the second generation of British industrialists lacked the drive and energy of their fathers, there existed enough hungry individuals ready to take their places in the struggle for markets and profits.

The failure of overarching cultural theories advanced by Weiner and other proponents of the so-called 'British disease' thesis has pushed social scientists in a different direction when dealing with the problem of industrial decline. In an important article, Kilpatrick and Lawson have argued for a shift away from supply-side and entrepreneurial explanations of Britain's relative industrial decline towards a greater concentration on the 'role of collective bargaining and the strength of job-based worker organisation'.[17] They argue that during the process of industrialisation the British economy relied on craft labour to a much greater extent than elsewhere. The emerging labour movement in the nineteenth century thus became organised on the basis of skill differences rather than industrial categories. Not only did this lead to a multitude of small craft unions, which created an inevitable problem in regard to demarcation, but also the reliance of employers on skill-intensive methods of production allowed the workers a large degree of control over the labour process. A system of collective bargaining was built round these realities.

Since 1945 the long economic boom and the full employment policies of successive governments have shifted the balance of power in industry further towards the unions and increased their control over the labour process. In the context of expanding union power and strength, collective bargaining is seen by Kilpatrick and Lawson as having consequences for the introduction and diffusion of new techniques in the workplace and for establishing manning levels above what is deemed necessary by the technology. It also establishes norms in regard to pay and conditions of work which constrain management in adjusting to new competitive environments, as any

---

[17] A. Kilpatrick and T. Lawson, 'The Strength of the Working Class', *The Economic Decline of Modern Britain*, p. 250.

attempts to erode past gains in these areas are resisted by the workers. Interestingly, they argue that it is the ability of workers 'to further or defend those interests [which] partly explain[s] systematic divergencies in patterns of development'.[18] Thus, the success or failure of industries, and even specific firms within an industry, may be determined by the distribution of power within the workplace.

The outcome of the Kilpatrick/Lawson thesis on industrial decline is to situate the problem within the site of production, and in particular within the system of industrial relations. This view has similarly been articulated within the context of the debate on the decline of the Scottish cotton industry by the Swedish economic historian, Per Bolin-Hort. In a recent study of child labour in the British cotton industry, he rejects Robertson's argument regarding entrepreneurial failure, and instead claims that the reasons for decline in Scotland are to be found in the failure of the employers and workers to establish a coherent system of industrial relations. Bolin-Hort argues that productivity remained low in the Glasgow mills because the operatives lacked organisational means to defend wage increases. Their main objective was to attain the customary wage level; beyond that they had no further expectations.[19]

Bolin-Hort's intervention draws attention to the importance of studying the workforce itself. After the 1840s there exists no detailed analysis of the age and sexual composition of the labour force in the Scottish cotton industry and how these changed over time. The relationship of household structure to the labour supply is also ignored, as is the question of how this variable influenced the state of industrial relations in cotton after 1850. In spite of the importance of these factors in furthering our understanding of the Scottish cotton industry's development, as an explanation of the industry's decline Bolin-Hort's thesis has certain deficiencies. As Chapters 2 and 6 of this book show, the female weavers may have been unorganised, but the male workers engaged in preparatory or supervisory positions in the labour process were highly organised in small

---

[18] Ibid, p. 251.
[19] P. Bolin-Hort, *Work, Family and the State: child labour and the organisation of production in the British Cotton Industry, 1780–1920* (1989), p. 260.

craft societies. In spinning, too, despite the defeat of the 1837 strike, there existed a system of industrial relations in which the male spinners' union negotiated with employers, although admittedly from a weakened, but not entirely hopeless, position. Thus, explanations of low productivity have to be located in the gender divisions which existed in the industry, rather than simply in the male-bounded system of industrial relations. However, perhaps a stronger criticism of Bolin-Hort lies in the fact that little consideration is given by him either to the way in which the market imposed constraints on the employers, or the way it determined the labour process; a point which can be more generally levelled at the Kilpatrick/Lawson thesis. Product and labour markets have a major role in explaining decline since the choice of technique, as well as the quality and quantity of labour available to the industry, was largely determined by them.

The control of markets as a crucial ingredient in influencing the success of an industry or firm is most strongly associated with the analysis of Britain's relative economic decline put forward by Elbaum and Lazonick. In a recent publication a number of industries, including cotton, were subjected to intensive scrutiny by the latter and a number of other economists and business historians.[20] Although each industry had its own particular history and sets of problems, it is fair to say that Elbaum and Lazonick have distinguished four features common to all which in themselves constitute the basis of an explanation of Britain's relative industrial decline. Firstly, British firms are highly competitive, exercising little market power; secondly, the average size of the firm is small, and mainly family controlled, compared to overseas practices; thirdly, markets rather than managerial hierarchies link the specific stages of production and the industries lack vertical integration; and, finally, reliance on labour-intensive production methods has ceded control over shopfloor organisation and new technologies to highly unionised groups of workers. According to Elbaum and Lazonick, the solution to the problem of industrial decline lies in the minimising of internecine competition through integration and in the long-term planning of

---

[20] Elbaum and Lazonick, *Decline*.

markets and investment. Lazonick himself states that the 'development of the firm's ability to mass distribute is a necessary condition for the development of its incentive to mass produce. Firms' control over markets must precede, or at least emerge simultaneously with, the development of large scale, standardized production'.[21]

This appeal to apply the 'visible hand' to Britain's industrial problems has been rejected by supply-side economic historians, most notably by Kirby in a recent review article.[22] He points to the failure of collusive agreements in British industry in the 1930s to improve productive efficiency. Furthermore, the price paid for such agreements was the suppression of competition and a reliance on low value manufactured goods destined for imperial markets, all of which reinforced managerial and shopfloor complacency. Although the Second World War masked these weaknesses, the collapse of empire and the exposure of British industry to the fierce draught of world competition in the 1950s demonstrated how cartelisation, or other means of regulation, had allowed the nation's industrial structure to ossify. Rather than planning markets, which only serves to buttress institutional regidities, Kirby calls for more exposure of British industry to market forces. Although he has some valid criticisms to make of the Elbaum/Lazonick thesis, the highly competitive world of laissez-faire capitalism Kirby trumpets as the best cure against industrial decay is in historical terms more fictional than real. The history of economic development in Britain and elsewhere is about the elimination of competition and the triumph of regulation, rather than the story of Smith's hidden hand.

However, even if the macro-economic application of the Elbaum/Lazonick thesis to the problem of relative industrial decline is fraught with problems, its relevance at the micro level is still of immense importance. Indeed, when analysing the varied sectoral performance within the Scottish cotton industry over the period 1850–1914, the regulated market model seems, with some modification, to provide a better means of dealing with the process of decline and renewal

---

[21] Lazonick, 'The Cotton Industry', p. 42.
[22] M. Kirby, 'Institutional rigidities and economic decline: reflections on the British experience', *Economic History Review*, xlv (1992), pp. 637–60.

than other historico-cultural explanations. Retention and/or expansion of market share and price competitiveness determined the category a firm would fall into: loser, hanger-on or winner.

Losers, that is spinning and combined spinning and weaving enterprises, tended to operate in elastic labour markets in which the adoption of ruthless policies of cost-cutting, particularly in regard to wages, had the opposite effect to that which was intended. Market share decreased and labour, particularly male, drifted to other industries. Faced with competition from other industries for labour Scottish spinners were placed in a strategic cul-de-sac. To raise wages would further undermine market share by raising product prices; to refuse to do so would lead to the migration of the best workers to other industries. By opting for a strategy based on integration and regulation, competition would have been reduced and cost-cutting minimised. This would have allowed firms to produce more enlightened policies towards their workforces in respect of wages and conditions to stem the drift of labour, increase productivity and reduce the amount of worker resistance to change.

A strategy of this kind was, however, largely inoperable for reasons discussed in Chapter 2, but it had much to do with the divisions within the employer class, and the fact that these sectors had been associated with craft unionism and traditions of worker resistance against the imperatives of industrial capitalism, not the least being the cotton spinners' strike of 1837.

Winners, on the other hand, tended to operate in the tight labour markets associated with smaller towns and country districts, where a particular employer or firm was dominant, as well as in regulated product markets. Pursuing a paternalistic managerial strategy, firms such as Coats of Paisley were able for most of the period to buy employee commitment and loyalty at a relatively low cost. Since the thread industry was feminised from the outset, with women employed as winders and the spinning done elsewhere, there were no craft, male traditions to defend. Consequently, thread employers throughout the nineteenth century faced little worker resistance to changes in the organisation of working methods or wage rates. Through takeovers and mergers they also created a highly integrated structure which, through agreements with other firms, extended to the control of output and price.

The hangers-on included firms with a limited product range who were able to regulate output in accordance with market demand. Competition for work in the 'weaving jobbing system', as it was known by contemporaries, was fierce and in times of depression this led to wage cuts and labour drift to better paid employment. Survival meant a steady supply of trained labour, but instability in the labour market made this increasingly uncertain. Not surprisingly, as the nineteenth century progressed and occupational opportunities expanded, young workers looked for better prospects in other sectors of the economy.

The tripartite division of the cotton industry in Scotland into losers, hangers-on and winners highlights the need for a sectoral analysis if the process of decline and survival is to be understood. As we have seen such an analysis has to be set firmly within the structure of industrial relations and show how the operation of local labour and product markets affected the character of the former. This understanding will also be enhanced by adding a comparative dimension. Reference to the experience of other cotton producing countries or regions will enable us to pinpoint more accurately the peculiar failings of Scotland, particularly as regards the important question of labour productivity and the feminisation of the industry. The structure of the book will follow from these considerations.

Chapter 1 will deal with the general economic background to the development of the Scottish cotton industry, with particular attention to the occupational structure, the level of output and investment. Chapter 2 will focus on the development of cotton machinery and how this affected the nature of the work process in the factory. Chapter 3 will examine the wages and working conditions of cotton workers. Chapter 4 will deal with the way management responded to the changing fortunes of the industry at both the level of action and organisation. Chapter 5 will deal with the formation and development of trade unionism and the way this affected the balance of power in the factory through an analysis of strikes and lockouts.

The Conclusion will attempt to lay out the preconditions of failure and success in the Scottish cotton industry, and how these might be linked to the wider problem of de-industrialisation. For if the polar opposites of industrial decline and growth are outcomes of human choices and decisions and, therefore, problematic, we must make clear the circumstances which allowed thread to flourish and the others to decline, both absolutely and relatively.

Paisley thread winders, c.1890s. Note the brooding presence of the male overseer. (photograph courtesy of Renfrew District Council, Paisley Museum).

CHAPTER ONE

The Economic Development of the Scottish Cotton Industry, c.1850–1914

WHEN examining the progress of the Scottish cotton industry one is struck by a number of outstanding economic features. Firstly, from the early decades of the nineteenth century the development of the Scottish cotton industry was unstable and subject to a violent cycle of boom and bust. Thus the years 1835–46, 1856–61, and the 1870s were periods of growth in employment. However, they were followed by periods of depression. Particularly bad years included 1835, 1856, the cotton famine of the early to mid-1860s, 1867–71, and 1885 through to 1895, with the latter year marking the entry of the spinning and weaving sectors into terminal and irreversible decline. Secondly, unlike Lancashire, the industry was dominated from a relatively early stage by female workers. How far this contributed to decline is a subject of some interest. Thirdly, the discontinuities in the experiences of the various sectors of the cotton industry created the threefold division into losers, hangers-on and winners. By examining the structure of employment, investment and output we can establish a basis for understanding these distinguishing features, although the reasons for success will only be appreciated through further analysis of other aspects of the Scottish cotton industry's development.

1. *Employment*

When examining the structure of employment in the cotton industry, the historian has two invaluable sources from which to draw:

the Factory Returns and the Census. The former is useful in comparing sectoral trends within the industry; the latter provides a means of interpreting changes in the level of employment in cotton with those taking place within the economy as a whole. Both sources provide data on the age and sexual composition of the labour force. There are, of course, major difficulties when using the Census. The most important of these are the changing system of classifying occupations and the shifting boundaries of cities and counties, which can at times appear rather arbitrary. Maintaining consistency in the face of changing systems of classification is difficult, and because of this a number of decisions have had to be made regarding boundaries and occupations. Although the study focuses on Glasgow and Paisley as the main centres of the cotton trade in Scotland, material regarding employment is presented for the counties of Lanark and Renfrew. As parts of what is now regarded as Glasgow proper, such as Pollockshaws and Eastwood, were not included under the returns for the city of Glasgow, it was felt more appropriate to examine the returns for the counties. However, it should be borne in mind that the majority of cotton workers were employed and lived in Glasgow and Paisley. The problem of interpreting data concerned with occupations led to equally hard decisions, although some problems were insurmountable. When comparing the numbers employed in cotton with, say, shopwork over the nineteenth century in Lanark and Renfrew one is faced immediately with the problem of the definition of a shopworker. For instance, the category baker may mean a person working on the retail or the production side of the trade. Therefore, as we will see, the figures for shopwork are probably on the low side, since only those occupations which were unambiguously connected with the retail trade have been included. Also within the cotton trade itself, the Census offers little distinction between the various branches of the industry. Until the 1901 Census most workers are grouped together under the heading 'cotton manufacture'. Furthermore, there are a number of rogue classifications such as 'weaver undefined'; although on the positive side it does have a separate entry for thread manufacture. Given these, and other problems with the Census, too numerous and tedious to mention, what follows should be treated with some caution.

If we look at the following graph illustrating the sexual distribution of employment in the cotton industry in Scotland as a whole over the period 1850–1914, it would appear that men were replaced by women to a significant extent in the years following the failure of the 1837 cotton spinners' strike, but after the cotton famine of the 1860s their numbers remained steady at around 17 to 18 per cent of the total.

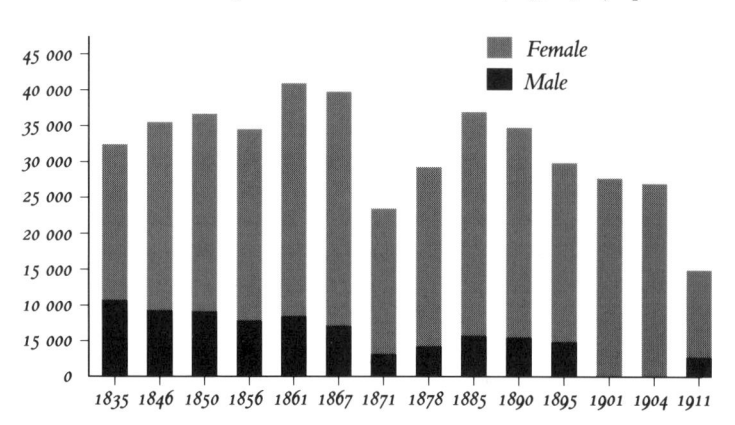

Table 1. *Number of cotton workers in Scotland (1835–1911) by sex.*

The employment returns would certainly appear to confirm 1837 as a turning point in restructuring the sexual composition of the cotton industry. However, total employment data provide a misleading account of the shift in the sexual distribution of labour in the cotton industry. Power loom weaving from the outset was predominantly a female occupation, with males employed as supervisory workers, or tenters, and making up only around one-sixth of a total labour force in 1850 of 9,176.[1] By 1861 the share of weaving employment going to male workers had fallen to 14 per cent, and thereafter varied between 12 and 14 per cent. Similarly, thread manufacture was from the beginning an almost exclusively female occupation. Therefore, it is the spinning sector which is

---

[1] Factory Report, PP, 1850, xx.

most relevant when analysing the changing sexual composition of the industry.

After the collapse of the 1837 spinners' strike, the Scottish employers were of the opinion that the introduction of the self-acting mule and the coupling of existing mules would drastically reduce the number of male spinners. A prominent master spinner claimed that if his machinery were run on self-acting principles, he would be able to dismiss all his male spinners.[2] However, the scope for such radical action was limited, as the following graph shows:

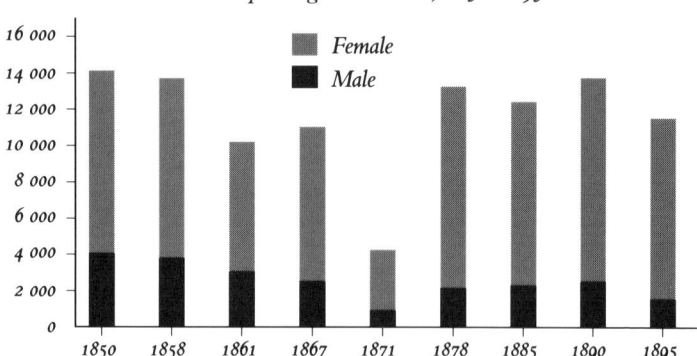

Table 2. *The sexual distribution of workers in cotton spinning in Scotland, 1850–1895.*

[Source: Factory Returns (1836–1895)]

Changes in the labour process were able to effect only a small initial fall of 8 per cent in male employment over the thirteen years after the 1837 strike. Thus it was the cotton famine of the early 1860s, rather than earlier industrial conflict, which marked a turning point in the sexual composition of the labour force in spinning. However, another important transitionary stage was during the period of the so-called 'Great Depression' of 1873–1896. Hard times forced male workers out of cotton and into the expanding heavy industries of the West of Scotland. The Factory Report for 1884

---

[2] Evidence of Charles Todd, manufacturer, First Report of the Select Committee on Combinations of Workmen, PP, 1837–8, VIII, qs. 521–3, p. 24.

estimated that between 1871 and 1881 the number of men employed in cotton manufacture in Glasgow declined by 50 per cent, while the number of women increased by over three times in the decade.[3] However, by using the very depressed year of 1871 as a base year, the Report overestimated the decline of male labour in cotton spinning, since by 1890 it had recovered its share of employment at 20.2 per cent. However, the shifting sexual balance of labour in the spinning mill in favour of women was welcomed by the cotton masters, as it reduced production costs in times of depressed trading conditions. As we shall see later, it also signalled a profound change in the labour process.

An important question to consider, in the light of the feminisation of the cotton industry, is how far the age composition of the labour force changed in the course of the nineteenth and early twentieth centuries. Did the employers respond to recurring economic difficulties by recruiting low-paid young female workers? Andrew Ure's study of the early cotton industry showed that, in 1834, 57.5 per cent of the combined male and female workforce, or 28,676, were over the age of eighteen, and that 29.3 per cent, or 13,721, were between the ages of thirteen and eighteen, the rest being made up of children under thirteen.[4] Thus, just under half the workforce was made up of young people.

Using the more detailed Factory Returns after 1850, and in the light of the factory acts of the 1840s, it would appear that the legislation was successful in reducing substantially the number of workers, both male and female, under the age of thirteen by 1850. The Factory Return of that year shows that in Scotland, out of a total labour force of 36,325, only 580, or 1.6 per cent, were in that age group, and although the figure grew to around 3 per cent with the expansion of the thread industry, low-cost child labour was rarely used in significant quantities by Scottish employers. The only exception to this was the thread-making sector, which was a noted employer of half-timers from 1860 onwards.[5]

---

[3] Factory Report, PP, 1884, XVIII.
[4] A. Ure, *The Cotton Manufacture of Great Britain*, 2 vols (1836), p. 357.
[5] Factory Report, PP, 1860, XXXIV, p. 10.

This, of course, tells us nothing regarding the employment of young workers. Until 1895 the Factory Returns aggregated female labour over the age of thirteen, making it impossible to calculate the ages of the majority of workers. There are figures for young male workers between the ages of thirteen and eighteen, but this is not helpful since that cohort at no time after 1850 made up more than seven per cent of the total workforce, and averaged only three per cent from 1850 to 1895. From the 1895 Factory Return it would appear that female workers in this cohort accounted for only 21.2 per cent, or 6,433 out of a total workforce of 30,262, the respective figures for women over eighteen being 59.5 and 17,999. Whether this represented a loss of this particular cohort from the industry to better and more regular work in other occupations as claimed by the 1884 Factory Report is, on these figures, difficult to say. However, using a different system of classifying age groups, the Census provides a somewhat different picture for the county of Lanark. As the following bar chart shows, the proportion of female workers in cotton manufacture under twenty remained fairly consistent from 1850 to 1901:

Table 3. *The ages of female cotton workers in Lanarkshire, 1851–1901*

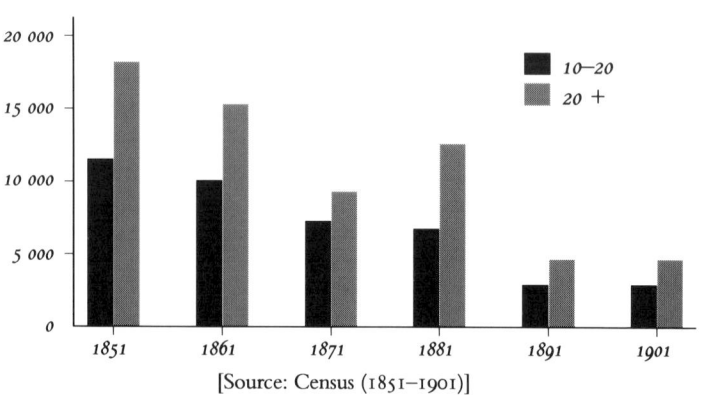

[Source: Census (1851–1901)]

Adult female labour remained favoured by employers, but on a diminishing total number of workers. This raises the issue of how important employment in the cotton industry was for women in Lanarkshire, as well as Renfrewshire, as the nineteenth century progressed. Using the decennial census of occupations to analyse this question is, as we mentioned above, fraught with difficulties surrounding the classification of work. To establish consistency, the categories used in the 1851 Census have been applied to those which follow it. Furthermore, in arriving at the total occupied female workforce in the two counties for the censuses of 1851, 1861 and 1871 the number of wives, widows, daughters, other relatives and scholars of no specified occupation has been deducted from the total female population. For convenience, it has been decided to present the figures for each occupation in percentage terms only.

Table 4. *The distribution of female employment in Lanarkshire, 1851–1901*

Occupation	1851	1861	1871	1881	1891	1901
Cotton Manufacture	23.0	23.6	13.2	15.8	5.5	4.7
Domestic Servant	12.7	16.6	13.5	21.5	22.4	16.8
Millinery/Dress/Stays	5.4	7.5	7.3	10.1	12.0	9.6
Farm Servant	2.2	2.4	2.4	2.3	1.1	1.2
Retail *	0.9	2.4	2.4	4.3	5.1	4.4
Woollen Manufacture	0.2	0.7	1.6	1.4	0.9	0.7
Thread Manufacture	0.4	0.5	0.4	0.7	0.7	—
Weaver (Undefined)	—	2.6	5.8	1.5	4.2	2.2
Muslin Manufacture	—	0.9	0.6	—	—	—
Factory Hand (Textiles)	—	—	5.8	2.0	2.0	1.1
Others	55.2	42.8	47.0	40.5	46.1	59.3

[Source: Census (1851–1901)] * Includes shopkeeper, milkseller, butcher, fishmonger, greengrocer and fruiterer, grocer.

The data clearly show the declining importance of textiles as an employer of labour in Lanarkshire, but chronicling that process is made difficult by the arbitrary introduction of occupational categories such as weaver (undefined) and factory hand (textiles). If we were to assume that these occupations were part of the cotton industry, which is not unreasonable given the low levels of participation in other branches of the textile industry, and include such trades as thread-making and muslin manufacture, then the figures for cotton manufacture would be higher and the decline less dramatic after 1881. The readjusted figure for employment in cotton manufacture in percentages would be 23.4 in 1851, 27.6 in 1861, 25.8 in 1871, 20.0 in 1881, 12.4 in 1891 and 8.0 in 1901. Although cotton fell behind domestic service as the largest employer of female labour after 1871, it was still the second most important in 1891, and, in spite of a large contraction of the industry after 1895, it still ranked third behind domestic service and millinery and dressmaking in 1901. Cotton manufacture, then, remained a major employer of female labour in Lanarkshire in the nineteenth century. However, it would appear that the growing diversity of employment, as represented by the category 'others', accounting for 59.3 per cent of employment in 1901, gradually siphoned labour away from the volatile cotton industry. This also had implications for labour relations in the industry, as we will see later.

Table 5. *The distribution of female employment in Renfrewshire, 1851–1901*

Occupation	1851	1861	1871	1881	1891	1901
Cotton Manufacture	25.0	18.5	8.6	6.3	5.3	3.7
Domestic Servant	11.7	12.3	11.1	20.9	16.5	14.4
Millinery/Dress/Stays	5.3	5.5	5.0	5.0	8.3	6.7
Thread Manufacture	3.5	5.4	7.0	11.1	16.5	—
Farm Servant	3.3	3.1	2.0	2.6	2.3	2.0
Flax/Linen Manufacture	1.9	2.8	2.3	5.0	4.1	3.7
Retail ★	1.9	1.9	3.1	4.2	4.4	4.3
Woollen Manufacture	0.9	1.0	2.0	1.4	2.3	2.0
Weaver (Undefined)	—	1.0	4.2	3.0	1.6	1.4
Muslin Manufacture	—	—	2.0	—	—	—
Factory Hand (Textiles)	—	—	8.8	11.7	6.7	1.9
Others	46.5	45.4	43.9	28.3	32.0	61.9

[Source: Census (1851–1901)]   ★ Includes shopkeeper, milkseller, butcher, fishmonger, greengrocer and fruiterer, grocer.

The occupational statistics for Renfrewshire highlight the growing importance of the thread industry for women in the economy of the county. From a mere 3.5 per cent of total female employment in 1851, by 1891 it had increased to 16.5 per cent. The absence of an entry in the 1901 Census is due to the introduction of a new category of occupation – 'fancy goods (textiles), small wares, etc.' – which accounted for 20 per cent of total female employment. In contrast to Lanarkshire, Renfrewshire in the course of the nineteenth century witnessed a narrowing of the structure of female employment as represented by the declining numbers placed under the category 'others', notwithstanding the rather strange figure for 1901. On the other hand, if we combine the figures for the various branches of the cotton industry (that is, cotton manufacture, thread making, weaver, muslin manufacture and factory hand), its dominance of the labour market is impressive. In 1851 cotton accounted for 28.5 per cent of total female employment, and in the following decades the respective figures were 28.0 in 1861, 29.0 in 1871, 28.1 in 1881, and 30.1 in 1891. The fact that so many females and their families relied on cotton for their living and the absence, outside domestic service and millinery and dressmaking, of alternative employment produced a particular structure of industrial relations in Renfrewshire which, as we will see, was markedly different to Lanarkshire's.

The employment statistics can also be used usefully to highlight the cyclical nature of the cotton industry's development in Scotland after 1850, and to show how this phenomenon was experienced in each sector.

Table 6. *An index of employment in the Scottish cotton industry, 1835–1911 (1835=100)*

Year	Employment
1835	100
1846	108
1850	111
1856	106
1861	127
1867	122
1871	71

1878	91
1885	114
1890	107
1895	93
1901	83
1907	85
1911	46

[Source: Factory Returns, (1835–1907)]

The table confirms the point made earlier in the chapter regarding the cyclical decline of cotton. This, of course, tells us nothing about how the process of decline was experienced in the various sectors of the industry. To understand this we must examine the share of employment by sector.

Table 7. *The share of employment in the Scottish cotton industry by sector, 1850–1895*

Year	Spinning No.	%	Weaving No.	%	Spinning and Weaving No.	%	Other Processes No.	%
1850	14057	38.7	9176	25.3	11212	30.9	1880	5.1
1856	13730	39.6	8013	23.1	11731	33.8	1234	3.5
1861	10175	24.7	11737	28.5	14155	34.3	5170	12.5
1867	10961	27.5	16971	42.6	11617	29.2	260	0.7
1871	4400	14.2	9565	30.9	9132	29.5	7863	25.4
1878	13510	45.4	7903	26.5	8124	27.3	238	0.8
1885	12747	34.3	16347	44.0	5874	15.8	2199	5.9
1890	13928	40.0	15336	44.0	4627	13.2	982	2.8
1895	11384	37.6	16020	52.9	1820	6.0	1038	3.5

[Source: Factory Returns, 1850–1895]

Clearly the sector which suffered earliest and most severely in the process of decline was the combined spinning and weaving trade. The more specialist branches of the trade did better after

1871 and survived longer as they were best able to adjust production as markets and trade changed. Weaving grew to become the most important branch of the cotton industry in terms of employment because it faced the least number of constraints. It was not dependent on yarn produced locally, but could buy in the cheapest markets, mainly Lancashire. Being tied to the higher end of the trade in ginghams and zephyrs, Scottish weavers also had the advantage of flexible production systems based on small batches. Switching production to suit changing tastes was relatively easier than for those weavers in the plain cloth sector of the market. As one employer explained in 1893: 'Glasgow is a huge pattern shop for coloured work buyers come to Glasgow for small orders, and having in this way got samples of the goods they give their large orders to Lancashire and America'.[6]

Therefore, if we use employment statistics as a yardstick for measuring the importance and progress of an industry, the Scottish cotton industry was a classic example of dynamic cyclical growth and decline. The final turning point was almost certainly after 1885, rather than the 1820s as Campbell has argued. In spite of declining fortunes it still remained an important employer of female labour as late as 1901. This was more true of Renfrewshire, where the thread industry grew rapidly as the century wore on, than of Lanarkshire, which experienced greater diversity in the female labour market and, thus, provide more scope for women to find other jobs outside the industry.

2. *Investment and Output*

Campbell, among others, has argued that the early technical leadership established by the Scottish industry was soon lost and that by the 1830s a pattern of what might be called de-investment or

---

[6] Quoted in A. J. M. Albert, 'Patterns of Employment of Working-Class Women in Glasgow, 1880–1914' (unpublished MA thesis, University of Victoria, Canada, 1985), p. 175.

stagnation had set in. The decision by Houldsworths, cotton manufacturers and machine makers of Glasgow since 1790, to shift their capital out of cotton and into ironmaking in 1837 is used as evidence, as well as the fact that between 1838 and 1843 several large mills were destroyed by fire and none of them was rebuilt.[7] Although new capital was still being invested in cotton after 1850 there was a net fall in the level of investment. Of the 24 mills and 24 extensions to existing mills built between 1850 and 1856, 38 were closed down over the same period.[8] Without additional data regarding plant size, the number of workers, the number of spindles and/or looms, and the level of output, the figures are meaningless. There is no way of knowing whether additions compensated for closures in terms of adding to fixed capital formation, or whether they altered the ratio of capital to labour. Moreover, as Crouzet pointed out, in regard to the relationship between capital formation and industrialisation, it is not the quantity of capital which is important, but its usage and quality.[9] Less may have meant bigger and more. A study of employment in the British cotton industry shows that during the nineteenth century a Scottish mill employed on average 50 to 100 per cent more workers than a Lancashire mill, and between two-and-half to four times that of a Yorkshire mill.[10] Thus a closer investigation of investment and output seems to be called for if a clearer understanding of these issues is to be achieved.

There are a number of factors we can examine to give us some indication of the level of investment in the industry, even if monetary statistics are hard to find. Firstly, we can examine the transformation of the power source of the industry. As the stacked bar chart shows there was a massive surge in the amount of steam power in the industry in the 1850s and '60s as the water-powered mills became obsolete.

---

[7] A. J. Robertson, 'The Decline of the Scottish Cotton Industry, 1860–1914', *Business History*, 12 (1970), pp. 117–18.
[8] Robertson, 'Decline', p. 118.
[9] F. Crouzet, 'Introduction', in *Capital Formation in the Industrial Revolution*, ed. F. Crouzet (1972), p. 18.
[10] D. T. Jenkins, 'The Cotton Industry in Yorkshire, 1780–1900', *Textile History*, 10 (1979), p. 76.

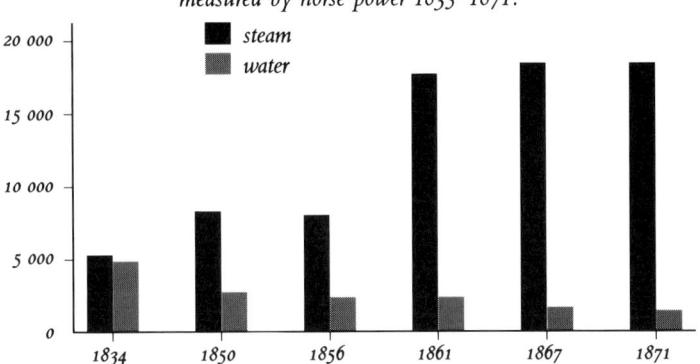

Table 8. *The ratio of steam to water power in Scottish cotton mills, measured by horse power 1835–1871.*

[Source: Factory Returns (1835–1871)]

A considerable shift from water power to steam was also taking place between 1835 and 1850, and again between 1850 and 1867. But what is very striking is the large increase in horse power in Scottish mills during the period 1856 and 1867, which increased from 9,971 hp to 20,470, or by 105 per cent, in total. However, if we examine the increase in steam power for the period 1856 to 1871 the rise is even more dramatic, increasing from 7,641 hp to 18,625, or 144 per cent. If we refine the figures further to take account of the fluctuating number of factories during this period, the following picture emerges:

Table 9. *The amount of moving power per Scottish cotton mill, 1834–1871*

Year	Total HP	No. of factories	HP per factory
1834	10152	134	75.8
1850	10554	168	62.8
1856	9971	152	65.6
1861	19970	163	122.5
1867	20470	131	156.2
1871	20122	98	205.3

[Source: Factory Returns (1835–1871)]

These figures can be interpeted in a number of ways. For example, the rise in horse power may not have effectively increased the level of investment in the cotton industry, as it might simply be the result of improvements to existing machinery. In spite of this, there is no doubt that the amount of capital per worker increased in this period. The percentage increase in the workforce over the period 1835 to 1871 was only 22.0 per cent, compared to a 48.5 per cent rise in total horse power. However, if we take the increase in steam horse power during the same period the figure shows a remarkable 249 per cent rise over the 1835 level, from 5,330 hp to 18,625 hp. At the same time in the spinning sector the number of spindles per worker grew from 83 in 1850 to 113 in 1861. This would tend to suggest that, in spite of periodic setbacks, investment continued to grow in the industry.

Even in the years after the cotton famine the industry, particularly the spinning sector, was still seen as a sound investment. Out of forty-three cotton spinning companies listed in *The Glasgow and Greenock Commercial List* in 1870/1, twenty-seven, or 63 per cent, were listed as establishments of 'good standing', while a further nine, 21 per cent, were considered a 'reasonable risk'. Only 27 per cent of the total number of weaving firms listed were considered companies of good standing.

After 1871 the level of investment fell as cotton entered a period of sustained depression. Employers responded to their economic difficulties by increasing the ratio of labour to capital. Like their counterparts in shipbuilding and iron and steel, the Scottish cotton producers faced with fluctuating international markets opted for labour-intensive methods of production. In spite of the increase in the number of workers per spinning mill, rising from 220 in 1871 to 435 in 1890, the number of spindles per worker fell from 150 to 76 over the same period. By comparison the number of spindles per worker in the Lancashire cotton industry grew from 194 in 1878 to 218 in 1890, in spite of the average number of workers per mill being lower.[11] The lack of investment in new machinery was seen by the Webbs as the root cause of the spinning sector's

---

[11] Jenkins, 'The Cotton Industry in Yorkshire', p. 76.

economic decline. They noted that 'Most concerns [were] reported to be unable to compete with Lancashire owing to old fashioned machinery'.[12] This view was shared by MacIntyre, who also pointed out in 1901 that 'The machinery in Scotch mills became archaic . . . and few, if any, serious efforts were made to restore anything like the equality in economy or speed of production'.[13]

However, there are a number of exceptions in this otherwise gloomy scenario to take into consideration. The spinning sector witnessed an increase in the number of doubling spindles, from 186,000 in 1867 to 541,000 in 1901, a rise of 191 per cent. Doubling spindles' share in total spindleage over the same period grew from 12 to 49 per cent. In addition to this development, there was the introduction of ring spinning in the 1880s in the Coats works in Paisley. This spread to other mills and by 1903 the Scottish industry operated 166,994 ring and throstle spindles, or 15 per cent of the total number of spindles.[14] Investment also occurred in new plant and machines. The Oakbank and St Rollox mills of A. & A. Galbraith, Glasgow, were said to be 'filled with machinery of the finest and most recent construction'.[15]

New factories were also built. In the 1870s two new large enterprises were opened in Glasgow. The first in 1871 was Robertson's Newhall factory in Bridgeton, which was reckoned to be the largest of its kind in the world with 150,000 spindles and 3,200 powerlooms;[16] and the second in 1875 was the Clyde Spinning Company producing fine yarns for the thread industry. In the 1880s the massive Glasgow Cotton Spinning Company opened to supply high count yarns to the Turkey Red dyeing trade.[17] Firms which

---

[12] The Webb Collection on Trade Unions, (British Library of Political and Economic Science [BLPES]), Section A, xxxvii, Textile Trades, f. 429.
[13] R. MacIntyre, 'Textile Industries', in *Local Industries of Glasgow and the West of Scotland*, ed. A. McLean (Glasgow, 1901), p. 145.
[14] *Return of Cotton Factories*, PP, 1903, LXIV, p. 5.
[15] D. Bremner, *The Industries of Scotland: their rise, progress and present condition* (1969 edn), p. 291.
[16] *Glasgow Herald*, 19 Jan. 1871.
[17] A. J. Robertson, 'Textiles', in *Dictionary of Scottish Business Biography, 1860–1960*, Vol. 1: the staple industries, ed. A. Slaven and S. Checkland (Aberdeen, 1986), p. 247.

had closed during the depression of the late 1870s and early 1880s re-opened with upgraded machinery. The Linwood Cotton Mill, at a standstill from October 1882, re-opened in March the following year with 'the whole of the machinery . . . overhauled or replaced by something more in keeping with the age'.[18] The thread industry of Paisley also went through a major expansion of fixed capital in this period. The firm of Coats experienced a large increase in plant and machinery over the period 1872 to 1878 from £60,000 to £157,000, with £58,000 laid out in 1878 for a new finishing mill.[19]

These bright spots could not disguise the otherwise depressing outlook for the spinning sector after the expansion of the 1880s. The number of spindles fell from 1.487m in 1878 to just under a million in 1903, and for the first time in the history of the cotton industry Renfrewshire had overtaken Lanarkshire as the main centre for spinning cotton. In 1871 933,000 spindles were in operation in Lanarkshire, mainly in Glasgow, and 370,000 in Renfrewshire, mainly in Paisley; by 1903 the situation had been totally reversed, with only 321,054 spindles in operation in the former and 542,000 in the latter.[20] As a reflection of this transformation the number of spinning firms in Glasgow collapsed. According to the Glasgow Post Office Directory, there were forty-nine cotton spinning firms operating in Glasgow in 1870; the number fell to twenty-nine in 1880–1, then increased to thirty-five in 1890–1 thanks to the boom of the mid-1880s, before decreasing dramatically to eleven in 1900–1. And while the number of firms in Paisley experienced a similar contraction, from nine in 1880 to four in 1906,[21] this was the result of the aggressive expansionary policy of the firms of Clarks and Coats rather than any inherent weakness in the thread industry.

The sector of least investment was weaving. In spite of the initial costs of establishing a power loom factory, the employers tended to rely on labour-intensive methods of production with very little

---

[18] *Paisley and Renfrewshire Gazette*, 18 Mar. 1883.
[19] A. K. Cairncross and J. B. K. Hunter, 'The Early Growth of Messrs J. & P. Coats, 1830–1883', *Business History*, 29 (1987), p. 173.
[20] *Returns of Cotton Factories*, PP, 1871, LXII and PP, 1903, LXIV.
[21] Kelly's Textile Directories (1880, 1906).

change in the ratio of looms to worker over the nineteenth century, as the following tables show:

Table 10. *The ratio of looms and workers to factories in the cotton weaving trade at selected dates*

Year	No. of factories	No. of workers	No. of looms	Looms per factory	Workers per factory
1850	49	9176	14391	294	187
1856	40	8037	12475	312	201
1861	54	11737	16796	311	217
1867	60	16971	20694	345	283
1871	36	9565	14398	400	266
1878	30	7903	13649	455	263
1885	63	16347	23282	369	259
1890	58	15336	22047	380	264

[Source: Factory Returns (1850–1890)]

Table 11. *The ratio of looms to workers at selected dates*

Year	Ratio
1850	1.6
1856	1.5
1861	1.4
1867	1.2
1871	1.5
1878	1.7
1885	1.4
1890	1.4

[Source: ibid.]

Obviously the ratio errs on the conservative side since it is based on the total number of workers in the trade and does not distinguish between the actual weavers and their assistants, or supervisors. The most common estimate puts the number of looms at two per weaver and this figure is confirmed by the 1886 Wage Census. From this source it would appear that of the 3,772 recorded power loom weavers, 18.0 per cent worked on three looms, 80.7 per cent tended two, and the remaining 1.3 per cent operated one loom each.[22]

The reasons for this failure by the weaving sector to increase the capital/labour ratio substantially lie in the economics of the cotton industry. Firstly, weavers had far lower fixed costs than spinners and it was far easier to increase the number of looms in a mill than it was to put on more spindles. *The Textile Recorder* estimated that in 1856 the cost of a weaving shed per loom was £15, including buildings, boilers, engines, gearing and accessories. Fifty years later the cost had increased by only £11, or by 73 per cent. In contrast, a spinning mill cost 45–50 shillings per spindle in 1856, and although by the latter date costs had fallen, at 19–21*s*. for mule spinning and 36–42*s*. for ring spinning it still involved more capital and was still relatively more expensive to carry on that weaving.[23] Given the relatively low cost in increasing the number of looms weaving manufacturers preferred variable to fixed costs. Moreover, extra looms and power could be rented if demand increased substantially. Secondly, weavers were reluctant to add to their stock of fixed assets as they were normally at a competitive disadvantage to spinners. As Ellison points out, 'So long as the manufacturer keeps his looms going he must have yarn no matter what the price, but in dull times, when demand is small and stock large, he must, if he wishes to sell, take the best price'.[24] In a fiercely competitive and unstable market weavers saw the flexibility of labour-intensive production as far more advantageous than lavishly appointed sheds with a high ratio of capital to labour. Finally, as the most time-consuming tasks in weaving were supplying the looms with weft shuttles and repairing broken warp threads, both of which involved stopping the machine, the lower the number of looms per weaver, 'the faster each could be run, the higher the output per loom, and the lower

---

[22] P. Bolin-Hort, *Work, Family and the State: Child Labour and the Organisation of production in the British Cotton Industry, 1780–1920* (1989), p. 121.
[23] 15 Mar. 1906.
[24] T. Ellison, *The Cotton Trade of Great Britain* (1886), pp. 78–9.

the total factor cost'.[25] This, of course, does not explain why the ratio of looms to weavers in Scotland was lower than in Lancashire, where three or four looms per weaver was the normal load, which is an issue which we will address later. However, it does help to explain how, when spinning in Glasgow was in terminal decline, the weaving firms were able to hang on. From 1880–1 to 1900–1 the number of weaving firms in Glasgow grew from forty-four to forty-eight, the latter representing a rise of 29 per cent over the figure for 1890–1.[26]

How far was output affected by the fluctuating levels of employment and investment? Unfortunately, data regarding the output of Scottish cotton firms are sparse, particularly after 1867. The tendency of the Board of Trade not to disaggregate the output of the cotton industry by region means that we have no specifically Scottish figures until the 1907 Census of Production. However, if we are to judge the decline of the industry in terms of the consumption of raw cotton, as Campbell does, then the spinning sector was in decline from 1840 onwards. In that year estimated consumption of raw cotton was running at 2,346 bales per week. According to Campbell, thereafter it was stable until 1866 when consumption reached 2,500 bales per week, falling back the next year to 1,700, and stagnating in the 1870s at around 1,500–2,000.[27] The truth of the matter is that between 1840 and 1867 the figures for consumption fluctuated wildly, reaching above 2,000 bales per week in only seven years. The average weekly consumption for the period 1840 to 1849 in Scotland was 2,002 bales, with the peak year being 1840 at 2,346 bales per week, and the worst being 1847 at 1,551 bales per week. In the following decade the average weekly consumption was 1,889 bales, with the highest year being 1852 at 2,245 bales per week, and the lowest being the years 1858 and 1859 at 1,538 bales per week. The latter years of the 1850s represented a short-term depression compounded by the cotton famine of the early '60s

---

[25] W. Lazonick and W. Mass, 'The Performance of the British Cotton Industry, 1870–1913', *Research in Economic History*, 9 (1984), pp. 25–6.
[26] Glasgow Post Office Directory (1880–1, 1890–1, 1990–1).
[27] R. H. Campbell, *Scotland Since 1707* (1985 edn), p. 89.

which makes comparison with early decades impossible. As Campbell points out, however, consumption increased to a peak of 2,500 bales of raw cotton per week in 1867; thereafter, it was estimated at 1,800 bales per week until 1879. After the latter date the figures are less precise and consumption figures for the 1880s are given as between 1,500 and 2,000 bales per week. At this point published information ceases regarding consumption of raw cotton in Scotland.[28] However, the wildly cyclical character of cotton spinning in Scotland is clearly shown by the figures, although the question of how consumption related to output is unclear.

On the basis of these figures alone one would have to assume that the cotton spinning sector was in terminal decline from 1840 onwards, since that year represented the peak in terms of the consumption of raw cotton. But such an assumption would have to take into account the rise in employment and fixed capital taking place in the period after 1850, which we discussed above. Moreover, it does not take into consideration the change in the quality of the product. The 1850s witnessed a shift from low, bulky qualities of yarn to much finer counts. This meant that the same or more output could be realised from less raw cotton. Thus a fall in the consumption of raw cotton did not necessarily imply a corresponding fall in output. As the *Commonwealth* pointed out:

> A spinner may have the same number of spindles, and may spin the same length of thread, but if he spins 80s in place of 40s, that is to say, every hank he spins now weighs only half the hank he used to spin, it is obvious that although he produces as many hanks as formerly, he will consume only one half the quantity of cotton.[29]

Unfortunately, testing this hypothesis is made almost impossible by the absence of separate figures for Scottish output. Historians have relied on the export data provided by David Bremner's study of Scottish industry in the 1860s and the much more comprehensive 1907 Census of Production to estimate the condition of the cotton industry in Scotland.

---

[28] Connal & Co., Clyde Market Reports (1835–1885).
[29] *Commonwealth* (1855), p. 237.

According to Bremner, the volume and value of yarn exports from Scotland in the period 1861 to 1867 were as follows:

Table 12. *Scottish yarn exports, 1861–7*

Date	lbs (000s)	value (£000s)
1861	6.555	468
1862	5.516	504
1864	5.828	831
1865	5.787	653
1866	7.733	848
1867	9.495	842

[Source: D. Bremner, *The Industries of Scotland* (1969 edn) p. 288]

However, this tells us nothing regarding the total output of the spinning sector in these years. This is where a number of assumptions have to be made in order to arrive at some sort of measure of total output. What we have to assume is that the division of output between home and overseas markets was the same in Scotland as it was for the UK. In 1861 and 1867, 19.3 per cent of UK production was exported, leaving 79.7 per cent for home consumption.[30] Applying this statistical division to the Scottish spinning sector, in 1861 a total of 34.3m pounds of yarn was produced, and this increased to 49.4m in 1867. If we divide total output by consumption, the relationship between the two may become slightly clearer. In 1861 consumption of raw cotton for Scotland was estimated to be 80,000 bales, which when divided into total yarn output for that year produced 429 lbs of yarn. The respective figures for 1867 were 130,000 bales producing 380lbs of yarn. These figures are open to a variety of interpretations. The higher output per bale of consumed raw cotton in 1861 may have been connected with its quality and type, or it may have had something to do with worker productivity,

---

[30] The figures for the UK were 947m lbs of yarn in 1861, of which 183.1m lbs, or 19.3 per cent, was exported; in 1867 the respective figures were 909m and 175.5m, or 19.3 per cent. (G. T. Jones, *Increasing Return* (1933), pp. 275–6; B. Mitchell, *British Historical Statistics* (Cambridge, 1978), p. 356.)

or the type of yarn demanded by the weaving sector. Although we cannot resolve these questions, from these data it would appear that consumption of raw cotton was not correlated directly with output and using only the former as a way of analysing the fortunes of the industry, as Campbell does, should be guarded against. It also says nothing regarding the weaving branch of the cotton industry.

Using Bremner's data it would appear that in terms of export volume and value the weaving trade grew in the 1860s, from 150,754,000 yards of piece goods worth £2.644m in 1861, to 206,395,000 yards worth £5m in 1867. By the time of the publication of the Census of Production some forty years later output had fallen to 108,758,000 yards of piece goods valued at £1.714m. Over this period the workforce had contracted along with output, which begs the question of whether productivity fell also, which is something we shall consider later.

From the foregoing discussion, however, it is clear that previous accounts of the development the Scottish cotton industry are in need of revision and refinement. The lack of evidence on such important matters as investment and output means that what exists can be open to several conflicting interpretations. In spite of this, it would appear that the decline of the industry in Scotland was neither predictable nor linear, but discontinuous and partial, experienced in different ways by individual sectors in a boom and bust development cycle. The partialness of decline is evident in the progress of thread manufacture, but it can also be seen in the statistics for sectoral employment, and less so in the extant data on investment and output. What conditioned the extent and rate of decline was the relationship between labour and capital, which itself was the result of the workings of the wage/effort bargain, the capital/labour ratio and the level of investment. However, these issues can only be understood by examining the labour process and the material conditions of the workers themselves.

CHAPTER TWO

Technological Change and the Labour Process

THE publication of Harry Braverman's seminal study – *Labour and Monopoly Capital* (1974) – marked a turning point for labour and social historians. Since then they have increasingly concerned themselves with the nature of the labour process in industrial capitalism. Central to this concern has been the debate on de-skilling and the destruction of craft control over the labour process and its subordination to the imperatives of capitalist accumulation. Braverman has been strongly criticised for the one-sidedness and simplicity of his account of this development. Among the weaknesses identified in his thesis is the omission of any mention of class struggle, or worker resistance to technical change;[1] the failure to grasp how de-skilling can be mediated and, therefore, modified through labour, market and product particularisms;[2] the lack of detailed analysis of the transformation of formal to real subordination (in the Marxist sense) of labour to capital – the process occurs automatically;[3] and, the failure to realise how formally skilled workers can continue to occupy a privileged position in the workforce through either the mechanism of custom, or by their strategic placing in the production process, or both.[4] Crucially, Braverman fails to appreciate how

---

[1] T. Elger, 'Braverman, Capital Accumulation and Deskilling' in *The Degradation of Work?*, ed. S. Wood (1982), pp. 25–53.
[2] J. Zeitlin, 'Craft Control and the Division of Labour: engineers and compositors in Britain, 1890–1930', *Cambridge Journal of Economics*, III (1979), p. 272; R. Penn, 'Skilled Manual Workers in the Labour Process', in *The Degradation of Work?*, pp. 99–100.
[3] Elger, 'Braverman, Capital Accumulation and Deskilling', p. 28.
[4] P. H. Sadler, 'Sociological Aspects of Skill', *British Journal of Industrial Relations*, VIII (1970), pp. 29–30.

gender affects the distribution of work and, hence, rewards. Feminist critics of his work have shown how gender structures the labour market and leads to the sexual division of labour.[5] The labelling of women's work as unskilled or, at best, semi-skilled regardless of the tasks involved allows employers to pay a lower rate of wages. At the same time, it creates a workplace hierarchy of skills, which reinforces masculine concepts of authority and power found in the wider society and, in turn, leads to the subordination of women both economically and socially.

These concerns are central to any discussion of the development of the labour process in the Scottish cotton industry. However, in analysing the changing distribution of skills and the restructuring of workplace hierarchies, it has to be remembered that in each sector of the industry – spinning, thread and weaving – we are dealing with a different labour process. In the nineteenth century technological changes and their impact on the labour force were more far reaching in spinning than in weaving. Because of this we shall take each sector in turn, examining the extent and rate of technological change, the impact this had on the nature and character of work, and, finally, what this meant in terms of the sexual division of labour.

1. *Cotton Spinning*

Regardless of the level of technology, the spinning of cotton involves a series of simple processes involving the drawing and twisting of raw fibres to a required degree of fineness, then winding them on to a cop. The degree of fineness is measured in counts, which is determined by the number of hanks, each of 840 yards in length, obtainable from a pound of yarn: the lower the count (that

---

[5] See, for example, V. Beechy, 'The Sexual Division of Labour and the Labour Process: a critical assessment of Braverman', in *The Degradation of Work?*, pp. 54–73; A. Phillips and B. Taylor, 'Sex and Skill; notes towards a feminist economics', *Feminist Review*, 6 (1980), pp. 79–88; J. West, 'Women, Sex and Class', in *Feminism and Materialism*, ed. A. Kuhn and A. Wolpe (1978), pp. 220–53.

is, less than 50s) the coarser the yarn; the higher the count ('medium' being 50s–90s, 'fine' being 80s–150s, and 'superfine' being 150s–300s) the finer the yarn.[6] While essentially a simple operation, cotton spinning, as the nineteenth century wore on and production was mechanised and housed in factories, became an increasingly complex operation. The pre-industrial domestic spinner working at home on a simple jenny gave way, under the impact of power-driven machinery, to a complicated division of labour, a bewildering number of processes, and machinery of a highly sophisticated nature. Although the basic process of drawing and stretching remained, the transformation of raw cotton into yarn for weaving or sewing was divided into four stages, each with its specialist machines and operatives.

The first involves operations for opening and cleaning, which is carried out by machines known as bale breakers, openers, scutchers and carding machines. The workers manning these machines mix the cottons into the required proportions and then remove impurities from the raw cotton. By the time the raw cotton reaches the second stage of the process there is nothing to be removed except knotted pieces, short fibres and other small impediments, and the material is formed in long coils or strands held in cans.

The second stage is concerned with laying the fibres parallel to each other and attenuating the collected strand. The drawing frames used in this part of the process produce a sliver not much thinner than that achieved on the carding machine, but the fibres are all lying parallel, which is essential for the third stage of twisting. If the yarn is to be especially fine then combing will be introduced before the drawing process. Combing increases the parallelisation of the fibres and results in a large amount of waste, because of which it was rarely used.

In the third stage the sliver is further attenuated and twisted. This is performed by slubbing, intermediate and roving frames, and, in the case of fine yarns, jack frames. The slubbers draw the slivers out to their fullest extent without damaging the strength of the

---

[6] J. Mason, 'Cotton spinning in the Industrial Revolution', in *The Barefoot Aristocrats: a history of the Amalgamated Association of Operative Cotton Spinners*, ed. A. Fowler and T. Wyke (Littleborough, 1987), p. 2.

fibres, and as they emerge from the rollers they are given a slight twist, then wound on to bobbins. These bobbins are passed to an intermediate frame, being placed in the creel above the frame, and then fed to the roving frame. Each stage sees a reduction in the thickness of the coarsely twisted yarn, and a corresponding decrease in the size of the bobbin on to which the yarn is wound.

The fourth stage is the actual spinning and twisting of the yarn itself into various counts on either mule, ring or throstle spinning machines. A further sophistication of spinning yarn is doubling, by which two or more strands of yarn are twisted together. As this process was strongly connected with thread making we will say more about this later.

The production stage which has caused most controversy and which underwent the greatest change is spinning. The transformation of cotton spinning began with the application of power to drive the machinery and obliged a transition to factory production. Most of the early cotton mills were dependent on water power and were thus located in the countryside, near fast flowing rivers. These mills adopted Arkwright's water frame for spinning, which was later adapted to throstle spinning. Most of the early ventures employed women and children since the work was light, even if the hours were long. The invention of Crompton's mule allowed for the use of steam power and facilitated the erection of cotton mills in urban areas. Rather than bringing workers to isolated rural parts, cotton masters could now tap in to the labour supply of the towns and cities. The power mule was dominated by male spinners as it demanded great physical strength. In spite of power assistance in the putting up of the carriage developed in 1825, as late as 1837 it was estimated that a mule spinner had to put up a 1,400lb carriage 5,000 times in twelve hours, or seven times a minute, which was the equivalent of raising 160lbs vertically over a distance of six feet in three seconds.[7] Such demanding effort made women unlikely

---

[7] I. Cohen, 'Workers' Control in the Cotton Industry: a comparative study of British and American mule spinning', *Labor History*, 26 (1985), pp. 62–3; W. Lazonick, 'Industrial relations and technical change: the case of the self-acting mule', *Cambridge Journal of Economics*, 3 (1979), pp. 231–62.

competitors in this line of work, although there were seventy female mule spinners in Glasgow in 1837.[8]

Another reason why males dominated hand mule spinning was that the work involved the supervision of other workers. Each spinner was assisted by three or four piecers, usually little girls, whose job it was to repair broken threads and remove the cops when formed.[9] Other assistants were also female. The creeler placed the rovings from which the yarn was spun in the creel, and the scavengers removed the cotton waste, or 'fly', and kept the machines clean.[10] Around three-quarters of the labour force in a spinning flat of a mill were adolescents and children.[11] The piecers were recruited and paid by the adult male spinner, and employed in the various stages of spinning according to age.

The 'inside' piecer was the youngest at between eight and ten years of age. When a few years older the child would progress to 'outside piecing'. Although there was no formal apprenticeship system, young male piecers would learn the art of spinning from seventeen onwards.[12] By this system of inside contracting the employers were spared the problems of recruiting labour and the added costs of supervision, all of which were borne by the adult spinner. The disadvantage of such an arrangement for the employer was that the supply of labour and the production process were dependent upon the spinner. The great power of the spinner to disrupt production was recognised at an early stage by Andrew Ure, who wrote in 1836 that:

> ... proprietors of cotton mills were ... subject to great disarrangement of business, and consequent loss, from the frequent turn-outs and other acts of insubordination by 'spinners', by which acts not only were their assistants thrown out of employ, but also

---

[8] First Report of the Select Committee on Combinations of Workmen, PP, 1837–8, VIII, q. 1339, pp. 66–7.
[9] Webb Collection on Trade Unions (BLPES), XXXIV, f. 406.
[10] A. Ure, *The Cotton Manufacture of Great Britain*, vol. 2 (1836), pp. 194–5.
[11] J. Butt, 'Labour and Industrial Relations in the Scottish Cotton Industry during the Industrial Revolution', in *Scottish Textile History*, ed. J. Butt and K. Ponting (Aberdeen, 1987), p. 142.
[12] *Combinations of Workmen*, qs. 411–19, p. 18.

in respect of each 'spinner', three or four other persons employed upon machines required to prepare the cotton previous to being spun . . .[13]

Control of the labour process became the major issue of confrontation between the masters and men prior to the strike of 1837. Short of breaking the spinners' union, the employers experimented with altering the balance between the various methods of spinning, and thereby altering the structure of workplace relations. The first of these was to encourage the spread of throstle spinning, which would allow women to replace men in increasing numbers. The throstle was based on Arkwright's water frame and was ill-equipped to spin all but the coarsest counts. The machines were driven by water power and for that reason had to be located in country areas. These drawbacks encouraged the displacement of the throstle by the hand mule and by the opening years of the nineteenth century it was claimed that 'very few water frames or throstles were left in the country'. However, the progress in power loom weaving saw an upsurge in demand in the 1830s for water twist, which, because of its 'strength and wiry smoothness', was particularly well suited to the warps of the power loom. The throstle underwent a number of improvements and it was hoped by some manufacturers that in years to come it would supersede the hand mule on all counts of 50 and under.[14] As it was light to operate its popularity increased the demand for women and children.

These hopes were not realised in full as improvements in the hand mule saw it outstrip the throstle in terms of costs, efficiency and output. The hand mule was worked by the spinner without an external source of power. This gave way to machinery propelled by steam power, with the exception of putting up the carriage, and working the guide for the building of cops. Even the lower cost of employing women on throstles could not compensate for the advantages to be gained from mule spinning. Firstly, the cops of the power mule held three times that of the throstle, which involved

---

[13] Ure, *Cotton Manufacture*, vol. 2, p. 195.
[14] J. Montgomery, *The Theory and Practice of Cotton Spinning* (Glasgow, 1836), p. 169.

less labour for the winders, and less time in doffing the cops; secondly, the power required for spinning was found to be two to one in favour of the mule, as was the quantity of oil used in lubricating the machinery; and, thirdly, the wear and tear on throstle bobbins was greater than on mule cops.[15]

Although the physical demands of mule spinning made the occupation a male monopoly, women spinners as we have seen were not unknown. However, employers were of the opinion that the labour of women was inferior to men's and that they turned out less.[16] In an influential article, Friedfeld has recently argued that it was also the policy of the union to exclude women from mule spinning, and because of this they denied them membership at their congress of 1829 and refused to train girl piecers as mule spinners.[17] But the evidence for Scotland is somewhat contradictory during this period. Testimonies from both employers and trade unionists before the Select Committee on Combinations of Workmen (1837–8) pointed to the fact that while the spinners' union found the employment of women disagreeable, owing to the arduous nature of the work, their main concern was to ensure that women were not paid 'at under the rate of wages' for men.[18] The union dispensed advice to the women on how to calculate their piece rates and even suggested they go on strike from time to time.[19] As Peter McNaught, cotton master, pointed out the union had not interfered with the employment of women since 1825 as many of the female spinners were relatives of the males.[20] However, it was also noted by another employer that the number of female spinners was declining.[21]

This meant that women were reduced to finding work as piecers. Cohen, in an influential article, has argued that male spinners

---

[15] T. Ellison, *The Cotton Trade of Great Britain* (1886), p. 38.
[16] *Combinations of Workmen*, qs. 642–3, p. 29.
[17] M. Friefeld, 'Technological change and the "self-acting" mule: a study of skill and the sexual division of labour', *Social History*, 11 (1986), p. 334.
[18] *Combinations of Workmen*, q. 1341, p. 67.
[19] *Combinations of Workmen*, qs. 1341–2, p. 67.
[20] *Combinations of Workmen*, qs. 638–9, p. 29.
[21] *Combinations of Workmen*, q. 1344, p. 67.

preferred male piecers to female for two reasons: firstly, it was from the males that the future generation of spinners was to come; and, secondly, piecing on a mule for twelve hours a day was too physically demanding for a female, since it involved, on long mules, walking the equivalent of twenty-five miles a day.[22] However, in a Scottish context what this meant was that the labour of children under the age of thirteen was abandoned for that of young men and women above that age. From accounting for 13.3 per cent of the total workforce in 1836, the number of children fell to just 2.1 per cent in 1847.[23] Bolin-Hort has claimed that this was due to the reluctance of the Glasgow employers to take on the responsibility of educating their young workers as laid down in the Factory Acts and to the relatively good supplies of adolescent labour.[24] However, employment returns would show this explanation to be misleading. In 1836 the age cohort 9–13 accounted for 16.6 per cent of the total workforce in cotton spinning, while the age group 13–18 numbered 30.3 per cent, with those over eighteen accounting for the rest.[25]

If Bolin-Hort's explanation is valid then we should witness over the next ten years a significant increase in the medium age cohort. However, Factory Returns for 1847 point in a very different direction. Although the Returns only provide employment data for the whole of the industry, rather than sectoral totals, they are still useful since we know that very few children were employed in power loom weaving. The Return of 1836 accounts for 1,103 children under thirteen employed in combined spinning and weaving factories, while in the more detailed Return of 1850 there were only five, compared to 250 in spinning.[26] If change of any magnitude in the age profile of the industry occurred it was likely to have taken place in the spinning sector. Therefore, the Returns for 1836 and 1847 are comparable.

From the latter Return it would appear that it was the age cohort

---

[22] Cohen, 'Workers' Control', p. 63.
[23] Ure, *Cotton Manufacture*, vol. 2, p. 357; Factory Returns, PP, 1847, xlvi.
[24] P. Bolin-Hort, *Work, Family and the State: child labour and the organisation of production in the British Cotton Industry, 1780–1920* (Lund, 1989), pp. 249–51.
[25] Factory Returns, PP, 1836, XLV, pp. 89–90.
[26] Factory Returns, PP, 1850, X.

18 + which experienced the largest increased share of employment, as the following table shows:

Table 13. *The distribution of employment by age groups in the Scottish cotton industry in 1847*

Under 13	%	13–18	%	18 +	%	Total	%
745	2.2	11,707	33.3	22,664	64.5	35,116	100

[Source: *Factory Return*, PPXLVI (1847), p. 8]

The oldest cohort had increased its share of employment by 11.4 per cent in the period 1836 to 1847, almost exactly the equivalent fall in the under-13 cohort. Until 1853, furthermore, legislation was rather vague regarding the definition of a working day for children. Employers could work children for the legal limit any time between 5.30 a.m. and 8.30 p.m., while adult females had a regulated working day of 6 a.m. to 6 p.m., or 7 a.m. to 7 p.m.[27] However, in spite of the incentive of more flexible working arrangements, employers preferred the labour of older to younger workers. Therefore, distribution of skills was based on the technical characteristics of the machinery rather than on relative wages, educational requirements or the supply of adolescent labour.

However, in Scotland most of the piecing duties were performed by women. Indeed, the view expressed by Cohen that women were somehow incapable of performing physically demanding or, indeed, skilled work in the cotton industry is suspect. Evidence shows that in the 1820s women in Scotland were working short mules of 250 spindles,[28] and most mules in Glasgow until 1837 were 200–300 spindles.[29] Whereas previously it was thought that 80 spindles were too many for a woman to cope with, the invention in 1825 of power assistance in putting up the carriage overcame problems

---

[27] B. L. Hutchins and A. Harrison, *A History of Factory Legislation* (1966 edn), pp. 108, 111.
[28] Fiedfeld, 'Technical change', p. 334.
[29] W. Sloan, 'The supply of labour for cotton spinning in Scotland *c*.1780–1836' (Undergraduate dissertation, Department of History, University of Strathclyde, 1980), p. 31.

connected with strength in spinning and opened the way for the employment of more women. Moreover, the skill in guiding the cop was something which could be performed by women, as in matters of dexterity there was and is little to choose between men and women. As Lazonick points out in regard to the English cotton industry, it was less the requirements of strength and dexterity which kept women out of spinning, than the internal contracting system, which established a workplace system of hierarchy and authority.[30] The spinners were responsible for the hiring and payment of their piecers, and it was felt by management that only men were capable of performing supervisory roles in the factory. Thus, it was less a question of skill and strength, and more the maintenance of patriarchy which kept women from spinning in large numbers. However, before leaving the question of women and work, it is important to point out that according to Andrew Ure the most physically demanding task in the process of turning raw cotton into yarn was battening cotton by hand (similar to threshing corn). This was a task wholly performed by women.[31]

The superiority of the power-driven mule over the throstle only served to increase the power of the male workers over the labour process and the supply of labour. The Glasgow cotton master, J. Houldsworth, spoke of an informal apprenticeship system by which young boys entering the mill at the age of nine were trained gradually until the age of seventeen or eighteen when they qualified as spinners.[32] As most of them were the sons or relatives of existing spinners, the adult male spinners were able to control and regulate the supply of labour. Advances in spinning technology had enhanced the power of labour in the workplace. Because of this many attempts were made 'to invent a mechanism which would dispense with the labour of the "spinner", or render the mule what is termed "self acting" '.[33]

The first successful self-acting machine was invented by Richard

---

[30] Lazonick, 'Industrial relations and technical change'.
[31] Ure, *Cotton Manufacture*, vol. 2, p. 311.
[32] *Combinations of Workmen*, qs. 411–19, p. 18.
[33] Ure, *Cotton Manufacture*, vol. 2, p. 196.

Roberts of Manchester in 1825, and further improved in 1830. Andrew Ure defined a self-acting mule as one which self-acts in the sense that 'steam or other power, not manual . . . cause[s] the mule to go through the whole of its required movements to spin the yarn, retain[ing] only the subordinate persons to piece the threads, fill the creels, clean the mules, etc'.[34] With the self-acting machine there was no requirement to put up the carriage or guide the cop building, which meant, in fact, there was 'no spinner required'.[35] This view was shared by some employers in Glasgow. Charles Todd, master spinner, when asked by a member of the Select Committee on Combinations of Workmen (1837–8) were his machinery based on the self-acting principle would he be able to dismiss all his spinners, replied: 'Every one of them'.[36]

In spite of its obvious advantages over the hand mule, the universal adoption of the self-acting mule was impeded by several factors. Technically, there was still scope for improving the efficiency and output of existing mules. Employers in the 1830s and, particularly, the 1840s began to couple mules together and to introduce longer mules. Short mules were coupled in groups of three by having the drawing gear adjusted so that the movement in one was transmitted to the other two. This meant that six mules, or three pairs, were worked by one spinner. Newer mills introduced long mules, which saw the number of spindles increase from an average of 200–300 before 1837, to an average of 600 after this. This not only reduced the number of female spinners, but it also saw wages fall for mule spinners. In the case of Glasgow, mule spinners saw their wages only slightly increase from 22s. a week for 300 spindles to 24s. for 600, in spite of a doubling of productivity.[37] As Watson noted, the 'reduction in the cost of spinning helped to retard the introduction of the self-acting mules for some time'.[38]

Running costs and technical problems of adapting the self-actor to spinning anything other than coarse counts also retarded the

---

[34] Ure, *Cotton Manufacture*, vol. 2, p. 196.
[35] J. Watson, *The Art of Spinning and Thread Making* (Glasgow, 1878), p. 254.
[36] *Combinations of Workmen*, qs. 521–3, p. 241.
[37] Friedfeld, 'Technical change', p. 335.
[38] Watson, *The Art of Spinning and Thread Making*, pp. 254–5.

spread of the new machine. The self-actor, as it revolved 5,000 times per minute, not only needed more power, but also more oil to lubricate it. The greater intensity at which the machine was run involved more repair work than on the hand mule. Breakages were more frequent and, in general, wear and tear were greater.[39] Moreover, it was found that hand mules were better on fine spinning than self-actors. Many employers retained the throstle for spinning coarser counts, particularly in the country mills. New Lanark in 1851 operated 22,800 throstle spindles.[40] Because of this, it was not until the late 1850s that the self-actor mounted a serious challenge on the medium counts, and not until the 1880s did it supersede the hand mule on counts up to 90s.[41] A cotton operative was able to write in 1854 that the 'mania for self-acting has been succeeded by that of long mule hand spinning, and the labour and responsibility of the operative greatly augmented'.[42] The usefulness of the hand mule in spinning finer counts gave it a working life greatly beyond what might have been expected from it. According to the Webbs, the last hand mules in Glasgow were done away with around 1887.[43]

For Andrew Ure the impetus behind the introduction of the self-actor was the desire of some of the employers to discipline 'refractory' spinners and limit their ability to disrupt production.[44] This view has been recently reiterated by Mason, who argues that the self-actor was introduced as a 'strike breaking weapon at Preston and Glasgow'.[45] Although there is some evidence which points to the introduction of self-actors of 250 spindles in Glasgow in the period 1835–40 being operated by young men and women with child piecers,[46] this is to misunderstand the issues behind the strike

---

[39] Watson, *The Art of Spinning and Thread Making*, p. 257.
[40] J. R. Hume, 'The Industrial Archaeology of New Lanark', *Robert Owen: prince of cotton spinners*, ed. J. Butt (Newton Abbot, 1971), p. 242.
[41] Mason, 'Cotton spinning', p. 5.
[42] *Glasgow Sentinel*, 18 Feb. 1854.
[43] Webb Collection, xxxiv, f. 413.
[44] Ure, *Cotton Manufacture*, vol. 2, pp. 195–6.
[45] J. Mason, 'Spinners and Masters', *The Barefoot Aristocrats: a history of the Amalgamated Association of Operative Cotton Spinners*, ed. A. Fowler and T. Wyke (Littleborough, 1987), p. 37.
[46] Webb Collection, xxxiv, f. 406.

and underestimates the economic incentives for employers in installing self-actors. The strike of 1837 was not about the introduction of new technology, or the employment of women, but was initiated by the employers' decision to couple existing mules, which would reduce wages proportionately and employment absolutely.[47] With the union effectively defeated after the strike the employers had a free hand to dismiss male spinners and introduce women and young men on self-actors, but as we have seen the latter machine was slow to spread. However, coupling had the effect, according to Houldsworth, of dismissing 'thirty or forty spinners' in Glasgow[48] – a rather paltry number considering there were estimated to be a thousand male spinners in Glasgow at this time.[49]

The introduction of the self-actor was more a matter of economics than anything else. The self-actor even in its unrefined state was superior to the hand mule on the spinning of counts below 18. Under the latter method the work was laborious, involving the spinner walking many miles every day,[50] something which was avoided by the former method. Moreover, early meticulous studies undertaken by Montgomery into the relative costs of the two methods seemed to point to greater cost savings on the self-actor. Montgomery obtained comparative statements as to costs and output from several Glasgow manufacturers who were operating both self-actors and hand mules. After making allowances for the extra charges and insurance on installing self-acting machines, Montgomery was of the view that the saving made by the spinning master in using self-actors to produce 359,424 hanks of yarn was £13.[51] Therefore, it would appear that the cost savings were a strong inducement to replacing the hand mule with the self-actor, providing the technical difficulties, which, as one Glasgow manufacturer pointed out, gave 'considerably more trouble with the self-acting, than with the hand

---

[47] *Combinations of Workmen*, q. 808, p. 39.
[48] *Combinations of Workmen*, qs. 336–9, p. 15.
[49] W. H. Fraser, 'The Glasgow Cotton Spinners, 1837' in *Scottish Themes*, ed. J. Butt and J. T. Ward (Edinburgh, 1976), pp. 81–2.
[50] Watson, *The Art of Spinning and Thread Making*, pp. 257–8.
[51] J. Montgomery, *The Cotton Manufacturing of the USA compared with that of Great Britain* (Glasgow, 1840), p. 80.

mules',[52] could be overcome. And as we have noted above in a relatively short period of time the long hand mule was more favoured by employers.

The technical problems with the self-actor meant that it was never automatic in Ure's sense, in as much as it could substitute young, low skilled piecers for skilled adult labour. Kurte Neste in his production manual, *The Mule Spinning Process* (1865), stated that the adjustment of the quadrant nut on the self-actor still had to be performed by hand, a skill similar to that of controlling the faller wire on the hand mule.[53] As Friedfeld points out, additional tasks such as the detection of improper roving on yarn production, the fixing and repairing of band straps, and so on, all fell within the remit of the spinner's work load.[54] Thus the desideratum of a deskilled workforce was still some way off and it was not until 1885 that the process was simplified.[55] The premium placed on skill in spinning on self-actors saw men, particularly in England, continue to monopolise the position of spinner and retain craft status. Why and how they were allowed to do this is a matter of some debate among historians, since on the surface it was more economically rational for employers to use lower-cost female labour now that the self-actor had obviated the need for strength as a criterion for the job.

Various theses have been advanced to explain the continuing domination of the spinning process by male workers. Cohen has argued that it was the power of the unions and their control of the apprenticeship system which led to the exclusion of women from the highest paid employment.[56] On the other hand, Lazonick points to the supervisory functions carried out by the males over their helpers and their ability to recruit labour which 'secured the occupation of mulespinning for men'.[57] These views have been rejected

---

[52] Montogomery, *Cotton Manufacturing*, p. 79.
[53] H. Catling, 'The development of the spinning mule', *Textile History*, 9 (1978), p. 51.
[54] Friedfeld, 'Technical change', p. 327.
[55] Catling, 'The development of the spinning mule', p. 51.
[56] Cohen, 'Workers' Control'.
[57] W. Lazonick, 'The subjection of labor to capital: the rise of the capitalist enterprise', *Review of Radical Political Economics*, X (1978), p. 9.

by Friedfeld, who argues that the unions were weak during the years 1837–42 and 1846–9, the crucial period of the self-actor's introduction, and were therefore not in a position to enforce apprenticeship restrictions.[58] Friedfeld also dismisses Lazonick's thesis for exaggerating the loss of skill among mule spinners in operating the self-actor.[59] Rejecting the theses offered by Cohen and Lazonick as inadequate, Friedfeld puts forward an alternative thesis based on skill transmission. She argues that the coupling and lengthening of mules which took place in the 1820s in England and after 1837 in Scotland effectively displaced women from spinning positions. 'Male strength', she claims, 'was . . . preferred by mill owners on these longer mules because men produced a greater quantity of yarn.'[60] The removal of this female stratum from spinning meant that at the vital stage of the introduction of the self-actor 'a cohort of women had not been trained in the mechanical skills of mule-spinning for a decade. In essence, a breakdown or discontinuity in skill transmission had occurred'.[61] Thus while in Scotland the majority of workers in a mule spinning room 'were women . . . they were unskilled piecers, not "minders" '.[62]

Persuasive as these interpretations might seem, they have little or nothing to offer in the case of Scotland. After the failure of the 1837 strike the spinners' union in Scotland was a pale shadow of its former self and lacked the power to enforce rules regarding apprenticeship. The cotton industry in Scotland was noted more for union weakness than strength. The Friedfeld thesis regarding the breakdown in skill transmission also has little applicability to Scotland. Although Scottish employers followed the example of their English competitors and coupled and lengthened mules, the survival of throstle spinning meant there was still a relatively large pool of trained female labour, particularly in the country mills, such as New lanark and Catrine. In 1857, for example, James Finlay's Catrine mill employed 145 mule spinners, of which eighty-nine,

---

[58] Friedfeld, 'Technical change', p. 339.
[59] Friedfeld, 'Technical change', pp. 319–20.
[60] Friedfeld, 'Technical change', p. 335.
[61] Friedfeld, 'Technical change', p. 337.
[62] Friedfeld, 'Technical change', p. 340.

or 61 per cent, were women. Additionally, there were ninety women spinning on water frames.[63] Moreover, by only concentrating on the final stage in the spinning process, that is, the actual spinning of the yarn, Friedfeld has neglected intermediate stages, such as slubbing and roving, which also involved some spinning skills.[64] According to the 1886 Wage Census, these preparatory tasks were performed, at least in Scotland, by women, and had been for a long time.[65] The extent of piecing duties performed by females is also of importance when considering recruitment into the ranks of spinning. A bank of skills still existed in the Scottish industry, which, in spite of coupling and lengthening, could be tapped into and adapted without too much difficulty by employers and female workers alike. Such a large discontinuity in the process of skill transmission from one generation of female cotton workers to another seems unlikely to have occurred in Scotland or, indeed, England.

However, more contentious is Friedfeld's claim that women in Scotland were confined to piecing and did not operate self-actors. The Webbs are clear that the first self-actors brought to Glasgow after the 1837 strike were worked by 'young lads and women' assisted by child piecers.[66] Employment returns make clear that there were as many female as male minders in Glasgow, with women working the shorter mules.[67] Writing in 1854, a cotton spinner anxious to prove the flexibility of spinners towards new technology, referred to the 'great mania that prevailed eight to ten years ago for self-actors . . . [which] the spinners in tens and in scores seen their places filled up with boys and girls and they submitted both patiently and intelligently'.[68] Although the mania for self-actors declined somewhat in the late 1840s and in the 1850s, the aftermath of the cotton famine saw an increase in their number and in the

---

[63] Historical Accounts of James Findlay & Co. (Business Archives, University of Glasgow, UGD 91/19).
[64] J. Nasmith, *Modern Cotton Machinery – its principles and construction* (1890), p. 147.
[65] Return of Wages in the Textile Trades, PP, 1889, LXX, p. 60.
[66] Webb Collection, XXXIV, ff. 381–6.
[67] Bolin-Hort, *Work, Family and the State*, pp. 257–8.
[68] *Glasgow Sentinel*, 18 Feb. 1854.

amount of females operating them. The industrial correspondent of the *Glasgow Herald*, describing the opening of Robertson's Newhall cotton factory in Bridgeton, Glasgow, in 1871, stated that while in the past a 'greater part of the work [in cotton spinning] used to be done by hand labour, various circumstances led to the introduction of self-acting mules, and now the thing is done by machinery under the supervision of girls'.[69] This observation is underscored by an earlier report of a strike in October 1863 at J. and W. Scott's cotton factory in Bridgeton. It was reported that a meeting of self-acting spinners and piecers was mainly made up 'of young women'.[70] The Returns of Wages for 1866 mentions for the first time women in Glasgow minding self-acting machines spinning counts from 4–24 and from 25–40 and earning between 13*s*. 6*d*. and 19*s*. 6*d*. a week.[71] On the other hand, there seems little evidence to suggest that male spinners operated anything other than hand mules. The Returns of Wages for 1866 does not list men minding self-actors, although a later return for 1886 lists them as minding those machines spinning 40–80 counts.[72] Thus, if men operated the self-actor, they certainly did not establish a monopoly over it.

With women working alongside men as spinners, it is also clear that the internal subcontracting system, which was the bedrock of patriarchy and the hierarchical workplace structure of cotton spinning, did not operate in the Scottish industry in the same way as it did in England. The Scottish employers prohibited their mule spinners from taking piecers under the age of thirteen and refused them the right to pay and hire and fire them. The *Glasgow Sentinel* in 1861 described the authority structure in mule spinning in Scotland thus: '... the masters had the entire power of employing and paying off piecers, and ... their number and wages are settled by an arrangement between the master and the spinner at the starting of the wheels'.[73] As Bolin-Hort concludes, mule spinners in the Glasgow district 'had very little influence in the subcontracting

---

[69] *Glasgow Herald*, 19 Jan. 1871.
[70] *Glasgow Sentinel*, 24 Oct. 1863.
[71] Returns of Wages, 1830–1886, PP, 1887, LXXXIX, p. 58.
[72] Returns of Wages, 1830–1886, p. 59.
[73] *Glasgow Sentinel*, 29 June 1861.

relationship and a low degree of authority over recruitment compared to the Lancashire operatives'.[74] These factors serve to emphasise the peculiar development of the spinning sector in Scotland, and the importance of the struggle between labour and capital in shaping the labour process, and the system of workplace relationships based upon it. Had the spinners, rather than the masters, been successful in the 1837 strike the future structure of the industry would have been very different.

The labour process in spinning was to undergo further changes in the post-1860 period. The industry was forced to recruit more and more female labour as rival industries siphoned off existing male labour. As early as 1860 factory inspectors were speaking of a crisis in the supply of labour. In spite of booming conditions and rising wages, the Factory Report was forced to conclude that the 'scarcity of hands is everywhere severely felt, and much machinery standing for want of workers'.[75] Failure to recruit male workers into the trade in sufficient numbers saw the introduction of what the Webbs described as the 'multi-pair system' in the 1880s. The system was first introduced around 1880 in Grant's mill, Glasgow, primarily 'out of economy',[76] and spread to other mills. Instead of minders and piecers, the new arrangement was based on doffers and piecers. Under it a male doffer supervised four pairs of mules with two women each acting as piecers in weft, and also five and a half pairs of mules with three women piecers in warp.[77] The restructured labour process redefined the sexual division of labour in spinning and led to the deskilling of female labour. The technical skills of adjusting and repairing the machinery, as well as supervision of the piecers, were appropriated by the male doffers. The women piecers, or 'guiders', were divided by age and task into those responsible for 'spinning', and those responsible for rove piecing, in a ratio of three to one in favour of the former.[78]

The other important change in the labour process, although

---

[74] Bolin-Hort, *Work, Family and the State*, pp. 256–7.
[75] Factory Report, PP, 1860, XXXIV, p. 10.
[76] Webb Collection, XXXIV, f. 431.
[77] Webb Collection, XXXIV, f. 413.
[78] Webb Collection, XXXIV, f. 429.

occurring on a smaller scale, was the introduction of ring spinning from the United States in the 1870s. Ring spinning was based on the same principles as old-fashioned throstle spinning,[79] but was revolutionary in the sense that it was much faster and more continuous than the mule. On the mule winding and spinning were intermittent actions, while on the ring frame they were both simultaneous and continuous. Ring spinning also offered cost and other advantages. The machines took up half the space of the mule and, therefore, could produce more yarn per square foot of plant as the latter. A trial lasting ten weeks demonstrated that 6560 Rabbeth ring spindles produced 17.25 ounces of yarn per spindle per week, while 3,592 mule spindles, occupying the same floor space, produced only 13.07 ounces.[80] Moreover, being less complex in construction the ring frame was less liable to break down. A greater amount of time was saved in piecing on the ring frame as a result.[81] Beyond these technical considerations, the other advantages related to labour costs. Ring frames required only unskilled labour and, therefore, could be operated by cheap female and child labour with very little training.[82]

Given the degree of feminisation which had occurred in the cotton spinning sector in Scotland, ring spinning had obvious attractions for employers. Indeed, Scottish employers were more ready to adopt the new technology than their English competitors, although on a much reduced scale. Excluding doubling spindles, the total spindleage in operation in Scotland in 1901 was 558,471. Of this number 166,994, or 29.9 per cent, were ring spindles, the rest being mule spindles. The equivalent figures for England and Wales were 43,314,641, of which 6,151,161, or 14.2 per cent, were ring spindles.[83] Counties and individual firms had ratios of rings to mules higher and lower than those included in national figures. In 1901 Lanarkshire boasted a ratio of just under four mule spindles to one

---

[79] Nasmith, *Modern Cotton Machinery*, p. 234.
[80] Ellison, *Cotton Trade*, p. 34.
[81] M. T. Copeland, 'Technical Development in Cotton Manufacturing since 1860', *Quarterly Journal of Economics*, XXIV (1910), pp. 126–7.
[82] Copeland, 'Technical Development', p. 127.
[83] Factory Return, PP, 1903, LXIV, p. 4.

ring, while in Renfrewshire, thanks to the predominant position of thread manufacture, the ratio was under two to one in favour of mules.[84] In the most advanced cotton spinning works in Glasgow, the Glasgow Cotton Spinning Company, the ratio was 93,000 mule to 36,000 ring spindles, about the average for Lanarkshire.[85]

Although Scottish employers were quicker to embrace the new technology than their English counterparts, the question remains as to why they did not go further than they did. The cost savings in ring spinning over mules were of such a magnitude that a revitalised and competitive spinning sector in Scotland was not inconceivable. The development of the Japanese cotton industry after 1890 showed how a predominantly young and inexperienced female workforce, who by modern standards were clearly 'children',[86] operating a small number of ring spindles per worker could be highly successful.[87] With replacement of mules by rings the output of cotton yarn in Japan doubled between 1899 and 1913 to over 670m lbs, and by 1913 the country was exporting a quarter of the world's exports of cotton yarn and half of its own output.[88] However, there remained strong barriers to the wholesale adoption of ring spinning even in the more favourable conditions existing in Scotland. These barriers were the result of a series of inter-connected factors which included the labour supply, the product and its market, the economic and technical aspects of cotton spinning in late nineteenth-century Scotland.

---

[84] Factory Return (1903), p. 4.
[85] Worrall's Textile Directory: Ireland, Scotland and Wales (Oldham, 1900–1).
[86] G. Saxonhouse, 'Two forms of cheap labour in textile history', *Research in Economic History*, Supplement 3 (1984), p. 6. The annual turnover rate was 420–460 per 1000 female employees in the Japanese cotton spinning industry; see G. Saxonhouse, 'A tale of Japanese technological diffusion in the Meiji period', *Journal of Economic History*, XXXIV (1974), p. 164; A. S. Pearse, *The Cotton Industry of Japan and China* (Manchester, 1929), p. 100.
[87] G. Saxonhouse and G. Wright, 'Rings and mules around the world: a comparative study in technological choice', *Research in Economic History*, Supplement 3 (1984), pp. 289–90; Factory Returns, PP, 1878–9, LXV, pp. 3–4; PP, 1884–5, LXXI, pp. 3–4; PP, 1898, XIV, p. 209.
[88] J. Hunter, 'Recruitment in the Japanese Silk Reeling and Cotton Spinning Industries, 1870s–1930s', *Proceedings of the British Association for Japanese Studies*, 9 (1984), p. 65.

Ring spinners in Japan achieved high returns on their investment by employing 'child' labour for long hours, using a shift system, on sophisticated technology. Clark's study of the world cotton industry shows that in 1910, when compared with England, Japanese mills operated hours which were three times longer; its manufacturing costs were just over one half; and its implied profit rate over three times greater.[89] Labour utilisation on this scale was denied to Scottish producers as they had to depend on half-timers. As we have seen, however, the system where children spent half their day in class and half in the factory never gained a strong foothold in Scotland. It was only the thread factories of Renfrewshire which used child labour in significant amounts, but even here the number was declining as the nineteenth century wore on. From a peak in 1878 of 7.4 per cent, or 1,002, of the total number of workers employed in spinning, children under the age of thirteen declined to 5.8 per cent, or 739, in 1885, and fell again to 633, or 5.5 per cent in 1895. Of the latter total, 562 half-timers were employed in Renfrew.[90]

The Education of Scotland Act of 1872, which introduced compulsory education for working-class children between the ages of five and thirteen, and the subsequent improvements to it, affected potential supplies of child labour. Although it was possible to gain an exemption (or Labour Certificate) from the provisions of the 1872 Act for children over ten years of age if they showed proficiency in the fifth standard, this loophole was closed with the passing of the 1901 Scottish Education Act. The legislation ended the practice of exemption by examination and this was only granted in necessitous cases by school boards.[91] By 1909 Margaret Irwin claimed that 'we have no half-timers in Glasgow', and the only large centre of half-time employment in Scotland was the Dundee jute industry.[92]

Any attempts to revitalise the Scottish cotton spinning sector along the lines of the Japanese industry were obstructed by the

---

[89] G. Clark, 'Why isn't the whole world developed? Lessons form the cotton mills', *Journal of Economic History*, 47 (1987), p. 126.
[90] Factory Returns, PP, 1878–9 LXV; 1884–5, LXXI; 1897, XVII.
[91] S. Cooper, *The 1872 Education Act in Lanarkshire* (Hamilton College of Education Publications, 3, c.1973).
[92] *The Woman Worker*, 21 April 1909.

growth of state intervention in education. Factory legislation had also brought in the recognised working day of 6 a.m. to 6 p.m. or 7 a.m. to 7 p.m. for women which made shift working in cotton mills, except for adult males, illegal. Moreover, the supply of cheap adolescent labour for the Japanese mills had predominantly come from rural areas, where expectations were low, and waged work was sought simply to provide a dowry.[93] Rural depopulation in Scotland had made the countryside an unlikely area of recruitment for Scottish mills. From 1851 onwards less than three per cent of the total occupied female labour force in Lanarkshire and Renfrewshire was employed in agriculture (see tables 3 and 4, pages 22, 23) Scottish employers were forced to compete with other trades for relatively more expensive labour in the urban areas. Thus, the potential productivity gains to be had from employing young workers on ring spinning were denied to Scottish employers.

Replicating the Japanese recipe for success through the use of cheap labour on ring spindles was also inhibited in Scotland by product/market concerns. Since Scottish weavers had been in the process of abandoning the production of coarse and plain fabrics before 1860 in favour of finer and fancier cloths,[94] spinners tended to concentrate on yarns of higher counts. This favoured mule spinning as the greater strain on the ring frames militated against it being used for spinning higher counts.[95] Also, given the collapse of the combined spinning and weaving factories and the increased specialisation in the later part of the nineteenth century, labour and transport costs became an important factor in deciding the choice of technique. Ring spinning used wooden bobbins, while mules used paper cops. As the cops held more yarn than the bobbins they required less doffing, which meant a saving on labour time. If the yarn was sold away from the place of production the freight charges on bobbins was much higher than that of mules since they held less, and weighed more than cops. Moreover, they also had to be

---

[93] Saxonhouse and Wright, 'Two forms of cheap labor', p. 5.
[94] A. J. Robertson, 'The Decline of the Scottish Cotton Industry, 1860–1914', *Business History*, 12 (1970), p. 122.
[95] Copeland, 'Technical development', p. 126.

returned, which was an additional expense. A contemporary estimated that the cost of carrying mule cops was 10 per cent of the freight charge on the yarn, while that of bobbins was 200 per cent.[96] Scottish producers faced increased freight charges on the bobbins in shipping weft yarn; therefore, it was only integrated spinning and weaving mills which could maximise benefit from the adoption of ring spinning as was the case in the United States.[97] The cyclical nature of cotton production also made it unlikely that Scottish employers would add to sunk costs by investing heavily in new technology. A cotton mule had a life expectancy conservatively estimated at sixty to seventy-five years.[98] To commit oneself to a replacement meant expressing a vote of confidence in the future of the industry, something Scottish employers were not prepared to do in a major way. As we have seen in the last chapter they preferred to experiment with altering the mix of variable capital, rather than add to fixed assets.

Thus, the potential lifeline offered by the introduction of ring spinning in the period after 1880 was spurned in the main by Scottish entrepreneurs. They had taken it up more enthusiastically than English spinners, but the impediments to universal adoption were too great to overcome. Spinners in Scotland fell back on the cheap labour of women organised in a labour process after 1880 which reinforced their subordination to men, but did little to increase their productiveness. In spite of using a greater amount of female labour than English spinners, at lower rates of wages, the factory inspector for Scotland was forced to conclude that 'Even though lower wages may be paid in Scotland, it is doubtful if the cost of production is not even greater'.[99]

---

[96] Copeland, 'Technical development', p. 126.
[97] Copeland, 'Technical development', p. 130.
[98] Saxonhouse and Wright, 'Rings and mules', pp. 281–3.
[99] Factory Report, PP, 1884, XVIII, p. 45.

2. Weaving

The process of turning yarn into woven cloth comprises an interdependent series of stages. Before weaving can take place the yarn has to be wound, warped, beamed, sized, dressed, drawn and twisted. As each stage in the process requires its own peculiar set of skills weaving, like spinning, involves a complex division of labour. However, weaving differs from spinning in as much as there is a clearer sexual bias in the distribution of work and rewards and a horizontal system of occupational hierarchy which intensified the subordination of women in the workplace. As we shall see, although women did the actual weaving, the labelling of women's work as unskilled allowed men to appropriate the 'skilled' jobs and to be paid craft rates. The refusal of employers and male workers to recognise the skills of the women power loom weavers and to pay them accordingly led to output constraints. This gradually undermined the competitiveness of the cotton weaving industry of Scotland and saw it lose out to the more productive weavers of Lancashire, especially in the area of plain cloth production, but also increasingly in the production of fine or fancy cloths. The refusal of the women weavers of Scotland to operate more than two looms, while those of Lancashire were working three and four, was seen by contemporaries, and by more recent observers, as perhaps the major cause of the industry's decline in the late nineteenth century.[100] The 'two loom' question thus becomes a major issue in understanding the decline of cotton weaving, but the intransigence of the weavers can only be appreciated through an understanding of the labour process.

The first stage in preparing yarn for weaving is winding or, more correctly, re-winding. The winders re-wind the yarn from bobbins or cops on to cone shaped spindles, a process which also has the effect of cleaning the threads and correcting bad piecing. This work was carried out exclusively by women and young girls.[101] The next stage is warping, in which a sufficient number of bobbins are placed

---

[100] Factory Report, PP, 1890–1, XIX, p. 7; Robertson, 'Decline', p. 124.
[101] Returns of Wages in the Textile Trades, PP, 1889, LXX, pp. 60–1.

in a bank, with the number determining the breadth of the web. The warper is also responsible for making sure that the yarn is put on to the beam in the right quantity. Once accomplished it is the task of the warper to keep a watchful eye for broken threads and to repair them as quickly as possible. The job was mainly carried out by men, but women were also employed in a ratio of two women to three men.[102] After warping had been completed, the web was sized, that is, starched or glued before beaming. The beamer put the warp on to the beam. The task was an exclusively male one, as reflected in the formation of a small craft society of beamers – the Glasgow Power Loom Beamers' Society. The final preparatory tasks involved the drawing and twisting of the thread on to the headles before going on to the reed, and were also performed by males. The loom was then ready for weaving; a task carried out exclusively by women and girls.[103]

According to the 1886 wage sample census, the organised male craft workers received nearly three or four times as much in wages as women weavers. The average weekly wage rate for male beamers on piecework was 29s. 11d., while male tenters received 42s. 7d. By contrast women weavers working two looms received 10s. 10d. a week on piecework.[104] The existence of differentials of these magnitudes poses several questions relating to the relationship between skill and the level of reward. Were the low wages of the women weavers the result of minimal skill requirements, or were they a pertinent example of the way that skill in the workplace is socially constructed? The resolution of these issues is important in understanding the unwillingness of the female weavers to operate more than two looms.

There seems little doubt that plain or coarse weaving on power looms, involving only one colour, was little more than machine minding. *Griffin's Book of Trades* (1854) remarked that steam looms only required to each pair of looms 'a boy or a girl to mend such

---

[102] Returns of Wages in the Textile Trades, pp. 59–61.
[103] Returns of Wages in the Textile Trades, p. 60; J. Watson, *The Theory and Practice of the Art of Weaving by Hand and Power* (Glasgow, 1863), pp. 156–77.
[104] Returns of Wages in the Textile Trades, pp. 59–61.

threads as may be accidentally broken'.[105] However, as Robertson pointed out, from the 1850s the policy of the Scottish weavers was to turn from coarse to fancy goods production.[106] Indeed, it was said that since 1870 in the fancier aspects of weaving, that is, coloured and white check goods, lappets, harness work and flushed beads, 'there is no country in the world that can, as yet, compete with Glasgow'.[107] Writing in the late nineteenth century, Margaret Irwin was of the opinion that production of ginghams and zephyrs needed 'much technical knowledge' on the part of the weaver.[108] Her views were shared by other commentators both inside and outside the industry. An old female power loom weaver, in a letter in early March 1874 to the newspapers regarding the shortfalls in the labour supply, claimed that:

> few young girls have gone to learn the looms for some years past, for it will now take months to learn instead of weeks . . . for the style of work and the machinery now are quite different from what they were in my day. It was plain white work with one shuttle box, but now . . . it is all fancy work . . . the looms are from two to six boxes, and some upwards. The work is so difficult that weavers will have nothing to do with learners, as they would only spoil the pattern and do other damage.[109]

Writing some twenty-six years later, the Scottish Council for Women's Trades described the occupation of weaver as one requiring 'health, strength, neatness, steadiness [and] intelligence. This industry employs a superior class of working women and is, on the whole, one of the trades to be highly recommended'.[110] This

---

[105] *Griffin's Book of Trades* (Glasgow, 1854), pp. 215–16.
[106] Robertson, 'Decline', p. 125.
[107] J. Campbell, *History of the Rise and Progress of Power Loom Weaving* (Rutherglen, 1878), pp. 10–11.
[108] M. H. Irwin, 'On the conditions of work in the textile industries of Glasgow and in the calico printing and turkey red dyeing on the Vale of Leven', *Royal Commission on Labour*, PP, 1893–4, pt. 1, XXXVII, p. 173.
[109] Campbell, *Rise and Progress of Power Loom Weaving*, p. 15.
[110] Scottish Council for Women's Trades, *Occupations for Girls: a guide to girls in selecting an employment* (Glasgow, 1900?).

assessment was shared by the women weavers themselves, who were said to feel that they were 'highly skilled worker[s]'.[111]

Although demanding a fair degree of skill and technical knowledge, power loom weaving of fancy goods did not require the female weaver to serve an apprenticeship. Skill transmission was achieved through a system of learnership based on family networks. Mary Paterson, factory inspector, provides some insight into how skill was transmitted from one generation to another when she remarked that, in the weaving sheds of the east end of Glasgow, 'I found that here more than elsewhere it was customary for the whole family (at least, the feminine portion of it) to be employed at the same work, generally in the same mill or weaving shed. The eldest sister brought in the younger ones in turn and gave them the necessary instruction in the craft'.[112]

The system was different to that of England as learning did not begin until the age of fourteen and the working life of a weaver was, in general, shorter.[113] South of the border, the half-time system socialised Lancashire children into the factory culture and allowed them to pick up rudimentary skills from an early age.[114] These tenters, as they were known, under the tutelage of an older weaver were gradually put on two looms, and after reaching a certain standard were made up to four looms by the overseer or the mill manager.[115]

Such a long, graded introduction to the work of a weaver was never adopted to any great extent in Scotland. A male machine dresser, giving evidence to the Factory Commissioners in 1876, claimed that during his working life he had never come across a

---

[111] M. Paterson, 'Memories of a Woman Inspector', *Scots Magazine*, 13 (1930), p. 366.

[112] Paterson, 'Memories', p. 366. This means of recruitment and training was also prevalent in the shipbuilding trades, particularly among riveters; see A. MacKinlay, 'The Inter-War Depression and the Effort Bargain: shipyard riveters and the "workman's foreman"', *Scottish Economic and Social History* 9 (1989), pp. 55–70.

[113] Irwin, 'On conditions of work', p. 173.

[114] Bolin-Hort, *Work, Family and the State*, p. 261.

[115] M. Savage, 'Women and Work in the Lancashire Cotton Industry, 1890–1939', in *Employers and labour in Textiles*, ed. J. A. Jowitt and A. J. McIvor (1988), p. 209.

half-timer in the Scottish power loom weaving trade.[116] His experience is borne out by sample studies based on census enumerator books for Bridgeton in 1851 and 1871. From a sample of 214 households in the Bridgeton area of Glasgow in 1851 containing at least one cotton worker a total of 101 females connected with power loom weaving were found, of these only six were found in the age cohort 10–14. Twenty years later, and using a slightly larger household sample, 16 out of a total number 210 workers in weaving were found to be in this age group.[117] The 1895 Annual Factory Return confirmed this trend, recording only thirty-nine half-timers out of a total workforce of 16,020.[118]

Moreover, the working life of a weaver in Scotland was shorter than her English counterpart. Irwin reported in the early 1890s that the working life of a female weaver in Scotland was only nine years, and that married women constituted only around six per cent of the total number.[119] The 1901 Census, the first to distinguish between the various occupations in the cotton industry, largely supports Irwin's findings. Sixty per cent, or 2,202 out of a total of 3,716 power loom weavers in Lanarkshire, were under twenty-five.[120] A later official return on employment in textile factories in Glasgow put the number of married women as only 836, or 11 per cent, out of a total of 7,396 female employees over eighteen years of age in 1907.[121] In this respect the position of Scotland contrasted sharply with England. Savage's study of women workers in the Lancashire cotton industry shows husbands and wives working together in the weaving sheds as weavers, an arrangement which accounted for the unusually low birth rates in towns like Burnley.[122] The family economy of the Lancashire weaving industry allowed manufacturers to retain the labour of their most skilled and

---

[116] Select Committee on the Factory and Workshops Act, PP, 1876, xxx, qs. 16557–60, p. 788.
[117] Census Enumerator Books: Bridgeton (1851 and 1871).
[118] Factory Return, XVII (1897), XVII, pp. 169–71.
[119] Irwin, 'On conditions of work', p. 173.
[120] Eleventh Decennial Census of Scotland, PP (1904), CVII.
[121] Returns of Employment in Textile Factories, PP, 1909, LXXXIX, p. 8.
[122] Savage, 'Women and Work', p. 211.

productive workers for longer periods, and ensured themselves of a regular supply of labour. By contrast, in Scotland the majority of the best workers left the industry before the age of twenty-five, and the employers constantly complained of the lack of trained labour, a fact noted by the correspondent of the *Textile Manufacturer*, who commented that 'The scarcity of hands is a curious feature in this decline in the trade'.[123] An attempt by an employer to introduce male labour into weaving was abandoned after the men left, being 'Unable to stand the ridicule to which they were daily exposed for taking up "women's work" '.[124]

The expansion of the labour supply in Scotland through increasing the employment of males was made impossible not only by the labelling of weaving as women's work, but also, and more importantly, by the existence of the tenters' society. Unlike in England, where tenter was the name given to a half-timer, a tenter in Scotland was a time-served male worker who enjoyed craft status. Once out of his apprenticeship the tenter performed a variety of functions in the weaving trade. He was responsible for overseeing the work of about eighty looms, putting in and taking out the web for the female weavers, as well as performing managerial tasks such as recruiting, disciplining and organising the female weavers. For the employers the tenting system of organising the labour force had its advantages and disadvantages. In the first area, as a low cost alternative to the erection of a middle tier of management it economised on expensive labour. One manufacturer in 1891 claimed that even if the tenters received an extra 10s. per week it would only amount to a half per cent on turnover.[125] Moreover, as the wages of the tenter were dependent on the output of those under his control it was in his interest to drive the women to meet production targets. The drawback in the system was that it afforded control of the labour supply to the tenters as employers had to apply to the latter's union for replacements.[126] The rules of the tenters' society allowed

---

[123] 15 May 1890.
[124] M. H. Irwin, 'Women's Industries in Scotland', *Proceeedings of the Philosophical Society of Glasgow*, XXVII (1885–6), pp. 72–3.
[125] *Glasgow Herald*, 7 May 1891.
[126] *Glasgow Herald*, 1 May 1891.

only women and young girls to work the looms, thus restricting the supply of labour and keeping out male workers, who might be promoted to overseers. The unscrupulous use by some employers of apprentice labour in the mid-1860s in tenting looms had led to the imposition of a highly restrictive ratio of men to apprentices or learners.[127]

The acceptance of a patriarchal mode of authority relations within the workplace by employers deprived them of the means to challenge the power of the tenters in the crucial areas of the supply and control of labour. Without an expansion in the numbers of tenters it was impossible to increase total employment. For an employer to do so arbitrarily would have disrupted production in a highly competitive industry as the tenters withdrew their labour. This was especially important in an industry which relied on highly profitable small batch production. The employers were faced with two options, both of which were connected. Firstly, they could increase the output per weaver by forcing them to operate more than two looms, or, secondly, adopt a new technology which would reduce their reliance on skill and allow workers to tend more looms. The latter option was made possible by the invention of the Northrop automatic loom in the United States, which was introduced to deal with the problem manufacturers had in 'obtain[ing] enough weavers'. The Northrop loom allowed for massive savings to be made on labour, with weavers tending from fourteen to thirty looms, whereas prior to its introduction they tended six to eight.[128] However, neither strategy seems to have been workable in the context of the Scottish weaving trade, which is surprising since by 1890 plain calico production had been lost to Lancashire,[129] and the dominance of the Glasgow manufacturers in the fancy end of the trade was threatened by the cheaper imitations of the former.[130]

---

[127] *Glasgow Sentinel*, 17 Feb. 1866. Alex Gray, apprentice tenter, employed by Robertson & Co was jailed for thirty days for refusing to tent ninety-six looms. Apparently there were 1,440 looms in the factory tented by ten apprentices and ten men. A similar situation existed in Preston (Savage, 'Work and Women', p. 210).
[128] Copeland, 'Technical development', p. 146.
[129] Irwin, 'On conditions of work', p. 173.
[130] Robertson, 'Decline', p. 122.

The ability of the employers to increase the number of looms per weaver was hamstrung by the militancy of the women on this issue. The tradition of two looms per weaver was maintained throughout the nineteenth century and into the twentieth. The 1886 Wage Census sample of 2,660 power loom weavers in Scotland showed that 2,100, or 79 per cent, operated two looms, and only 560, or 21 per cent, operated three looms.[131] Twenty years later an earnings survey found that of 1,178 power loom weavers, 967, or 82 per cent, tended two looms, the remainder operating three.[132] The stubborness of the women weavers on the two looms issue was the subject of much contemporary criticism. From 1890 onwards there were repeated attacks on the position of the female weavers made by the factory inspectorate. The weavers' attitude was depicted in the reports of the inspectorate as irrational, particularly when contrasted with that of Lancashire women. The hostility this induced in the inspectors towards the Scottish weavers is well captured in an extract from the 1890 report. The chief inspector, Henderson, remarked that:

> There are no operatives of whom I have ever had an experience who work with so much energy as the Lancashire people, and the contrast between a Scotch and a Lancashire weaving factory in this respect is very remarkable. The Lancashire weaver works with a will, she earns a high wage (on an average double that of her Scotch sister on the same class of work), and is anxious to maintain it. She will take charge of four power looms without hesitation; and, indeed, her energetic industry is not unfrequently an embarassment to the inspector, for it makes her indifferent to the provisions of the Act of Parliament which has been passed for her protection. She has practically to be driven from her work . . . In Scotland . . . it is common to find weavers of long experience with only two power looms, and it is with difficulty that they can be persuaded to take a third. Such is the recognised contrast between the two classes of cotton operatives . . .[133]

---

[131] Returns of Wages in the Textile Trades, PP, 1889, LXX, p. 61.
[132] Report on Earnings and Hours of Labour: 1. Textile Trades, PP, 1909, LXXX, p. 57.
[133] Factory Report, PP, 1890–1, XIX, p. 71.

For Henderson the inability of the Scottish weaving trade to compete with Lancashire lay not with the employers, but 'more with the workpeople'.[134] In the official version the feckless and lazy Scots workers were at the root of the problem.

Attempts had occasionally been made to force the female weavers to operate more than two looms. As early as 1858, A. & A. Galbraith of Glasgow attempted to restructure customary workloads by assigning one operative with the assistance of a young girl to tend four looms. The action provoked a strike which led to management backing down.[135] Another attempt was made by a Glasgow employer in 1890 to introduce a three loom per weaver system, but, in spite of the intervention of the Glasgow Trades Council and the Women's Protective and Provident League as mediators and the promise of higher wages for operating more looms, the weavers refused even to sanction an experiment.[136]

The position taken by weavers on the two loom issue raises questions regarding the irrationality of their behaviour and their weak commitment to the work ethic. As we have seen this is how their attitude was viewed by the factory inspectorate and by sympathetic labour bodies, such as the Trades Council. However, the psychological approach to understanding the two loom question obfuscates the issues involved because it is dominated by a shared subjective and value-laden concept of the work ethic on the part of middle-class professionals and respectable workers. It is also flawed because it abstracts the question of work from the realities of the labour process and the economics of the production system.

Charges of a workforce being lazy are very subjective. American weavers tended six to eight looms before the introduction of the Northrop automatic loom, which increased the load to anything between fourteen and thirty looms. When the Lancashire employers attempted to increase the number of looms to the pre-Northrop American equivalent in the early 1900s it led to a prolonged strike.[137]

---

[134] Factory Reports PP, 1890–1, p. 71; 1892, XX, p. 23; XVII, p. 102.
[135] *Glasgow Sentinel*, 14–21 Aug. 1858.
[136] Irwin, 'On conditions of work', p. 176.
[137] Clark, 'Why isn't the whole world developed?', p. 169.

Did the refusal of the English weavers to tend more looms mean that their commitment to the work ethic was of a lesser degree than their American counterparts, and that relative differences in technology, product and market played no part in deciding the loom load? It might also be appropriate to ask whether the situation in Scotland was highly unusual when compared to worker/loom ratios existing in other countries producing cotton cloth? As Clark points out in his study of the world cotton industry, there were various arrangements regarding the number of looms per worker: 'In India the struggle was over two looms per weaver as opposed to one, in Russia three versus two, in France and Mexico four versus three, and in Britain six versus four'.[138]

Although we might be able to decide which nationalities were the most productive, the differing ratios of looms per worker in each of the countries does not allow us to draw conclusions as to which of them worked hardest. Japanese mills operated twice as long as English mills, but the weavers there only tended 1.6 looms compared to 3.8 in England.[139] Therefore, the possibility of drawing conclusions as to the laziness or otherwise of Scottish weavers from looms operated per worker is negligible. It is also interesting to note that in the debates which took place in the *Glasgow Herald* and the *Textile Manufacture*, in the period 1889–1 regarding the relative decline of the Scottish weaving industry, none of the participants mentioned the loom question as a major cause of the industry's problems. Trade unions, the unwillingness of workers to assist each other, shortage of labour, higher transport costs, unfair competition from England, and inadequate machinery were given as principal reasons for decline.[140]

Leaving the question of aptitude aside as too subjective to be of much help in understanding the loom question in Scotland, we can turn to more productive areas concerned with the nature of weaving and the payments system based upon it. The weaver was responsible

---

[138] Ibid, p. 169.
[139] Ibid, pp. 147, 152.
[140] *Textile Manufacturer*, 15 May 1890; *Glasgow Herald*, 27 April 1889, 1 May 1889, 5 May 1889, 12 May 1889.

for rectifying the errors of all the workers who preceded her in the process of cotton manufacture. Whether it was the lumpy knots of the warper, or whatever, it was her job to put them right. The fancier the article, the more complex the pattern, the greater was the strain placed on the weaver, as failure to mend breaks or undo knots in the thread ruined the expensive finished product. Given that by 1890 Scottish manufacturers had almost given up producing plain cloth in favour of fancier goods, the attentiveness needed by a weaver in Scotland was far greater than that demanded of a plain cloth weaver in England.

By taking on more looms the stress on the weaver intensified, as did the risk of producing faulty work. Indeed, even under the two loom system there were recurring complaints by the women regarding fines for bad work, which occasionally led to strikes.[141] From the late 1850s the fear that the introduction of four loom working on fast machines would lead to more fines for bad work was expressed by the weavers.[142]

The problem, however, was compounded when the female weavers were supplied with inferior yarn. Mary Paterson, factory inspector for Glasgow, recalled that in 1901 the main complaint of the weavers 'was the steady deterioration in the quality of yarn'. Breakages were so frequent 'that they never got their heads up', and this had 'a lamentable effect on earnings'.[143] Bitterness over this issue led sometimes to industrial action, as in Paisley in March 1897, when weavers withdrew their labour.[144]

Increasing the number of looms to be tended also had to be set against a higher frequency of breakages and lost production in repair work. As Lazonick has noted, the higher the number of looms per weaver, the greater the number of stoppages. By reducing the number of looms to be tended the machines could be run at a faster rate with less interruption, leading to higher ouput per loom, and a lower total unit factor cost.[145] However, in England this

---

[141] See, for example, the strike at Henry & Son reported in *Glasgow Sentinel*, 7 Feb. 1863. See also *Glasgow Herald*, 17 May 1908, for more information on this issue.
[142] *Commonwealth*, 14 Aug. 1858.
[143] Paterson, 'Memories', p. 367.
[144] *Glasgow Evening Times*, 10 Mar. 1897.

option was unavailable to employers due to the strength of the weavers' union. Weavers, used to a relatively good wage, would not accept the kind of reductions in wages that this strategy involved. In spite of this, there was a tendency even in England to slow down the increase in looms per weaver. During the period 1870 to 1886 the number of looms per weaver was increasing by one per cent *per annum*, but over the next twenty years this fell to 0.2 per cent *per annum*.[146]

Scottish employers, working under fewer constraints with a younger, unorganised workforce, saw the economic benefits of a higher intensity throughput per loom. In 1908 the *Glasgow Herald* reported that while 'formerly one woman was given two or even three looms to look after . . . in many cases they are [now] confined to one'.[147] Accompanying this trend was the intensification of the work effort. From the 1890s onwards, to maintain wages women on piece work worked extra hours which contravened the Factory Acts. The extra work involved women working meal breaks or starting early in order to 'pick' the cloth, that is, prepare it for the warehouse, clean the looms, and carry out any other supplementary tasks.[148]

The mounting pressures on weavers in Scotland made them unlikely to accept a higher loom/worker ratio, particularly when they, unlike English weavers, had 'no real control over piece rates or wage levels'.[149] In the English trade the weavers had established price lists for weaving in the decades after 1850, and this was fairly uniform in Lancashire by the 1880s. As Bolin-Hort points out, the existence of price lists secured additional compensation for the weaver for taking on more looms.[150]

As we will see later, the absence in Scotland of any system of

---

[145] W. Lazonick and W. Mass, 'The performance of the British Cotton Industry, 1870–1913', *Research in Economic History*, 9 (1984), pp. 25–6.
[146] Lazonick and Mass, 'British Cotton Industry', p. 26.
[147] *Glasgow Herald*, 17 May 1908.
[148] Irwin, 'On conditions of work', p. 175; see also the *Glasgow Herald*, 17 May 1908.
[149] Bolin-Hort, *Family, Work and the State*, p. 263.
[150] Bolin-Hort, *Family, Work and the State*, pp. 263–4.

industrial bargaining made negotiation on this question impossible. Scottish weavers, as Margaret Irwin noted, lacked 'a uniform rate of wages for the same work throughout the trade'.[151] Individualised bargaining and the highly competitive nature of weaving manufacture in Scotland meant that wage rates varied from firm to firm, and that in most cases they were fixed on an arbitrary basis. An alteration in the customary workload of two looms per weaver brought no guarantees to the workers that they would be better off. Higher wages for tending more looms might have been followed by a lowering of piece rates, which would have made the weavers relatively worse off for accepting an increase in their workload.[152]

This view was expressed by the weavers during a strike in August 1858 at the works of A. & A. Galbraith, Glasgow. The weavers argued that although the adoption of a four loom load would lead to an immediate increase in earnings 'the rate at which they are now paid would be reduced in a short time'. There was also the subsidiary fear that the number of workers would be reduced.[153]

When these factors are taken into consideration the defence by the weavers of their customary workload seems far from irrational. In the absence of powerful bargaining structures, indeed, it appears a wholly sensible and logical strategy on their part. But if the employers failed to modify the two loom system, why did they not seek to restructure the labour process by adopting the automatic loom? The Northrop loom was developed in the United States to simplify weaving skills in order that manufacturers there could tap in to the large pool of unskilled labour. Before its invention, the expansion of output had been constrained through inadequate supplies of labour. The automatic loom also saved on labour since, as we noted above, it increased the worker/loom ratio.[154] As Scottish manufacturers had long suffered from the same problem, in theory, at least, it seemed as if the invention of the Northrop loom was

---

[151] Irwin, 'On the conditions of work', p. 174.
[152] Bolin-Hort, *Family, Work and the State*, p. 264.
[153] *Commonwealth*, 14 Aug. 1858.
[154] Clark, 'Why isn't the whole world developed?', p. 146.

the means of leading the industry out of its spiral of decline. Before 1914, however, the Northrop loom had made little inroad into Scottish and English weaving sheds. On the eve of the First World War automatic looms were only one or two per cent of the total number of British looms, while in America they accounted for 40 per cent.[155] While in the English case the reason may have had much to do with the power of the weaving unions to inhibit the spread of the new technology, the Scottiish manufacturers suffered far less in this respect. However, in spite of the obvious advantages in adopting the new weaving technology, the latter set their faces against this course of action.

The reasons are partly technical and partly economic. The complementary nature of spinning and weaving meant that a technical time lag in one process had a knock-on effect on the other. This was evident during the early industrial revolution when the mechanisation of spinning took place first, forcing the pace towards a similar breakthrough in weaving at a later date. Similarly, the automatic loom was dependent on the introducion of ring spinning on an extensive scale as the mule cop was not so well adapted to the hopper of the machine as was the bobbin of the ring frame.[156]

The delay in adopting ring spinning in a major way significantly inhibited the spread of the automatic loom. But the most important technical impediment to the widespread acceptance of the Northrop loom was the fact that, although it had gradually been adapted to weaving fine cloths, 'it is not adapted to the weaving of fancies'.[157] Since fancies were the staples of the Scottish weaving trade by this time, the loom appeared irrelevant to the Scottish manufacturers' needs. However, even if these technical difficulties could have been resolved, there still existed economic barriers to its installation in Scottish weaving sheds. As Copeland points out, the automatic looms were expensive to purchase and install.[158] Given the cyclical nature of the cotton industry in Scotland and the unpredictability

---

[155] Lazonick and Mass, 'British Cotton Industry', p. 2.
[156] Copeland, 'Technical development', p. 149.
[157] Ibid, p. 150.
[158] Ibid, pp. 147, 150.

of the market for fancies, which had witnessed the collapse of the embroidered muslin trade in 1857, Scottish weavers were unenthusiastic when it came to adding to their fixed assets. Another problem was the seasonal nature of the trade which rendered looms idle and threw weavers out of work. A jobbing weaver, in a letter to the *Glasgow Herald*, explained how the large manufacturers had taken advantage of the depression in the 1880s to engineer a greater move towards seasonality of production. He claimed that:

> In order to keep the looms going the goods of one season must be started before those of the previous season are finished, but that is precisely what the manufacturers take care to prevent. The policy they pursue is to hold back the orders of one season till the orders of the previous season are fulfilled; by this means they empty the looms, throw the workers idle, and coerce the weaver into taking prices that they know very well are far below what the goods cost to weave . . . then and only then the orders are sent out, and the usual result is that more orders are sent out in two months than can be woven in four months. But as the prices are fixed in advance the weaver cannot raise his prices.[159]

The exploitation of the jobbing or commission weaving branch of the trade by large manufacturers was a strong disincentive to holding anything resembling fixed capital. The commission weavers leased, rather than owned, weaving factories; they bought warps and wefts from manufacturers and wove them for a fixed price;[160] and sought to economise on capital rather than labour.

Failure significantly to reorganise the labour process, or to alter the customary workloads of the female weavers, resulted in the continuance of labour-intensive production, which, as we have seen, intensified, rather than declined, in the first decade of the twentieth century. Only by depressing wages, encouraging a greater throughput per loom, and operating within tight profit margins, were the Scottish weavers able to hang on to the fancy branches of the trade. However, it was on an unceasing downward spiral. Competition in the fine goods trade was already being experienced

---

[159] *Glasgow Herald*, 27 April 1889.
[160] *Glasgow Herald*, 27 April 1889.

from Lancashire, as well as from overseas countries, such as France in the North African market, and in the Orient from India.[161] This competition could only have been met by increasing productivity in the industry and by introducing new product lines. But by this time the weaving trade of Scotland was burdened with outdated machinery and a haemorrhaging of labour. Moreover, low wages and uncertainty of employment saw few new workers wishing to train as weavers. Starved of labour and capital the Scottish weaving industry atrophied.

3. *Thread*

The labour process in thread manufacture had strong affinities with cotton spinning, as much of the technology was shared, but the structure of the workplace hierarchy more closely resembled that of weaving. This was evident from the outset of the industry's development: a phenomenon which owes more to accident than design. It emerged during the Napoleonic wars when, after the promulgation of the Berlin decrees in 1806, the supplies of silk to the heddle-makers of Paisley were interrupted. Peter Clark, one of the founders of the famous Clark and Co., hit on the idea of using cotton as a substitute for silk in the production of heddles, and by doubling the yarn as in the process of making rope, he discovered a new material of the required durability and strength. The technology Clark used is something of a mystery, but by using fine cotton yarn instead of silk he had a cheaper input and a guaranteed supply. Thus, although originally viewed as a stop gap, cotton soon supplanted silk yarn in the making of heddles, and eventually superseded linen as the main sewing thread in Scotland and elsewhere.[162] With the later invention of the sewing machine the demand for thread increased enormously, as did the scope and scale of the producers'

---

[161] Robertson, 'Decline', p. 122.
[162] 'The origin and development of the J. & P. Coats organisation' (undated typescript, Kinning Park Collection), p. 2.

operations. Firms such as Coats and Clarks became multi-national companies with branches all over the world, employing by the end of the century one-eighth, or 10,000, of Paisley's population.[163]

However, from the vantage point of the early nineteenth century this seemed unlikely. In 1812 the Clark family had opened a factory in Seedhill, Paisley, to develop the new thread. The finished product was sold in hanks or skeins and it was left to the purchaser to wind it into balls for more convenience. James Clark made a breakthrough in 1814 by introducing the practice of selling spools to his customer and agreeing to wind the thread on to them for 1s. 2d.; a charge which was refunded when the customer returned the spool. The idea of a spooling machine was the work of James Carlile of Paisley. At this time, the thread was wound on the spools by men using a hand wheel, and it was not until 1846 that a self-acting machine for spool turning was introduced. Through subsequent improvements, particularly the application in 1858 of William Weild's self-acting spooler, production was speeded up. The new machine was first introduced at Coats' Ferguslie mill and was said to produce between seventy and eighty gross of spools per day, using the labour of a boy or girl at 7s. a week.[164] These inventions did away with the need for hand spooling on a large scale, and as a result altered the sexual composition of the labour force. By 1857 ten thread factories in Paisley were employing 3,000 workers, of whom 2,300, or nearly 77 per cent, were women.[165] The Weild self-actor was complemented by the Conant spooling machine, which raised the poductivity of the girls in the mill by some 50 per cent. By the mid-1870s Weild had developed an improved multiple spindle automatic spooling machine and this superseded the Conant in the spooling department for all standard threads and lengths, with the exception of one-off special orders.[166] The Paisley firms of Coats

---

[163] *Paisley and Renfrewshire Gazette*, 16 Mar. 1910.
[164] 'The origins and development of the J. & P. Coats organisation', p. 3; J. B. K. Hunter, 'Economic History of J. & P. Coats: excerpts relating to the USA' (undated typescript, Kinning Park Collection), p. 40.
[165] J. Parkhill, *The History of Paisley* (Paisley, 1857), p. 108.
[166] 'The origin and development of the J. & P. Coats organisation', p. 3; Hunter, 'Economic History', p. 40.

and Clarks were also first to import ring frames from the United States for the purpose of twisting sewing cotton; the first being installed in 1866. A year later eight sample ring frames of 238 spindles were ordered from a Manchester machine maker for doubling purposes, and this led to repeated orders in the succeeding years.[167]

The Paisley thread manufacturers were at the frontier of technological development throughout the century. It was said of Clarks that they 'leave no opportunity untried of improving their productive capabilities as manufacturers. . . . they test and examine practically every new improvement or invention that is brought out'.[168] This view was shared by the historian of the Paisley thread industry, Mathew Blair, who remarked that 'The newest inventions in machinery were . . . readily adopted, no matter at what cost. All obsolete machinery had short shrift'.[169]

In addition, the firms modified existing technology and made machines of their own manufacture for which they held the patent.[170] Closer integration, with the merger of Coats and Clarks in 1896 and the establishment of the Sewing Central Agency [SCA], which included the English Sewing Cotton Company [ESCC], led to the accumulation of more advanced technical knowledge. Among members of the SCA there was a free interchange of ideas and knowledge, as well as the obvious standard pricing policies for labour and thread.

A cooperative atmosphere of this kind was conducive to increased research and development as companies shared in the costs and benefits of experimentation with different machinery and processes. Continuous trials were conducted on existing machinery in an attempt to find the optimum speed for running it to gain the maximum output. For example, at the ESCC's mill at Neilston, near Paisley, extensive tests were carried out over a period of four

---

[167] Nasmith, *Modern Cotton Machinery*, p. 239.
[168] *British Mercantile Gazette*, 15 Oct. 1876.
[169] M. Blair, *The Paisley Thread* (Paisley, 1907), p. 61.
[170] Letter from Fuller, Horsey and Cassell, acutaries, valuers and surveyors, to J. & P. Coats, 25 July 1890 (Kinning Park Collection, Box A1/3).

weeks to establish the correct speed at which to run the rewinding machine.[171]

Through the company's extensive network of mills throughout Britain it was able to test results in one mill against another, thus gaining accurate data regarding worker productivity. Neilston copwinders' productivity working on yarn with no paper tubes was compared against workers in the ESCC's mills at Pendlebury and Matlock. From the results gathered in the trials it was found that the Neilston copwinders 'are regulating their production and earnings'.[172] Information gathered through these and other experiments were passed between members of the SCA. Coats, for example, wrote to the ESCC in January 1911 advising them of the unsatisfactory outcome of trials on the Moscrop machine for testing glace thread, and as a result the latter ordered two Nesbit single thread testing machines.[173]

There is also little doubt that the Paisley thread firms' expansion into the United States was beneficial in this respect. Although the Scottish manufacturers had been selling thread in the United States from the 1840s, the transportation costs and the American tariff made their product increasingly uncompetitive. Thus, both began manufacturing there. The Clarks established a mill at Newark, New Jersey, in 1864, and they were followed by Coats six years later at Pawtucket on Rhode Island. The Kerr Thread Company also established a presence in the Newark and Fall River areas.[174] Through establishing overseas plants the Scottish thread makers benefited from technology transfer, which put them at the frontier of technical change in Britain. Inventions in the United States were tested in the mills there before exportation to Paisley, which minimised set up costs and training. The advantage of this relationship was demonstrated when Coats and Clarks, frustrated because

---

[171] English Sewing Cotton Company (ESCC), Minutes of the Executive Committee, 13 Feb. 1911 (Manchester Central Library, file M127/1/1–6).
[172] ESCC, Minutes of the Executive Committee, 25 July 1909, 16 Sept. 1910.
[173] ESCC, Minutes of the Executive Committee, 16 Jan. 1911.
[174] Paisley Museum and Art Gallery, 'Notes on the history of J. & P. Coats', p. 4; D. Keir, The Coats' Story (unpublished history, Coats Vyella, 155 St Vincent St, Glasgow, 1964), vol. 1, p. 101.

of the difficulty in getting acceptable quality yarn in sufficient bulk, decided to begin spinning operations themselves in the 1880s. At first, the work was done by mules, as experience in America had shown that ring frames were inappropriate for spinning finer counts. The increasing sophistication of the ring frame, however, saw it conquer the higher counts, and by the end of the decade it was the dominant form of spinning in the Paisley thread mills, with the mule only used for the finest counts. Without the experience gained in the United States Coats would not have invested so heavily in ring spinning.[175] Indeed, between 1870 and 1883 Coats' owners were ploughing back 43 per cent of gross profit into the firm.[176]

Trading with the United States also encouraged firms like Coats to move towards specialised forms of production. The American clothing market, which in 1855 was taking 85 per cent of Coats' output of thread, was a highly standardised one.[177] For a firm like Coats this opened up the possibility of concentrating on producing a small range of threads, with all the savings in labour and capital that involved. Production runs were longer, and economies were made in both machines and skills, as well as in make-up materials like labels and wrappers.[178] This was to have an enormous impact on the labour process in the thread industry.

Prior to the introduction of ring spinning, the process of making thread differed depending on how the cotton yarn was spun. If it was throstle spun yarn then it was ready to be bleached or dyed immediately as it had already been wound on to bobbins. However, if the yarn was mule spun, it was delivered in cops, and therefore had to be wound on to bobbins or reeled. Since, until the end of the 1880s, most of the yarn was mule spun, the labour process was determined by it rather than the throstle spun yarn. The finished product was distinguished by the fineness of the yarn and the strength of the thread. For example, 30s three cord was made from

---

[175] Private information from J. B. K. Hunter, Department of Economics, University of Glasgow (24 Jan. 1991).
[176] A. K. Cairncross and J. B. K. Hunter, 'The Early Growth of Messrs J. & P. Coats, 1830–1883', *Business History*, 29 (1987), p. 169.
[177] Hunter, 'Economic History', p. 7.
[178] Keir, *Coats' Story*, vol. 1, p. 8.

three strands of 30s single cotton; 30s six cord was made from six strands of 60s single cotton, twice as fine as the former. However, regardless of whether it was three cord or six cord the finished product was of the same thickness.[179] In addition to subsidiary operations such as bleaching and dyeing, there were seven main stages in the making of thread of whatever dimension, each involving a different machine and set of skills. The reelers put the bundled yarn into hanks; the winders, of which there were two kinds – cop winder and hank winder – put the yarn on to bobbins; if the yarn was to be of a finer quality it was warped on to a beam and made into a chain, and this also was done for the purpose of polishing, which itself constituted the fourth stage; after polishing the yarn was doubled, which should not be confused with doubling of cotton yarn as it was the raw material for the latter; from there it was put on a twisting frame where it was turned into thread; the final stage saw the thread spooled on small bobbins or spools for distribution.[180]

Before the 1880s all the cotton yarn used in producing thread was brought in from elsewhere, mainly from Lancashire. A visitor to the Ferguslie mills of Coats was astonished that no yarn was spun at the mill and that 'considerably upwards of 1,000 employees were engaged in twisting and finishing'.[181] The absence of spinning meant that most of the work in the process of thread-making was unskilled machine-minding. This was certainly the view of the employers. Replying to a letter in Febuary 1883 from the Royal Commision on Technical Instruction regarding the benefit of technical education to industry, Clark and Co. stated that 'as our manufacture is very much manufacture' skilled labourers were 'without much opportunity of exercising their knowledge'.[182] If training periods on various processes and machines are anything to go by, the tasks involved in the making of thread were not very skilled, although they did involve a phased introduction to the work. At the age of thirteen

---

[179] Blair, *Paisley Thread*, p. 27.
[180] Watson, *The Art of Spinning and Thread Making*, p. 112; I. W., 'Cotton', in *Encyclopedia Britannica*, VI (Edinburgh, 1877), p. 502.
[181] Keir, *Coats' Story*, vol. I, p. 83; *Textile Manufacturer* (May 1887), p. 14.
[182] Royal Commission on Technical Instruction, PP (1884) (iv), XXXI, p. 660.

they became full time workers in one of the various departments in the mill. Similarly there was a gradual increase in responsibility and workload. A learner, for instance, in the twisting department was only given a maximum workload after twenty-one weeks' employment. The procedure was to give a new start one to two sides of the machine to mind after two weeks on the job, then increase this to two to three after six weeks, three to four after twelve weeks, reaching a maximum of four to five after twenty-one weeks.[183] Promotion was based on seniority and a female had to mark time until a vacancy arose in one of the mills before attaining the full load and the wages which went with it. However, most other jobs took around two to three days to learn and three months to become fully proficient.[184] Simplified work tasks were necessary as labour turnover was high. In the year 1902 to 1903, out of a total of 4,495 workers 1,245, or nearly 28 per cent, left the Ferguslie mill of Coats. The most affected age group was that between fourteen and twenty, accounting for 36 per cent of leavers, with the next largest fall in the cohort twenty to twenty-five.[185]

Recruitment to millwork was achieved through family and kinship networks and early experience of workplace socialisation through the half-time system. Thread works, unlike spinning mills and weaving sheds in Scotland, made extensive use of child labour. Although the figures varied from year to year, the half-timers comprised around 14–15 per cent of the total workforce.[186] Between the ages of ten and twelve boys and girls were employed in making boxes, sweeping floors, then were transferred to more responsible tasks, such as guide cleaner, odd worker, band drawer, labeller and spool carrier as they got older.[187] In spinning departments they were used for piecing duties. The half-timers worked alternate days and their hours of work were from 6 a.m. to 6 p.m., just like the older

---

[183] Promotion Book, Twisting Department, Anchor Mill, 1909 (PMAG, file 1/5/68).
[184] Advance Book of Coats' Spinning Department (PMAG, file 1/5/6).
[185] Letter Book of J. & P. Coats (Kinning Park Collection, Box A2/1, 1906).
[186] Irwin, 'Conditions of Work', p. 192.
[187] Coats' Promotion Book for Half-Timers, Jan. 1882 (PMAG, file 1/5/34); Letter, 21 Feb.1952 (Kinning Park Collection, Box HH3).

workers.[188] Their importance to the production system of the mill was such that it was claimed by management that for 'every two half-timers who are withdrawn, in the largest department, [it] cause[s] the stoppage of four to five full timers'.[189] The dependency of Coats and other major thread firms in Paisley on child labour saw the thread interest oppose any extension of the Factory Acts which would raise the age limit of half-time scholars.[190]

In spite of the unskilled nature of much of the work in the thread mill, there was a notional hierarchy of skills among the female labour force, and a clear division of labour based on gender. Wage data from Coats' Ferguslie mill in 1878 shows that all the ancillary, non-productive tasks were performed by males at substantially higher rates of pay than those earned by the females, who were mainly confined to productive work. Although from a half to a third lower that men's rates, wage levels for female workers were reflective of varied patterns of skill among them, as the following table shows:

Table 14. *Occupations and weekly wage rates at Ferguslie Mill in 1878**

Men		Women	
Foremen	28s.	Cop Winders	14s. 8d.
Storemen	23s.	Re-Winders	8s.
Mechanics	32s. 8d.	Twiners	10s.
Joiners	39s. 8d.	Slippers	8s.
Packers	25s.	Reelers	14s.
Firemen	21s. 8d.	Hank Winders	10s. 2d.
Enginemen	23s. 6d.	Spoolers	12s. 6d.
Wood Turners	25s. 8d.	Ticketers	13s. 2d.
Dyers	25s. 6d.	Bleachers	10s.

[* 56 hour week; Source: Letter Books of Coats 24/6/78]

---

[188] Letter, 21 Feb. 1952.
[189] Letter from Coats to Rev. Dr Hutton, Paisley School Board, 4 Oct. 1881 (Kinning Park Collection, Box HH3).
[190] See opposition to 1895 private members bill to raise the limit to twelve by Coats (Works Committee, Minute Book, 5 Mar. 1895, PMAG, file 1/10/1).

While the introduction of spinning in the 1880s added a further tier to the occupational hierarchy, it in no way altered the balance of the sexual division of labour, as the mule and ring spinners were female. The labelling of women's work as unskilled was of benefit to the thread manufacturers, and as their numbers increased the wage bill for the latter fell. Cairncross and Hunter estimate that wages as a fraction of total costs were stable at around 13 per cent until 1860, then fell under the impact of the high price of raw cotton to between 8 and 10 per cent, where it stayed, in spite of the resumption of cotton supplies from America after the end of the Civil War. The authors conclude that over the period 1830 to 1883 not only were wages a small proportion of total costs, but they were about a third lower at the end of the period than at the begining.[191] By using large supplies of relatively cheap female labour, initially bequeathed to them by the collapse of the Paisley shawl trade,[192] on the most up-to-date technology, the thread firms of Paisley were able to maintain cost competitiveness over rival firms in a manner, as we have seen, unavailable to Scottish spinning and weaving manufacturers.

This raises the issue of the division of the social product. Why in the face of the large profits made by the thread firms were industrial relations peaceful and protest muted?[193] Indeed, we might go further and ask why low wages were acceptable throughout the cotton industry in Scotland? These issues, however, cannot be resolved without first examining the historical development of wages and material conditions in the Scottish cotton industry in the period c.1850–1914, and it is to this we turn in the next chapter.

---

[191] Cairncross and Hunter, 'The Early Growth of J. & P. Coats', p. 175.
[192] Blair, *Paisley Thread*, p. 32.
[193] Coats made £250,000 profit in 1876 and only paid £1,500 in taxes (Cairncross and Hunter, 'The Early Growth of J. & P. Coats', p. 169).

CHAPTER THREE

Wages and Working Conditions

WAGE DATA have a number of uses when discussing the development of the Scottish cotton industry in the nineteenth and early twentieth centuries. It not only points to the comparative advantage producers in Scotland had over their English competitors, but also tells us something about the sexual division of labour in the factory. Along with the material conditions under which work was performed, wages also have a strong bearing on the ability of firms to attract labour. However, it is clear that the labour markets in which the branches of the industry operated were not similar. There was a substantial difference between those thread firms operating in the tight labour market of Paisley, with those spinning and weaving firms in the elastic market of the Glasgow conurbation. The latter employers were also faced with the problem of increased competition in a situation of relative decline, and because of this had to adopt a regressive wage policy, particularly in regard to women, adapted to meet the realities of their circumstances.

The thread-makers faced the very opposite: decreasing competition and expanding output. As one might expect, therefore, there was a great deal of variation in wages between the main sections of the Scottish cotton trade, and between firms. Given these differences, it will be necessary to examine each part of the industry separately, before drawing any conclusions regarding the industry as a whole. Before conducting such an examination, however, we have first to discuss the issue of whether the lower wages prevailing in Scotland gave producers here a cost advantage over their English rivals.

The best available source for examining this question is Wood's study of earnings in the British cotton industry during the period 1806 to 1906. Although of great value to historians, the study does have certain limitations, the most significant being the aggregated nature of the data. Because of this a number of deficiencies emerge;

firstly, wage rates in the different branches of the trade are aggregated, which distorts any analysis of sectoral productivity; secondly, no distinction is made between male and female earnings, which is an important omission considering the high proportion of female workers employed in the Scottish cotton trade; and, lastly, the data is only concerned with nominal rather than real wages; average rather than actual earnings. However, in spite of these omissions, Wood's data shows that wages in Scotland lagged behind those in England throughout the nineteenth and early twentieth century:

Table 15. *Estimates of average weekly earnings in the British cotton industry at selected dates.*

Date	Manchester	Oldham	Preston	Blackburn	Scotland
1833	10s. 3d.	10s. 7d.	—	—	8s. 0d.
1845	10s. 9d.	—	8s. 6½d.	8s. 11d.	8s. 6d.
1850	9s. 8d.	11s. 0d.	8s. 3d.	8s. 11d.	7s. 5d.
1860	10s. 4d.	13s. 7d.	10s. 10d.	12s. 3d.	9s. 0d.
1866	11s. 9½d.	14s. 9½d.	13s. 0d.	13s. 10d.	9s. 9d.
1871	13s. 4d.	—	13s. 10½d.	15s. 0d.	10s. 10d.
1880	14s. 0d.	16s. 9½d.	14s. 8d.	15s. 3d.	—
1891	—	18s. 5d.	16s. 9d.	17s. 6d.	14s. 0d.
1900	—	20s. 0d.	16s. 11d.	18s. 11d.	—
1906	16s. 3d.	21s. 0d.	18s. 6d.	20s. 8d.	14s. 9d.

[Source: G. H. Wood, 'Statistics and Wages in the Nineteenth Century, Part XIX, Cotton Industry', *Journal of the Royal Statistical Society*, vol. 73 (1910), p. 587]

If we take the lowest wage district, Manchester, and the highest, Oldham, over the period from 1833 to 1906 and compare them with Scotland, it would seem that from 1833 to 1850 that wages were higher in the former by 21 to 22 per cent and 24 to 33 per cent respectively. From 1850 to 1906 the differences fluctuated between 18 and 9 per cent in the case of Manchester, and by 34 to 24 per cent in Oldham. This is not altogether surprising since for most of the nineteenth century wages in Scotland, even for skilled workers, were generally lower than those in England,[1] and also taking into account the far higher rates of male employment in the English cotton industry. The extensive use of females as piecers and later as spinners, as well as the dominance of women in power loom weaving, inevitably meant that the wage bill for Scottish employers would be lower. Indeed it is the female factor which is the most important factor in explaining the large differentials between the cotton producing districts.

The wage census of 1886 found that the higher the proportion of men employed, the higher the average wage. Burnley, with males making up 35.4 per cent of the total number of cotton workers, had an above average wage of £42 *per annum* per head, while the respective figures for Halifax and district were 26.5 per cent and £36 (average), with Scotland below average with 10.6 per cent and £28.[2] In respect of male labour, according to the factory inspectorate, 'The difference in the rate of wages paid to men in Scotland and England is not great if indeed there is any difference. A self-actor minder [in 1884] – that is, a spinner – in Scotland will earn on average 28s. a week, and the amount in Lancashire would probably not be very different'. However, the inspector went on to say, that in regard to female employment, 'the wages of women and girls will average 50 per cent more in the textile districts of Lancashire and Yorkshire than they do in Scotland'.[3]

Whether this gave Scottish producers a competitive edge over their rivals in England is debatable. Historians of the Scottish cotton industry have generally been of the view that despite lower wages north of the border, English producers still held a competitive advantage because of the greater productivity of their spinners and weavers.

The basis of this claim is a comment made by the factory inspectorate in its 1883 report, when it claimed that 'Even though lower wages may be paid in Scotland it is doubtful if the cost of

---

[1] R. Rodger, 'Employment, Wages and Poverty in the Scottish Cities, 1841–1911', in *Perspectives of the Scottish Cities*, ed. G. Gordon (Aberdeen, 1985), p. 42.
[2] Return of Wages in the Textile Trades, PP, 1889, LXX, p. IX.
[3] Factory Report, PP, 1884, XVIII, p. 46.

production is not even greater'.[4] No historian, however, has provided any comparative statistical evidence regarding this issue. This is not surprising since the task is made particularly difficult by the paucity of disaggreagted data concerning employment and output in the British cotton industry in the nineteenth century.

In trying to provide a satisfactory answer to the question of productivity the years 1867 and 1907 have been chosen, because of the data available. To determine total output in England and Scotland the method outlined in Chapter 1 was used. Employment totals by sector were derived from the Factory Return of 1867 and from the Census of Production in 1907. The major problem with the Factory Return was that it provided employment data under three headings: spinning, weaving, and spinning and weaving combined. Estimating the share of employment in the combined sector was solved for the year 1867 by deducting the number of power loom weavers from the total number employed, and transferring the residue to the spinning sector. This probably inflates the number of workers in the spinning sector but there was little choice.

As the Census of Production of 1907 provides no disaggregated data for employment the division between employment in the spinning and weaving sectors had to be deduced from the 1901 Census, which in Scotland's case gave an 80 to 20 split in favour of the latter.[5] By comparing the two reference years a very rough guide to the level of productivity in the respective countries can be obtained.

The approach is twofold: firstly, to divide weekly output in pounds and yards by the number of workers; and, secondly, to take account of the wage effect, that is, multiply the average weekly wage rate [in pence] by the number of workers and divide this into the weekly output of spun cotton yarn [in pounds] and woven piece goods [in yards]. By doing so we should arrive at the amount

---

[4] Factory Report, 1884, p. 46 quoted by A. J. Robertson, 'The Decline of the Scottish Cotton Industry, 1860–1914', *Business History*, 12 (1970), p. 123.

[5] The respective figures were 2,455 in spinning and 12,380 for weaving, but unaccounted for are a further 4,687 weavers (undefined) and 4,210 factory hands (textiles). Eleventh Decennial Census of Scotland, 1901, vol. 11, PP, 1903, LXXXVI.

of yarn or piece goods produced per worker and by 1*d*. of labour per week.

Table 16. *Output, workers and wages in England and Scotland (Spinning)*

	1867		1907	
	England	Scotland	England	Scotland
Average wage (per week *d*.)*	160	117	237	177
No of workers †	200000	17000	219000	3000
Weekly output of yarn (in million lbs) ‡	17.5m	.950m	29m	.192m

['Sources: * An average of wages for Manchester, Oldham, Preston and Blackburn in Wood, 'Statistics and Wages'; † Factory Return (1867) and Census of Production (1907); ‡ compiled from D. Bremner, *The Industries of Scotland* (1969 edn)]

From these figures it would appear that in 1867, excluding the wages' effect on calculations, the English spinning industry produced 87.5 lbs of yarn per worker per week, while their Scottish equivalent produced only 56 lbs, giving the former a 56.2 per cent advantage over the latter. By 1907 the lead had grown enormously with the English turning out 132.4 lbs of yarn for each worker per week, while the Scots only produced 64 lbs, giving the former 107 per cent avantage in spite of higher wages. Interestingly, over the period in question both countries experienced a rise in productivity, although it was much greater in England than in Scotland, the respective figures being 60.3 per cent and 14.3 per cent. However, if we take account of wages and ask the question how much output did a penny of labour produce, then the true cost advantage between the two countries becomes clearer.

Using the formula of output divided by the sum of wages times workers, shows that in 1867 a penny of labour produced 0.55 lbs of yarn per week in England, while in Scotland it was 0.48 lbs, giving a reduced advantage to the English spinners of 14.6 per cent. Forty years later the English producers enjoyed an increased advantage of 40 per cent, although smaller than the simple total of output per worker. Despite the fact that the wages of Scottish spinners grew marginally faster than English spinners between 1867 and 1907, the massive gap in productivity cannot be explained by this factor alone, and we will look at other reasons below.

When compared to England the weaving sector in Scotland showed itself to be even less productive than the spinning sector, as the following table demonstrates:

Table 17. *Output, wages and workers in England and Scotland (Weaving)*

	1867		1907	
	England	Scotland	England	Scotland
Average wage (per week *d.*)	160	117	237	177
No of workers	153000	22000	304000	11000
Weekly output of piece goods (in million yds)	68.25m	5.192m	134m	2m

[Sources: the same sources were used as for table 16]

Employing the identical method of calculation used for measuring productivity in spinning, the English weaving sector in 1867 produced 446.1 yards of piece goods per week per worker, while in Scotland it was only 236 yards, which gave the former an 89 per cent advantage over their Scottish competitors. By 1907 the margin had considerably widened with the English sector producing 440.8 yards as against only 181.8 yards in Scotland, increasing the advantage the former had to 143 per cent. If the wage effect is taken into account then the cost advantage of the English weavers falls to 39.5 per cent in 1867, and to 84.5 per cent in 1907. Interestingly, both sectors experienced a fall in productivity, but again in the case of Scotland is was much steeper over the period than in England, the respective figures being 100 per cent and 33.7 per cent. Clearly, as in the case of spinning, whatever method is used for calculating productivity, English weavers were more productive than their Scottish counterparts. However, the comparison may be considered an invidious one given the particular economic disadvantages the Scottish producers faced, and, in the case of the weaving sector, the intricate nature of their product.

The superior technology of English producers and, in the case of weaving, the reluctance of female weavers in Scotland to operate more than two looms ensured higher productivity rates south of the border. However, it must be remembered; firstly, that weavers in Scotland tended to work on much fancier and complex patterns and this may have affected output; secondly, the high density of male workers in the English cotton industry allowed a longer working day and for shift working as the men's hours were not restricted by the Factory Acts in the same way as women's; thirdly, the excessive use of sizing in the English weaving sector distorted not only the figures for output, but articially raised the productivity of weavers there; and, lastly, with the demise of the cotton brokerage facilities in Glasgow, Scottish spinners faced higher raw material prices because of the added cost of transporting raw cotton from Liverpool to Scotland. Transport costs were not an insignificant burden since raw cotton accounted for 61 per cent of total factor costs in the industry in 1910.[6]

These qualifications point to the need to examine in detail the experiences of the various branches of the Scottish cotton industry in respect of wages and conditions if we are to gain a deeper understanding of the reasons why the Scottish trade fell so far behind England in the nineteenth and early twentieth centuries.

1. *Spinning*

Until their defeat in the 1837 strike, mule spinners in Scotland were inside contractors, working on piece rates and responsible for the recruitment and payment of their assistants. The adult spinner, prior to the coupling of wheels, would employ three piecers and pay them weekly from 2s. 6d. for the youngest, to 4s. 6d. for the inside piecer, and 6s. 3d. for the outside piecer.[7] After deducting the wages of the piecers from his earnings, the spinner might earn from between 25s. and 35s. a week in the 1830s. Working on piece rate, the wage of the spinner was determined by the quantity rather than

---

[6] G. T. Jones, *Increasing Return* (1933), p. 105.
[7] Evidence of James McNish, spinner, in First Report of the Select Committee on Combinations of Workmen, PP, 1837–8, VII, q. 1263, p. 64.

the quality of the yarn he produced. This method of determining wages stratified the workforce by earning power. The first grade, amounting to 12–13 per cent of male spinners, earned 35s. per week and was employed on heavy coarse spinning; the second, perhaps the majority, earned between 24s. and 25s.; and the third from 12s. to 16s.[8] The coupling of wheels after the end of the 1837 strike resulted in a doubling of productivity, but not a doubling of wages. According to James McNish, cotton spinner, spinners operating one pair of wheels of 300 spindles made around 40 lbs of yarn a week. Under the new arrangements he made 75 lbs, but saw his earnings increase by only 4s. 9d. a week.[9]

From this period onwards the evidence on spinners' wages is fragmentary and sometimes contradictory. Strang's contemporary study of wages in the west of Scotland suggests that spinners were earning 21–25s. per week in 1851, exactly what it had been ten years earlier, and this increased to 20–35s. in 1856.[10] Strang fails to take into account the way in which the spinning trade continued to be stratified by earnings and skill. First-class spinners earned 6s. 6d. a day, or 39s. a week, in the period 1856–8, while those in the second grade earned 5s. 6d. per day, or 33s., and the third grade only 18s.[11] Much depended on the number of spindles a spinner minded. The lower rate was probably earned by spinners minding self-actors of 500 spindles, whereas on the higher rate it might be as many as 1,500–2,000.[12]

However, the absence of strong trade unions combined with the operation of the trade cycle saw the wage structure determined largely by the employers. Gains made in one year could be wiped out in the next, as occurred in the period February 1850 to May 1851, when a ten per cent increase in wages granted in the former

---

[8] Evidence of Angus Semple, spinner, Combinations of Workmen, qs. 9948–54, p. 47.
[9] Evidence of James McNish, Combinations of Workmen, qs. 1255–62, p. 64.
[10] J. Strang, *Report on the Returns of Registrars of the City of Glasgow, 1855* (Glasgow, 1856), pp. 3–4; 'On the Money-Rate of Wages of Labour in Glasgow and the West of Scotland', *Journal of the Statistical Society*, XX (1857), pp. 308–9.
[11] Returns of Wages, 1830–1886, PP, 1887, LXXXIX, p. 56.
[12] Strang, 'Money-Rate of Wages', p. 309.

month was reduced by exactly the same amount in the latter.[13] Similarly a rise of five per cent given by the employers was followed by a 7.5 per cent reduction in the course of 1861.[14] The operatives, in a letter to the master cotton spinners, complained that they had 'received many wage decreases' since 1837 'which they deem[ed] unfair being as the burden to them is all the greater considering they have to pay piecers, whose wages . . . have advanced 25 per cent over the same period'.[15]

The intensity of the cotton famine also affected the earnings of the spinners, as inferior Indian cotton was substituted for high-quality American. The former was spun at a lower speed and needed an extra twist, which led to a fall in output and, as spinners were paid by quantity, a reduction in wages. Spinners were said to be earning a third less than in 1860, while still having to pay their piecers full wages for the time worked.[16] This led to an exodus of male labour out of cotton spinning into the high growth heavy industries of the west of Scotland. The *Glasgow Sentinel* reported that seven spinners in the employ of A. J. Walker, of Mile End, Glasgow, were earning 60s. per week, less payment for piecers, for operating self-actors of 1600+ spindles.[17] The onset of the cotton famine of the early 1860s saw the wages of the spinners plummet. Walker's spinners saw their wages fall to 10s. 9d. per week for full-time working over the period December 1863 to February 1864. The men, it was said, 'refused to starve and so left work'.[18] After a brief recovery in wage rates following the end of the cotton famine, reductions of ten per cent were once again introduced in 1870. By the time of the 1886 wage census there were few male spinners left, with the number of men employed in cotton manufacture in Glasgow declining by a half in the decade 1871 to 1881.[19]

---

[13] *Glasgow Sentinel*, 26 July 1851.
[14] *Glasgow Sentinel*, 27 Apr. 1861.
[15] *Glasgow Sentinel*, 4 May 1861.
[16] *Glasgow Sentinel*, 8 Nov. 1862.
[17] 27 Feb. 1864.
[18] *Glasgow Sentinel*, 27 Feb. 1864.
[19] Factory Report, PP, 1884, XVIII, p. 44.

For those who remained, the average weekly earnings for working counts of 40s. to 80s. was 25s. 5d. on piecework.[20]

Women's wages, as one might expect, were substantially lower than men's, although the evidence is once again sparse. It is highly probable that those spinners operating short wheels and earning 18s. a week in the 1850s were females, and of those operating self-actors of under 500 spindles at 21s. a week some would have undoubtedly been women. A survey of two firms in 1866 shows that women spinners were earning between 19s. and 19s. 6d. a week, although it is not clear whether they paid for piecing assistance.[21]

The restructuring of the labour process into doffers and piecers some time in the early 1880s effectively redefined the skill of the female spinner and allowed employers to alter the wage rate accordingly. The wage census of 1886, taken at a downturn in the spinning trade, lists no category for female spinner, and gives the average wage rate for women piecers as 10s. 2d. a week, although the majority earned only 9s.[22] According to the Webbs, the earning of female spinners had only increased to between 10s. and 12s., although ring spinners were earning an extra shilling on the higher rate.[23]

These latter rates, however, are contradicted by the findings of Margaret Irwin. Her investigations present a highly varied wage structure, which altered between firms and individuals. At Clark's mill in Paisley she found spinners to be earning between 9s. and 11s. a week on piece rate, while in the same town two-thirds of the spinners at the Coats' mill were on 14s. per week and one third on 12s.[24] Two firms visited in the Bridgeton district of Glasgow were paying their female spinners 14s. 9d. and 14s. 6d. respectively on time rates. In spite of the acknowledged variations in wage rates among female spinners, one cannot ignore the fact that they earned less than half that of male doffers, or overseers. Even the relatively

---

[20] Returns of Wages (1889), p. 59.
[21] Returns of Wages, 1830–1886, pp. 56–7.
[22] Returns of Wages (1889), p. 61.
[23] Webb Collection on Trade Unions (BLPES), XXXIV, Textile Trades, f. 427.
[24] M. Irwin, 'The Employment of Women', in Royal Commission on Labour, PP, pt.I, 1893–4, XXXVII, p. 192.

well paid spinners of Bridgeton earned between 21s. 6d. and 24s. 6d. less a week than their overseers.[25] However, within the world of female spinning there were gradations in earnings according to the type of machine operated and the age of the operative. Female throstle spinners, who were mainly young girls, earned substantially less than those minding self-actors. Wages were 9s. 6d. in 1866 or about half those of women on self-actors.[26] In the 1870s the differential between the throstle spinner and the mule spinner narrowed to around two shillings, or around 17 per cent,[27] and this was the position until the last recorded earnings of the former in 1886, although this, as we have seen, was the result of a regrading of the mule spinners into piecers.[28]

Regardless of the level of wages, spinning was considered a light, but a very unattractive occupation for women and girls. Irwin remarked that 'Scottish women spinners are usually a much less intelligent class than the women engaged in the weaving'.[29] This view was shared by employers, one of whom commented that 'Glasgow women were very poor workers . . . inferior . . . both in skill and regularity'.[30] Part of the problem lay in the fact that spinning was not considered a desirable occupation for females. In a handbook for young workers, the work was described as 'somewhat rough' and, because of the heat, 'exhausting'.[31] The heat in the spinning mills also raised issues regarding respectability. For ordinary spinning temperatures had to be maintained around 70 to 75 degrees Fahrenheit to avoid excessive breakages in the yarn; in fine spinning it could range from 84° to as much as 105°.[32] The greater the heat, the scantier the dress of the women. Also because

---

[25] M. Irwin, 'The Employment of Women', p. 193.
[26] Returns of Wages, 1830–1886, p. 58.
[27] Factory Report, PP, 1884, XVIII, p. 45.
[28] Returns of Wages (1889), p. 60.
[29] M. Irwin, 'The Employment of Women', p. 194.
[30] Webb Collection, XXXIV, f. 427.
[31] Scottish Council for Women's Trades, Occupations for Girls: a guide to girls in selecting an occupation (Glasgow, n.d.).
[32] Report on Proposed Wages, Hours and Ages of Employment in Textile Factories, PP, 1873, LV, p. 14.

of the movements involved in piecing, which to some were sexually suggestive, girls were felt to be demeaning themselves by doing this job.[33]

The other part of the problem was one of health and the working environment. In spite of the progress made in ventilating mills, the necessity of keeping out draughts and wind, and maintaining temperatures at levels to avoid excessive breakages, saw air vents blocked up and windows in winter permanently closed,[34] all of which created a stifling environment to work in. This was intensified by the pressure in spinning flats to maximise floor space for labour and machine, and by the use of gas lighting. Even in the best ventilated modern workplaces, Irwin noted that 'the majority of girls attending the mills are thin and colourless'.[35] The primitive sanitary provisions in many mills added to the poor quality of the working environment.

Irwin's investigations threw up three major areas of concern. Firstly, nearly all lavatories were situated in the workroom, which denied the women privacy and made them vulnerable to the prying eyes of male workers; secondly, many lacked flushing systems, and those that had them were in need of repair in many instances; and, finally, lavatories lacked proper ventilation, which added to the oppressive atmosphere of the spinning flat.[36] Working in stenchy and stifling conditions, the environmental position was made worse by dust particles which filled the mills and covered the clothes and hair of the workers.[37]

These conditions had to be endured for long periods. The working day was 56.5 hours a week for most of the period covered in this study, and was still 55.5 hours per week as late as 1914. Although two hours were given for meal breaks, the working day for women was from 6 a.m. to 6 p.m., or from 7 a.m. to 7 p.m., with a shorter working day on Saturday. This involved the women

---

[33] Report on Proposed Wages, Hours and Ages of Employment, p. 10
[34] Report on Proposed Wages, Hours and Ages of Employment, p. 14; M. Irwin, 'The Employment of Women', p. 176.
[35] M. Irwin, 'The Employment of Women', p. 194.
[36] M. Irwin, 'The Employment of Women', p. 177.
[37] Report on the Proposed Wages, Hours and Ages of Employment, p. 7.

being on their feet for at least ten hours a day in a very physically demanding occupation; one which had seen both the size and speed of the spinning machinery increase enormously over the course of the nineteenth century. The stress and the unhealthy atmosphere the female spinners worked in gave rise to a number of diseases. A medical study of the impact of dust on the health of British workers in spinning mills in the 1870s came to the conclusion that bronchial catarrh, anaemia, phthisis were common, and 'The most unfavourable cases were to be found amongst women'.[38]

Another investigation into death rates in the cotton industry in the period 1891 to 1895 found that in all age groups the death rate was higher among spinners than weavers, and in the age group 45–55 at 34.2 per cent it was more than double that of weavers.[39] It is hardly surprising that girls were not advised to enter the trade unless that were 'active and have a good amount of physical strength'.[40]

Given the slow growth in wage rates and the undesirable aspects of much of the spinners' working conditions, employers found it increasingly difficult as the century wore on to attract female workers of intelligence and good working habits. Spinning mills were losing out as women found more congenial, although not, as we will see, necessarily better paid work in shops and sewing factories.

2. *Weaving*

Much of the evidence we have on wage rates in the Scottish weaving industry, although surprisingly more voluminous than for spinning, remains patchy and contradictory. One author gives two different rates for average wages in 1851 in two separate

---

[38] Report on the Proposed Wages, Hours and Ages of Employment, p. 9.
[39] J. and F. Nasmith, *Recent Cotton Mill Construction and Engineering* (1909 edn), p. 128.
[40] Scottish Council for Women's Trades, Occupations for Girls.

publications.[41] This is perhaps inevitable in the absence of uniform wage lists for the industry, and given the highly individualistic process of wage determination which flowed from that. Margaret Irwin, in her work for the Royal Commission on Labour, noted the impossibility of getting accurate and comprehensive information regarding average weekly wages in weaving sheds in Scotland.

One of the impediments was the lack of cooperation from the employers; another was the fact that wages varied from one week to another, and among individuals and firms there were tremendous differences. To highlight this point Irwin cites the rates in three different factories. In factory one wages ran from 6s. to 22s. a week, in two it was from 7s. to 18s., and in three the figure quoted was from 14s. to 20s.[42]

In spite of the fragmentary nature of the wage data, one thing we can say is that over the course of the nineteenth century female power loom weavers earned much less than male workers in the industry. As they controlled no other forms of labour, as spinners did with piecers, but were themselves supervised by male tenters, their wages reflected this. The men appropriated the best paid maintenance, preparatory and supervisory positions and this was demonstrated in the large differentials in pay. At no time in the nineteenth century did power loom weavers earn more than a third of the tenter's wage, and invariably it was as low as one-quarter.[43] Moreover, as the following table shows, although power loom weavers earned slightly more than female winders, their wages were less than the weekly average in the Scottish cotton industry throughout the nineteenth and early twentieth centuries:

---

[41] J. Strang puts power loom weavers' wages at 7s. 3d. a week in 1851 ('On the Money-Rate of Wages of Labour in Glasgow and the West of Scotland', *Journal of the Statistical Society*, XX (1857), p. 309), while in another article ('Comparative View of the Money-Rate of Wages in Glasgow and the West of Scotland in 1851, 1856 and 1858', *Journal of the Statistical Society*, XXI (1858), p. 423), he puts them at 8s. 9d.
[42] M. Irwin, 'The Employment of Women', pp. 175–6.
[43] Strang, Comparative View of the Money-Rate of Wages, p. 4; Returns of Wages (1889), pp. 60–1; Report on Earnings and Hours of Labour: Textile Trades, PP, 1909, LXXX, p. 71

Table 18. *Average weekly wages [in pence] in the Scottish Cotton Industry and power loom weaving at selected dates.*

Date	Average * Cotton Industry	Average † Weaving	% Difference
1841	88	84	−5
1850/1	89	105	+18
1855	103	108	+5
1860	108	87	−20
1870/1	130	112	−14
1874/5	146	122	−17
1883	142	114	−20
1886	147	130	−12
1892	168	144	−14
1906	177	162	−8

[Sources: * Wood, 'Statistics and Wages' p587; † Compiled from Strang, *Report on the Returns of the Registrars*, pp. 3–4; *Returns of Wages* (1889), pp. 60–1; Webb Collection, vol. xxxvii, f. 291; *Report on Earnings and Hours of Labour* (1909), p. 71]

Although working the same number of hours, apart from a brief period in the 1850s, power loom weavers' wages were from a sixth to a fifth lower than the average earnings in the Scottish cotton industry. The lower wages of the weavers were the result of the interplay of three factors: age, effort and exploitation. As we have seen, the weavers' expectations were governed partly by the fact that most were under the age of twenty-five and unmarried. Higher wages might have been earned if the weavers accepted working more than two looms, but they stubbornly refused to allow the management to alter the customary workload, an attitude influenced by the exploitative behaviour of management, which bred resentment and suspicion: fining for so-called bad work, supplying inferior yarn, and refusing to pay for extra work, were all factors that confirmed the weavers' attachment to the customary workload.[44]

---

[44] M. Irwin, 'The Employment of Women', p. 174.

Weavers in the late nineteenth and early twentieth century were also subject to an intensification of the effort/wage bargain. 'Driving', as it was known, caused all sorts of infringements of the Factory Acts, particularly with respect to working hours. Denied the help of young assistants for cleaning looms and fetching and carrying duties, weavers were forced to work additional unpaid hours to carry out preparatory tasks to keep up their wages.[45] The 'driving' was made possible by the existence of the piece rate method of payment, which individualised the effort/wage bargain and divided the female spinners. As the *Glasgow Herald* noted, the 'women tending the looms do not assist each other',[46] being too busy earning a living under murderous piece rates.

Like spinners, weavers were also subject to cyclical interruptions to their earnings, but with one major difference. Spinning masters, with expensive fixed overheads, attempted to keep their mills in employment all year round. The more labour-intensive weaving trade was more flexible in adjusting its output and demand for labour. Moreover, the seasonal nature of the work of the commissioned weavers, referred to in the last chapter, as well as the rapidly changing demand for certain cloths, greatly affected the earning of the workers. The fickleness of the weaving economy can be grasped from examining monthly reports for the year 1895. In January and February trade was reported 'as bad', with most factories having a 'high percentage of looms idle' and workers on short time at thirty-three hours a week; in March and April the commission weaving trade in coloured goods was said to have shown 'a slight improvement', and other branches of the trade were 'moving on a fair pace', although one large factory north west of Glasgow 'had decided to close until trade resumes a condition which will give them a profit'; in May the cotton trade was said to be 'moving merrily along, most of the factories being fully employed'; in October the recovery was still being sustained and 'trade . . . maintains a highly satisfactory condition in all the various weaving factories'.[47]

---

[45] M. Irwin, 'The Employment of Women', p. 175.
[46] 1 May 1891.
[47] *Cotton Factory Times*, 18 Jan., 1 Feb., 15 Mar., 17 May, 18 Oct. 1895.

Although their earnings were unstable and relatively low in relation to other groups of workers in the cotton industry, and like spinners they worked without shoes or stockings,[48] weavers saw themselves as more intelligent and socially superior. This view was shared by factory inspectors such as Margaret Irwin and Mary Paterson. Irwin noted that in Bridgeton, where female spinners and weavers inhabited similar accommodation and shared the same social conditions, 'there is a quite remarkable difference in their appearance and habits, and there is little social intercourse between the two classes of workers'.[49] Irwin put this down to the fact that weaving was a cleaner and more skilled occupation than spinning. Paterson underscored Irwin's views, claiming that 'Bridgeton weavers were amongst the most interesting women with whom my official duties brought me in contact'.[50] One female in the trade claimed in the mid-1870s that power loom weavers in Scotland were more respectable as they 'were the daughters of managers, foremen, clerks . . . engineers and various other artificers'.[51] Perhaps, this was true of some of the female weavers, but the claim was an exaggerated one. A sample of census enumerator books for Bridgeton in 1851 shows that 73.4 per cent of heads of households in families bearing a connection to the textile trades were employed in that sector. Twenty years later it was still just under 60 per cent,[52] and as the century wore on the social status of the weaving girls became even more proletarian. By 1892 Irwin noted that the 'better educated and more socially ambitious of the girls frequently prefer becoming shop assistants, etc., even at a lower wage, because these callings give them a higher status'. The more feminine dress of the shop girl also embarrassed the mill girl, whose 'bit shawlie' and lack of a bonnet made her seem more masculine and somewhat rough.[53]

---

[48] *Forward*, 29 Oct. 1912.
[49] M. Irwin, 'The Employment of Women', p. 194.
[50] M. Paterson, 'Memories of a Woman Inspector', *The Scots Magazine*, 13 (1930), p. 336.
[51] *Glasgow Sentinel*, 26 June 1875.
[52] Census Enumerator Books: Bridgeton 1851 and 1871. The first sample contained 214 households and the second 271.
[53] M. Irwin, 'The Employment of Women', pp. 173–4.

These observations raise the question as to what kind of conditions did power loom weavers labour under?

Working conditions in the weaving shed were not as oppressive as those in spinning flats. As no special temperature was needed for weaving the atmosphere in the shed was determined by its proximity to other parts of the factory and whether the weavers chose to open or shut the windows. Only in the sizing room was the temperature high, but the use of apertures through the roof of the shed kept conditions bearable and far from stifling.[54] One of the unintended by-products of this system of ventilation was that it drew down cold currents of air and forced the worker to block the ventilators with paper. Weavers continually complained of the need for a ventilation system which would supply them with fresh air without causing bad draughts.[55] In spite of this, however, rather than heat being the problem, it was dampness. In weaving warp, especially with inferior yarn, the damper the conditions, the less the breakages in the yarn.[56] The Nasmiths noted the practice in some firms of flooding the floors of weaving rooms with water to improve the humidity.[57] But this was only practised in firms which sized their cloth excessively; the atmosphere in the bigger mills was thought to be free from moisture.[58] As to sanitation, all the defects Irwin found in the spinning mills applied also to weaving sheds, but the stench would not have been as powerful due to the cooler temperatures prevailing in the sheds. However, the instability of earnings and employment, the unwelcome aspects of the driving system, combined with unfeminine features of the weavers' apparel and working conditions, led to a continual movement of weavers away from the industry, looking for, as one trade paper put it, 'more constant and profitable employment'.[59]

---

[54] Report on the Proposed Wages, Hours and Ages of Employment, p. 14.
[55] M. Irwin, 'The Employment of Women', p. 176.
[56] Report on the Proposed Wages, Hours and Ages of Employment, p. 18.
[57] J. and F. Nasmith, *Recent Cotton Mill Construction*, p. 126.
[58] Report on the Proposed Wages, Hours and Ages of Employment, p. 20.
[59] *Cotton Factory Times*, 5 Apr.1895.

3. Thread

As the nineteenth century progressed the thread manufacturers of Paisley increasingly operated in different labour markets to those of the spinning and weaving enterprises of Glasgow. Before the era of cartelisation, thread companies were engaged in a fierce struggle for markets both in Britain and the United States and competitive wage policies reflected this. But with the formation in 1896 of the giant conglomeration of Clark and Coats the free market in labour, particularly for females, was virtually ended. The firm became directly responsible for the employment of 10,000 workers, or one-eighth of the total population of Paisley.[60] The control of the labour market this afforded the thread manufacturers allowed them to determine the level of wages free from the kind of competition faced by the cotton firms in Glasgow. In concert with the remaining thread firms, such as the ESCC, Clark and Coats were able to fix the wage rate which not only stabilised the labour market, but also prevented intra-firm competition for labour which would have bid up its price. Control of wages was facilitated by a system of information exchange between the companies. As the minutes of the executive committee of the ESCC shows proposals for raising wages or introducing new payments systems were discussed between themselves and J. & P. Coats before being implemented.[61] Therefore, after the merger of Clark and Coats in 1896 there existed only a nominal free market for female labour in Paisley and wages, unlike in Glasgow, were determined less by supply and demand, and more through the relative bargaining power of employers and workers. The question remains as to whether this situation led to substantially lower earnings for workers in the thread trade of Paisley?

Thanks to the preservation of company archives by the firm of J. & P. Coats, we have more information regarding wages than

---

[60] *Paisley and Renfrewshire Gazette*, 16 Mar. 1901.
[61] English Sewing Cotton Company [ESCC], Minutes of Directors, 31 May 1910, 16 Jan. and 27 Apr. 1911, 24 Jan. 1913 (Manchester Central Library, M127/1/1–6).

exist for cotton spinning or weaving, but even here most of the useable data is post-1890. Moreover, much of the material on earnings is preserved in the form of quarterly wage bills for full- and half-time workers, obscuring for most of the nineteenth century the occupational stucture of reward distribution. Cairncross and Hunter have shown that wages in the Coats' enterprise as a fraction of total costs were decreasing as the nineteenth century progressed, and that by the early 1880s they were a third lower than in 1833.[62] But this tells us nothing about actual earnings and their distribution between different groups of workers in the firm and how this was determined by the sexual division of labour, nor how they compared with other thread firms, or the kinds of conditions and hours of work in the thread industry. The reluctance of Coats to divulge information regarding these questions to the Board of Trade means that little can be retrieved from official reports or returns regarding wage rates in the thread trade. Therefore, what light can be shed on these questions is derived from fragmentary sources in company records and newspaper reports, as well as from contemporary observers.

However, it would appear that in the 1870s there was competition between Coats and other threadmakers for labour and that created intra-firm differentials for certain classes of labour. In May 1875 Coats wrote to J. & J. Clarks complaining that they were paying their twiners 21s. per fortnight, or a shilling more than the former.[63] Their is also evidence that foremen were actively poaching workers from rival firms by promising them higher wages. Three years earlier J. & J. Clarks wrote to the manager of Coats condemning its behaviour in this respect and the practice of their foremen in 'treating . . . workers in order to try and induce them to come to [you]'.[64] Competition for labour was of benefit to the workers concerned, but given the sexual division of labour in the thread factories, it was men, rather than women, who were favoured by

---

[62] A. K. Cairncross and J. B. K. Hunter, 'The Early Growth of Messrs J. & P. Coats, 1830–1883', *Business History*, 29 (1987), p. 175.
[63] Coats' Letter Books, 6 May 1875 (Kinning Park Collection, Box HH3).
[64] Coats' Letter Books, 15 Mar. 1872.

the distribution of rewards. As we saw in the previous chapter, the returns of wages paid at Coats' Ferguslie works in June 1878 gave men occupancy of the best paid positions in the firm, and women the worst. In spite of taking little or no part in the actual production of thread, the least paid male occupation, fireman, earned seven shillings a week more than the best paid female operatives, copwinders.[65] By comparing these rates with those provided in Margaret Irwin's study of employment in the Scottish textile trades in 1892, and the detailed wage bill of the Ferguslie mill for 1894, as well as the fragments found in the company records of the ESCC for 1910/11, we can produce a rough guide to the development of waged work in threadmaking since 1878, and, later, how this compared with other branches of the cotton industry.

Table 19. *Average weekly wage rates for selected occupations in the Scottish thread industry.*

Occupation	1878	1892	1894	1910/11
Copwinder	14s. 8d.	13s. 6d.	15s.	16s. 1d.
Rewinder	—	—	12s. 3d.	—
Reeler	14s.	14s. 6d.	14s. 4d.	—
Hank Winder	—	10s. 2d.	—	10s.
Spooler	12s. 6d.	15s.	12s. 10d.	—
Spinners	—	9s.	9s. 3d.	—
Ticketer	12s. 6d.	7s. 6d.	9s. 4d.	—
Twisters	—	9s. 6d.*	6s. 9d.*	—

* time rates, all other rates are for piecework.
[Sources: Coats' Letter Book 24 June 1878; M. Irwin, 'The Employment of Women', Letter from H. Walmsey to A. W. Guthrie, 3 May 1953 (PMAG, file 4/1/2); ESCC, Minutes of Directors, *passim* 1910/11]

The difference in pay rates within the various occupations can be explained by the age, experience and productiveness of the worker. Obviously, beginners and young workers could not hope

---

[65] Coats' Letter Books, 24 June 1878.

to earn the same wage as the more experienced hands, and those on time rates could not expect to earn as much as those on piece rates. According to Irwin's study, two-thirds of the time workers in the twisting department of Coats in 1892 earned only between 7s. and 12s. a week, half of them less than 9s., but even this is over generous as in the Ferguslie mill all twisters were on time in 1894 at the rate given in Table 19.[66]

The differentials in earnings between time and piece workers was a source of discontent and the management were faced with repeated requests from time workers to be placed on piece rates.[67] Of those working on piece rates in Irwin's survey there existed wide differences in take home pay. The best paid copwinders earned a maximum of 17s. per week, while the worst paid received 12s. 6d.; similarly, reelers could earn as much as 19s. 6d., and as little as 10s.[68] However, from the data dealing with average wages there appears to have been little improvement, if any, in the nominal wage rates for the lower class of winder between 1878 and 1910/11, and even the best paid copwinder only experienced a 10 per cent increase over the period 1878 to 1910/11, or a 19 per cent increase between 1892 and 1910/11. Compared to increases in the cost of living the result of increased nominal wages seems negative. However, the reward system used by Coats was biased to favour long-serving employees. Wage data from the twisting department of the Anchor mills shows that a twiner in 1909 minding eight sides received 21s. 6d. a fortnight, while a twiner performing the same task with ten years' service received 29s. 6d., and those with thirteen years' service 30s. 6d.[69] The ESCC had a practice of paying those with ten years' unbroken employment 6d. a week extra over other workers.[70] Loyalty may have brought its own rewards, but there still existed a certain amount of income instability. Like the other

---

[66] M. Irwin, 'The Employment of Women', p. 192; Letter from H. Walmsey, Coats, Paisley, to A. W. Guthrie, Coats, Glasgow, 3 May 1954 (Paisley Museum and Art Gallery [PMAG], file 4/1/2).
[67] Coats' Wage Complaints Book (PMAG, file 1/5/45).
[68] M. Irwin, 'The Employment of Women', p. 192.
[69] Coats' Wage Books, 1909 (PMAG, file 1/5/68).
[70] ESCC, Minutes of Directors, 24 Jan. 1913.

branches of the trade, thread manufacture was subject to depression. Short-time working and wage reductions were reported as one might expect in the famine years, but also in 1869,[71] and for most of the period 1883 to 1890,[72] and, after a sustained recovery, again in 1908.[73] However, wages, particularly of pieceworkers, could be affected by more mundane factors, but of no less significance for all their pettiness. The Wage Complaint Books of Coats are full of references to disruptions in earning power brought about by such minor things as inadequate supplies of bobbins, lack of spools, inferior yarn, soiled and knotted yarn, and so on.[74] In the face of these disruptions to earnings and the rather slow growth in wages, how was the general standard of living of the mill girl in Paisley perceived by contemporaries, and how did it compare with other branches of the cotton trade?

Evidence regarding the physical appearance and the social circumstances of Paisley mill girls is conflicting, but it does appear that things improved greatly towards the end of the nineteenth century and the beginning of the twentieth. The first series of reports on the standard of living of female thread workers came as a result of American interest. The debates taking place in the United States over free trade in the early 1880s generated interest in the activities of Paisley millowners, since they had established thread mills in Newark and Pawtucket. Comparison with wages and conditions in the United States with those existing in Scotland were made by both sides in the debate over the tariff. William Clark, of the Clarks O. N. T. thread works, Newark, a noted protectionist, said that 'In Scotland three-quarters of the girls go to the mills without bonnets and very many without shoes', while in America 'they are better clothed, better fed', and receive $4.50–6.50 a week compared to $2–2.50 in Scotland.[75] Clark's pessimistic view of the Paisley mill girls was contradicted by Col. C. D. Wright, of the United States Bureau of Statistics, a supporter of free trade. Wright

---

[71] *Paisley and Renfrewshire Gazette*, 25 Sept. 1869.
[72] *Economist*, 26 June 1890.
[73] Chairman's speech, 3 Dec. 1912 (Kinning Park Collection, Box HH3).
[74] Coats' Wage Complaints Books, 1907–9 (PMAG, file 1/4/45).
[75] *Paisley Daily Express*, 2 Nov. 1880.

claimed that 'In France the female operatives take pride in their dress and hair, and in the mills they look as bright and comely as do the bonnie operatives in the thread mills of Paisley . . . perhaps the finest body of operatives in the world'.[76]

Between the publication of these widly conflicting views, R. P. Porter, of the American Tariff Commission, visited Paisley and made house-to-house inquiries among mill workers. Admittedly this was during a slack period in winter with the mills operating on short time and average wages only 10s. a week. In spite of this, it remains a more balanced, and probably more accurate, account than the more partisan views of Clark and Wright. Porter found that there was a high incidence of single parenthood among the young women, and although, in the main, they were 'warmly clad', he observed that 'perhaps a score [of the mill girls] trudged through the cold slush without shoes. Not any of them had bonnets'. Compared to the females he had seen coming out of the mills in Manchester, the former were 'a superior class of girls', but 'they would not compare with the neatly dressed girls . . . coming out of the Merrimac mills at Lowell', Massachusetts.[77] This view is supported in a letter to *Scottish Fields*, which mentions 'the fine, clean and healthy looks of the female workers. Clothed with their drugget petticoats, and light coloured jupons, with good shoes and stockings and shawls'.[78]

There is little doubt that the standard of living improved substantially for female thread workers after Porter's report. In spite of the low wages continuing to be paid in some of the departments of the thread mills, by the first decade of the twentieth century the Rev J. B. Sturrock, in his book of reminiscences about Paisley, *Looking Back*, observed that in 1910 the mill girls of Coats were 'all tidily dressed, and never fail to impress visitors to the town with their smart appearance'.[79] The historian of the Paisley thread industry, Matthew Blair, also noted that:

---

[76] *Paisley Daily Express*, 23 June 1884.
[77] *New York Daily Tribune*, 27 Jan. 1883.
[78] July 1880.
[79] Typescript PMAG, file 4/1/9.

Gone are all the shoeless feet, the jupe, and the petticoat, the tartan shawl over the head, and the subdued air of hard times. Now there is a rush of young and hopeful life . . . Neat and comfortable in attire, with frequent touches of art and taste in dress . . . smart costumes of harmonious colours, and warm woollen 'tammies' . . .[80]

Although the evidence regarding the lifestyle of the mill girls is impressionistic, one thing which cannot be disputed is the improvement in working conditions and hours which took place in the thread works of Paisley in the latter decades of the nineteenth century. Much of this had to do with the continual upgrading of older parts of the mills and the construction of wholly new ones, such as the Atlantic mill of Clarks built in 1872 and complemented by the Pacific mill three years later, as well as Coats' new Ferguslie spinning mill in 1886. These mills were built on the most modern principle available and catered fully for the health and welfare of the workers. Margaret Irwin described the Clarks' mill as one of the 'finest in the kingdom', and together with Coats' Ferguslie mill, representing 'the highest standard I have met as regards sanitation and general internal appointments'.[81] The factory of the former was said to be well-ventilated and lit, with drinking wells and superior lavatory accomodation. And similar conditions were found in Coats, as well as dining rooms, recreation grounds.[82] By 1908 Coats' workers had also achieved the nine-hour day, which saw the working fortnight reduced from 111 hours to 99. The working day was reorganised on two four and half hour shifts, from 8 a.m. to 12.30 p.m. and from 1.30 p.m. to 6 p.m., with an hour for lunch, and was accepted by a ballot of the workforce. The factory inspector, Mr Cooper, said that the social gains from the new arrangements were 'considerable', and that he was 'favourable impressed with the healthy appearance of these workers'.[83]

The question which emerges from this discussion on wages and working conditions is whether the superior social amenities were

---

[80] M. Blair, *The Paisley Thread* (Paisley, 1907), pp. 190–1.
[81] M. Irwin, 'The Employment of Women', p. 191.
[82] M. Irwin, 'The Employment of Women', pp. 191–2.
[83] Factory Report, PP, 1910, XXVIII.

provided by the employers at the expense of wages? How did average wage rates in thread manufacture compare with other branches of the cotton industry and alternative forms of employment for females? The latter question also allows one to raise the issue of why the spinning and weaving branches of the trade found it difficult to recruit adequate supplies of labour. Was it the wage rate or the working conditions?

From the following table a number of features stand out; firstly, wages in a defined occupation in the thread trade were comparable to spinning, and far superior to weaving; and secondly, wages in the cotton trade were among the highest paid to female workers.

Table 20. *Average weekly wages for selected female occupations*

Occupation	1861	1886	1892
Cotton spinning	19s. 6d.*	—	14s. 6d.
Cotton weaving	10s. 6d.	10s. 10d.	12s. 0d.
Cotton copwinding	—	14s. 8d.†	13s. 6d.
Jute spinning	7s. 3d.	8s. 3d.	—
Jute weaving	9s. 6d.	12s. 6d.	—
Carpet weaving	—	11s. 10d.	—
Lace winders	—	10s. 5d.	—
Dressmaking	—	12s. 8d.	12s. 0d.
Shop work	—	—	10s. 0d.
Nursing	—	8s. 3d. ‡	—

[* refers to 1866; † 1878; ‡ majority of nurses earned £21 10s. per annum: Sources: Wages compiled from *Returns of Wages, 1830–1886*, PP, 1887, lxxxix; *Returns of Wages in the Textile Trades*, PP, 1899, lxx; *Returns of Wages in the Minor Textile Trades*, PP, 1890, lxviii; M. Irwin, 'The Employment of Women'; E. Orme, 'Conditions of Work in Scotland', in *R. C. on Labour*, pt.1, PP, 1893–4, xxxviii; *Report on the Wages of the Manual Labouring Classes in the UK*, pt. 2, PP, 1893–4, lxxxiii]

There are a number of features of the wages table which are in need of some further clarification. The declining rate for female spinners is explained above; however, it would appear that nursing and shopwork were the worst paid occupations, in spite of their appeal to socially aspiring girls from working-class backgrounds. Indeed, if one takes into account that in the early 1890s a gross working week of between 77 and 84 hours was normal for shop girls,[84] then their wages were even more appalling. Of course, nursing had a career ladder in which the talented could rise and this, and the caring image it carried, made it attractive to the ambitious daughters of skilled and middle-class families. However, given that between 1841 and 1911 65–72 per cent of women in Glasgow were employed in industrial work a career outside manufacturing was unusual.[85]

In the world of industry female cotton workers received wages which were comparable to any of the listed occuaptions in Table 20, and a good deal better in some instances. Moreover, there is little evidence to suggest that Coats' workers, outside of time workers, were somehow disadvantaged in respect of wages. The varied structure of skills and wages existing in a thread factory provided mobility for women which did not exist in weaving or, at a later date, in spinning, with the ending of the spinner/piecer system. In spite of this, it remained a fact that of the 3,245 females employed in Coats' Ferguslie mill in 1894, 1,736, or 53.5 per cent, of them earned 10s. or less per week.[86]

However, regardless of the level of wage, or the degree of job mobility, all women in the Scottish cotton industry were paid less than men. Indeed, in Scotland as a whole, women at the turn of the century received on average only about 42 per cent of the average pay for men,[87] and in this respect cotton was no different to other branches of industry. The large differentials existed as a result of a sexual division of labour in the cotton industry which placed women at the bottom of the workplace hierarchy. The individualising of the effort/wage bargain through the piece rate

---

[84] E. Orme, 'Conditions of Work in Scotland', pp. 312–6.
[85] Rodger, 'Employment, Wages and Poverty', p. 35.
[86] Letter (Walmsey to Guthrie), 3 May 1954.
[87] E. Gordon, 'Introduction', in *The World is Ill-Divided: women's work in Scotland in the nineteenth and early twentieth centuries*, ed. E. Gordon and E. Brietenbach (1992), p. 2.

payment system made collective protest against such disadvantages difficult, although not impossible, among female workers. Even as late as 1913, however, the female factory inspector for Scotland, Miss Vines, could say that she found 'Scottish women markedly more ready to endure hard conditions and contraventions than English workers and less willing to complain of them'.[88] Therefore, the method of payment and the way it harnessed women to a division of labour in which they were subordinated to men is highly significant for understanding the system of industrial relations which emerged in the Scottish cotton industry after 1850.

---

[88] Factory Report, PP, 1914, XXIX, p. 74.

CHAPTER FOUR

Employers, Strategy and Organisation

EMPLOYERS in the cotton industry have on the whole received a bad historical press. Excoriated in the first phase of the industrial revolution by writers, such as Carlyle and Dickens, and reformers, such as Lord Ashley, for their gross exploitation of women and children, their reputation as entrepreneurs in the Scottish context has also been damned in the period after 1850. In his influential article on the decline of the Scottish cotton industry, Robertson lays a large portion of the blame for the failings of the industry on the shoulders of the employers, arguing that this had a more serious impact on the 'industry's competitive position' than the 'inefficiency and restrictionism' of the operatives.[1]

Contemporary observers were of a similar opinion. The correspondent of the *Textile Trade Review* contrasted unfavourably the hard-working, practical men of the first generation of Glasgow cotton masters, with the dilettantes of the second generation schooled in the classical tradition of the landed gentry and with gentlemanly aspirations. 'Born with silver spoons in their mouths,' he claimed, had left the latter with 'little love for the practical work of their fathers.'[2]

Disinterest led to decay as many of the Scottish cotton owners failed to keep abreast of changing technical developments or to invest in new machinery and plant.[3] Margaret Irwin also accused

---

[1] A. J. Robertson, 'The Decline of the Scottish Cotton Industry, 1860–1914', *Business History*, 12 (1970), p. 124.
[2] May 1883, p. 4.
[3] May 1883, p. 4.

the Scottish cotton manufacturers 'of lacking in commercial enterprise'.[4]

However, just as the Gradgrind reputation of the early cotton master has been modified by more recent research, which has stressed the degree of welfarism practised in many of the mills,[5] criticisms regarding the quality of management in the Scottish cotton industry must also be reassessed. Recent and contemporary comments on this issue are based purely on casual observations with little regard paid to the backgrounds of the entrepreneurs, the constraints they operated within, or the strategies they employed in running their businesses and managing their labour forces. Unfortunately history prefers winners to losers. Therefore, most of our information regarding the social and business backgrounds of Scottish cotton employers derives from the biographies of the successes rather than the failures.

Drawing on the entries in volume one of the *Dictionary of Scottish Business Biography* and other biographical fragments, it would appear that successfully run firms were those in which the management possessed technical and financial expertise, and, possibly more important, had the strongest sense of family unity and purpose. The unity of purpose in the Coats family enabled it after 1850, according to one historian, to supersede the Clarks as Paisley's leading thread manufacturers as the latter's partnership in J. & J. Clark 'included members of two other families – the Kerrs and the Balderstones – [which led to] conflicts among the partners on questions of policy'.[6] Dithering and conflict among the partners whether to expand overseas meant that Coats established a lead in the American market.

---

[4] M. Irwin, 'Women's Industries in Scotland', *Proceedings of the Philosophical Society of Glasgow*, XXVII (1895–6), pp. 77–8.
[5] See, for instance, S. D. Chapman, *The Early Factory Masters: the transition to the factory system in the Midlands Textile Industry* (Newton Abbot, 1967); J. Butt (ed.), *Robert Owen: Prince of Cotton Spinners* (Newton Abbot, 1971); P. Joyce, *Work, Society and Politics: the culture of the factory in later Victorian England* (1982), pp. 134–57; A. Howe, *The Cotton Masters, 1830–1860* (Oxford, 1984); R. S. Fitton, *The Arkwrights: Spinners of Fortune* (Manchester, 1989).
[6] D. Keir, 'The Coats Story', vol. 1 (Glasgow, 1964, unpublished history, a typescript of which is held at Coats Vyella, 155 St Vincent St, Glasgow), p. 67.

Clarks, however, survived and eventually amalgamated with Coats at a later date, and this is due in large part to the quality of its management. As we have seen the founder of the firm, James Clark (1747–1829), was the first to adapt cotton for the purposes of sewing thread, and his technical abilities were found in later generations. John Clark (1791–1864) was educated at Paisley Grammar School before serving an informal apprenticeship to Robert Guthrie, shawl manufacturer of Paisley. Clark's knowledge of cotton machinery was considered first rate, and while in charge of the bobbin turning department he spent his time 'improving old, and inventing new machines'.[7] Peter Kerr, a partner in the firm, was described as a 'brilliant technician'.[8]

The founder of the firm of J. & P. Coats, James Coats (1774–1857), came from several generations of Paisley weavers. He retired in 1830 giving the firms over to his two sons – James (1803–1845), a manufacturer, and Peter (1808–1890), who had a mercantile background. Their brother Thomas (1809–1883), an engineer, was later admitted, as was Andrew, who opened up the American market for the firm.[9] Although we have very little biographical information on successful entrepreneurs in the spinning and weaving sectors, fragmentary evidence would point to similar characteristics in both the ownership of the firms and their management. John Colville (1844–1924), chairman of A. & A. Galbraith, spinners and weavers of Glasgow, was the son of a Campbeltown banker, and a nephew of the founder of the firm;[10] James Paterson (1834–1909), a partner in the company of James Paterson and Co. and, later the Clyde Spinning Co., came from a family of prominent textile manufacturers;[11] David Blyth Anderson (1872–1944), of D. J. Anderson's, was the son of John Anderson, cotton manufacturer; Henry Birkmyre (1832–1900), owner of New Lanark from 1881, was the son of William Birkmyre, partner in the Gourock Rope Works;

---

[7] Local Memorabilia (Kinning Park Collection, Box HH3).
[8] N. J. Morgan, 'John Clark', in *Dictionary of Scottish Business Biography*, vol. 1, *The Staple Industries*, ed. S. Checkland and A. Slaven (Aberdeen, 1986), p. 326.
[9] M. Blair, *The Paisley Thread* (Paisley, 1907), p. 44.
[10] N. J. Morgan, 'John Colville', in *Dictionary*, p. 337.
[11] N. J. Morgan, 'James Paterson', in *Dictionary*, p. 383.

Alexander M. Fleming (1826–1905), worsted spinner, was the son of James Fleming, bleacher and merchant; and, lastly, John Muir (1828–1903), a partner in James Findlay of Catrine and Deanstone and a graduate of the University of Glasgow, was the son of James Muir, an early partner in the Findlay enterprises.[12] These, then, were men with either strong, practical training in the cotton trade, or a university education which prepared them to engage in the financial as well as scientific aspects of production and distribution. The dilletantish image seems quite out of place when these characteristics are taken into consideration.

One social characteristic of these entrepreneurs which stands out is membership of the non-established churches of Scotland. They were either members of the Free Church or the United Presbyterian Church (UPC), or, when they amalgamated in 1900, the United Free Church (UFC). Robert Balderstone, manager of Clark and Co., was a member of the Thread Street UFC, Paisley;[13] Archibald Coats financed the renovation of St James' UFC, Paisley, of which he was a manager; and Alexander M. Fleming had a long connection with the St Andrews Free Church, Gourock. Among the prominent members of the UPC were Henry Birkmyre, John Clark and John Muir.[14] Thomas Coats, a deeply religious man, was a member of the Baptist Church.[15] All of them translated their religious beliefs into practical action on behalf of the churches and their missions towards the working class. John Clark spent £30,000 on construction of a UPC in Largs; Birkmyre built the Clare Park UPC near his Gourock Rope Works; Archibald Coats with his two brothers helped to finance the renovation of St James' UFC in Paisley;[16] and Thomas Coats financed the building of the Memorial Baptist Church, Paisley.

Religious benevolence was complemented by philanthropic activity, as employers such as Clarks and Coats spent large sums in municipal building programmes. Paisley's George Clark Town Hall

---

[12] *Dictionary*, pp. 305, 315, 362, 375.
[13] *Paisley and Renfrewshire Gazette* (PRG), 31 Aug. 1912.
[14] *Dictionary*, pp. 315, 331–2, 362–3, 375–6.
[15] J. B. K. Hunter, 'Thomas Coats', in *Dictionary*, p. 334.
[16] *Dictionary*, pp. 315, 328, 331–2.

was financed by the Clarks, and substantial sums were given to the Paisley Infirmary,[17] whose chairman was the firm's manager, Robert Baldestone. The Coats family were also important civic benefactors in Paisley. Thomas Coats contributed £10,000 to the building of Royal Alexandra Infirmary, and provided the finance to extend the Paisley Museum which was built by Peter Coats. Money was also donated by Coats for the building of the North, South, East, West and Ferguslie schools in the town. And school bags were given to children, with the initials 'J.C.' printed on them. He also arranged for boots to be made for the barefooted children of Paisley.[18]

Indeed, it was almost impossible for a worker in Paisley to escape the presence of the Clarks or the Coats. Their imprint was placed on practically every educational, recreational and medical development in the town. In addition to those acts of public benefaction mentioned; the Fountain Gardens were provided by Thomas Coats in 1866; the Museum and Library were built by Peter Coats the following year; the Coats' Observatory was built by Thomas Coats in 1882.

The physical manifestations of the power and wealth of what might be called a 'threadocracy' were as socially overwhelming as were the giant thread mills themselves. Just as the cathedrals of the medieval and early modern period were designed to contrast the power of God and the Church with the insignificance of human beings, these icons of capitalism's civic gospel served to underscore the weakness of the workers in the face of a hegemony which extended well beyond the narrow perimeters of the factory walls.

Thus, philanthropic activities and the religious conviction which underscored them were to play important parts in the evolution of a paternalistic strategy towards the labour force, particularly among the large thread manufacturers of Paisley. Paternalism as a means of social control had developed within the relatively closed parameters of landed society and was used as a means of managing the tensions which arose from the existence of huge inequalities in

---

[17] *Dictionary*, p. 328.
[18] 'James Coats: a life well spent', *Life and Work* (Supplement, Mar. 1987).

the distribution of power and wealth within this mode of production.[19] The operation of the system was based on both parties in landed society recognising the reciprocal rights and duties involved in the relationship. In return for the acceptance of the unquestioned right of the landowner to exercise authority and power in his sphere of ownership, the subordinate members of landed society expected to have work for life and to be protected against exigent problems, such as famine, and other pressures resulting from the growing commercialisation of agriculture in the eighteenth century.

Recent historical research has applied the concept to the wider arena of class relations in capitalist society, as well as industrial enterprises, most notably Patrick Joyce's study of the Lancashire cotton towns.[20] Joyce argues that the implementation of a paternalist strategy by employers was fundamental to understanding the stabilisation of class relations in the mid-Victorian period. As employers moved away from a policy of confrontation and the intensive quest for accumulation, a civic gospel emerged which stressed the virtues of philanthropy and of awarding recognition to labour. Although this did not abolish conflict between capital and labour, it modified it and made it more manageable. The outcome was the acceptance by the working class of the liberal capitalist framework of society and the consequent stabilising of what during the first phase of industrialisation had seemed to be an inherently unstable society. In more detailed studies of individual industrial enterprises, historians have shown how paternalism encouraged worker identification with the goals of management and assisted in the recruitment and retention of labour through establishing strong links with worker families and firms. However, if the concept is to have relevance for the study of social relationships in an industrial/urban environment some appreciation of its limitations and weaknesses is necessary.

---

[19] H. Perkins, *The Origins of Modern English Society* (1969), pp. 17–62, 182–92; P. Laslett, *The World We Have Lost – further explored* (1983), pp. 22–80.

[20] See, for example, P. Joyce, *Work, Society and Politics*; H. I. Dutton and J. E. King, 'The limits of paternalism: the cotton tyrants of northern Lancashire', *Social History*, VII (1982), pp. 59–74; M. Huberman, 'The economic origins of paternalism: Lancashire cotton spinning in the first half of the nineteenth century', *Social History*, 12 (1987), pp. 177–92.

Firstly, as Newby et al., have observed, paternalism in landed society was based on tradition, which legitimised the right of the person embodying it to control subordinate labour forms. This enabled power relations to become moral ones as the subordinate classes accepted the dominant class's definition of their social situation.[21] However, the moral authority of the landowner was not easily transferable to a capitalist society, where social relationships were governed less by intimate, personal bonds, and more by what Carlyle called the cash nexus. The authority of the capitalist was established through the wages' system and worker dependence, rather than by custom or tradition. Job security and protection from exigencies were seen as barriers to the free movement of capital and labour, and in a price conscious society the antithesis of the laws of supply and demand.

Secondly, the intimate nature of the class structure of landed society was missing in industrial capitalism after its pioneering phase. Social distance increased between the worker and the employer both in the workplace and the community. The defection of the middle class from the disease-ridden and overcrowded inner-city areas for the cleaner and healthier suburbs profoundly reconstructed residential patterns on explicitly class lines.[22] The workers became alienated from other social classes and only came in contact with their superiors in the course of their work, but even here this was becoming rarer as industry grew and employers withdrew from the sphere of production, devoting their energies towards the sphere of distribution. As plant size increased the construction of a bureaucracy was unaviodable, and this development placed several more tiers of authority between the owner and the workers.

Thirdly, the impersonal nature of production in capitalist society made expectations of deferential behaviour unrealistic among the working class. As Joyce notes, the desire for self-respect among workers meant that the deferential aspect of the paternalistic

---

[21] H. Newby, et al., *Property, Paternalism and Power: class and control in rural England* (Wisconsin, 1978), pp. 27–8.
[22] S. G. Checkland, 'The British Industrial City as history: the Glasgow case', *Urban Studies*, 1 (1964), pp. 34–54.

relationship was missing in an industrial setting. He also noted that the desire for self-respect was also reciprocated by the employers, many of whom disliked being called 'Sir', aware of the need to combine the aloof with the familiar.[23] Indeed, during the 1830s the thread firm of Coats employed technical staff who were addressed as 'Mr Young and Mr Arrol' by the employees, while the owner's sons were called by their christian names. James Coats informed his technical staff that in his Bible men were to call 'no man master', and from then on it was to be plain John Young and Thomas Arrol.[24]

Finally, industrial society also lacked the social guarantees of landed society. Security of employment was problematical in a dynamic economy in which wealth was as much destroyed as it was created through the continuous cycle of boom and bust.

Such factors as these restricted the operation of paternalism to specific locations and production sites. Glasgow, for instance, with its massive and continually shifting labouring population, its varied occupational structure and cosmopolitan culture, lacked the community stability needed to cement paternalistic relations. Although some of the larger spinning and weaving firms in Glasgow adopted a policy of company welfare, the scope was limited and the rewards negligible.[25] This is borne out by other research. Employers in the textile industry south of the border found the strategy to be unworkable in the large towns such as Manchester and Liverpool, where it was not possible to carve out a community isolated from the world outside.[26] In small towns and isolated industrial villages, where the employer(s) had a near monopoly in the labour market, controlled housing, and through symbolic acts of public benevolence,

---

[23] Joyce, *Work, Society and Politics*, p. 164.
[24] Keir, *Coats Story*, vol. 1, p. 45.
[25] E. Johnston, *Autobiography, Poems and Songs* (Glasgow, 1867), contains some contemporary accounts of paternalist practices in Glasgow cotton enterprises.
[26] See, for example, Joyce, *Work, Society and Politics*; H. Bradley, 'Technological change, managerial strategies, and the development of gender-based job segregation in the labour process', in *Gender and the Labour Process*, ed. D. Knights and H. Wilmott (Aldershot, 1986), pp. 54–73; J. Lown, '"Not so much a factory, more a form of patriarchy": gender and class during industrialisation', in *Gender, Class and Work*, ed. E. Gamarnikov, *et al.* (Aldershot, 1985), pp. 28–45.

was able to extend the workplace authority beyond the walls of the factory, paternalism was, however, a realistic and, indeed, highly beneficial strategy. Paisley and the industrial villages of Catrine and New Lanark were classic examples of this. The thread mills of Paisley used paternalism to generate consent in the workplace for the imperatives of capital accumulation. This gave the thread manufacturers a free rein in using the most modern forms of textile technology to destroy craft-based skills and hence resistance, further increasing dependency on them among their workers; a phenomenon replicated in other branches of the textile trades in Britain, as the studies by Bradley on the Nottingham hosiery trade, Lown on Courtaulds, and Bursfield on the West Riding of Yorkshire wool trade, all show.[27] In Glasgow failure of the confrontational approach of management, as well as the general failure to invest in the most modern technology, complicated the move from the formal to the real subordination of labour which left a platform for organising resistance among workers. As we will see later, while Paisley for almost the whole of the period 1850–1914 was strike free, the Glasgow spinning and weaving mills experienced frequent expressions of industrial protest.

Part of the reason for the different workplace relationships experienced in Paisley and Glasgow may be connected with the stability of the workforce. A shifting working population as reflected in patterns of household formation was unlikely to be responsive to paternalist overtures since playing the market was more important than job security. While it is difficult to calculate the degree of in/out movement within an industry and/or district except by long and labour-intensive data collection over several censuses, an insight into this question can be gained by examining the birthplaces of heads of households in the main cotton producing district of Glasgow – Bridgeton – with Paisley over the course of the second half of the nineteenth century. If there proves to be a strong correlation

---

[27] Bradley, 'Technological change'; Lown, 'Not so much a factory'; D. Bursfield, 'Skill and the sexual division of labour in the West Riding Textile Industry, 1850–1914', in *Employers and Labour in the English Textile Industries, 1850–1939*, ed. J. A. Jowitt and A. J. McIvor (1988), pp. 153–70.

between place of birth and the occupational location we can assume that the working community was more cohesive and stable than one in which workers were drawn from many other places. In this respect textile workers in Glasgow appear to have been less homogenous in regard to their origins than their counterparts in Paisley.

Bridgeton cotton firms recruited workers mainly from outside Glasgow, especially from the west of Scotland and Ireland, while Paisley firms tended to rely on local labour for most of the period, as the following tables show:

Table 21. *Place of birth of heads of households employed by Bridgeton textile firms at selected dates*

	Glasgow	Rest of Scotland	Ireland	England	Total
1851	55 (36.0)	51 (33.3)	43 (28.1)	4 (2.6)	153
1871	46 (28.4)	70 (43.2)	43 (26.5)	3 (1.9)	162
1891	37 (40.2)	32 (34.8)	21 (22.8)	2 (2.2)	92

[Source: Census Enumerator Books: Bridgeton 1851, 1871 and 1891]

Table 22. *Place of birth of heads of households employed by Paisley textile firms at selected dates*

	Paisley	Rest of Scotland	Ireland	England	Total
1851	137 (77.0)	33 (18.5)	5 (2.8)	3 (1.7)	178
1871	122 (59.2)	72 (34.9)	7 (3.4)	5 (2.5)	206
1891	88 (44.9)	75 (39.2)	18 (9.3)	15 (7.6)	196

[Source: Census Enumerator Books: Paisley 1851, 1871 and 1891]

Although the growth of the thread industry necessitated a widening of the labour market as the century wore on, there still existed a core of worker households whose roots in Paisley were long established and might be expected to respond to paternalistic overtures from management.

The historian of the firm of J. & P. Coats underscored this observation when he claimed that 'their mill girls were sprung from parents and grandparents who had worked at either Ferguslie or at the Anchor Mills, and who themselves went into the mills almost by hereditary right.'[28] In Bridgeton, by contrast, the working population appeared more fragmented and less likely to establish the kind of stable households which formed the basis of the organic industrial community found in Paisley. And while it was not possible in a town like Paisley, with a population of around 51,000 in 1875, growing to nearly 86,000 during the next thirty years,[29] to exercise the close control found in industrial villages such as Catrine and New Lanark, where work and residence were intertwined,[30] the stability of the working community offset this drawback to applying a paternalist strategy.

However, although the thread employers did not own extensive housing units in Paisley, in the period 1871 to 1891 their ownership of domestic properties rose from 183 to 372, an increase of around 50 per cent. In spite of this housing was used in a highly subtle manner, extending the power and influence of the owners among key groups of workers. As one might expect the firms of Coats and Clarks showed the largest growth in domestic property ownership, with the former showing a rise over the same period in domestic property ownership from 100 to 171, and the latter more spectacularly from 21 to 119. From a tenuous relationship between tenant and mill in 1871, there was an increasing tendency to make the link, if judged by the occupation of the head of household, more direct. Thus, in 1871 just under 50 per cent of heads of households in Coats' tenancies had some connection with the mill; twenty years later the figure had risen to 65 per cent. It is clear that company housing tenanted by employees was used to reward loyal service and win the allegiance of key supervisory and managerial staff; a trend which grew over time, as the following table shows:

---

[28] Keir, *Coats' Story*, vol. 11, p. 113.
[29] Blair, *Paisley Thread*, pp. 182–3.
[30] S. D. Chapman, 'Workers' Housing in the Cotton Factory Colonies, 1770–1850', *Textile History*, 7 (1976), pp. 130–1, has some details of Catrine.

Table 23. *Main occupations of heads of households in tenancies of J. & P. Coats, 1871–1891*

Occupation	1871	1881	1891
Managerial	0	5	16
Foremen	3	1	16
Mill Worker	6	12	21
Weaver	11	7	4
Others	8	15	28
Total	28	40	84

[Source: SRO, VR66/39]

From just over 10 per cent of company tenancies in 1871 the supervisory/managerial stratum's share rose to just under 40 per cent in 1891, while mill workers' share only increased from 20 to 25 per cent. Housing, then, was being used to reproduce the status hierarchies of the workplace in the wider society, as well as to intensify the links between owners and their functionaries. The strength of these links can be demonstrated by sampling company tenancies owned by Coats over time through the use of valuation rolls. Of thirty-two families who first appeared at a particular address in 1891, the same number appeared at that address in 1901, and eighteen families were still there in 1911. These included nine mill foremen and five managers. Typical was John Cowie, foreman of 3 Ferguslie Buildings, who was recorded as living at the same address from 1891 to 1911.

A sample of the 1901 valuation roll shows that of twenty-six families living at a particular address all were still there ten years later, and of this number were five mill foremen and three managers. The bond between this stratum and the company was also strengthened by the increasing trend towards the recruitment of foremen whose links with the mill community were tenuous or non-existent. A sample of enumerator books of the main textile residential areas of Paisley found twenty-one supervisory workers in the census year 1871 and forty-one in 1891. It also showed that there was a marked shift towards the employment of outsiders for these important functions, as the following table makes clear:

Table 24. *Birthplaces of foremen thread workers in 1871 and 1891*

	Paisley	West of Scotland	Other Scotland	Ireland	England
★ 1871	10 (47.6)	8 (38.1)	2 (9.5)	1 (4.8)	0
† 1891	8 (19.5)	16 (39.0)	7 (17.1)	2 (4.9)	8 (19.5)

[★ Sample size 377 households; † 406 households]

For those engaged in the production process we can, by linking the data on valuation rolls to decennial census returns, say that there was a direct relationship between household and mill. All male heads of households connected with the thread or other branches of the textile trade had daughters or other female relatives working in the thread mills. Thread mill worker, William Adam of 2 Ferguslie Walk had two female relatives working in the mills in 1871, and by 1891 the number had increased to three. Those tenancies where the head of household had no connection with the mill on a street sample had no female relatives working in the mills.

Although housing was used more to cultivate links between the supervisors/managers and the owners, or as a form of investment, it could also be used as a source of labour for the mills or as reward to long-serving workers. However, ownership of domestic property was never large enough for the threadocracy to use it as the main thrust of a paternalist policy. Other means were used to further this strategy, particularly through the creation of what Joyce has called 'company cultures' and by intensifying worker dependency, all of which helped stabilise industrial relations. At the same time, the manufacturers worked to create a high degree of identification between employee and firm, which, as Putterman has noted, had the added advantage of reducing supervisory costs as firm-structured goals and incentives became internalised by the workforce.[31] The thread works were Newby, *et al.*'s, archetypal 'greedy institutions',[32]

---

[31] L. Putterman, 'On some recent explanations of why capital hires labour', *Economic Inquiry*, 22 (1984), pp. 175–9.
[32] H. Newby, 'Paternalism and Capitalism', in *Industrial Society: class, cleavage and control*, ed. R. Scase (1977), pp. 59–73.

whose antennae reached beyond the factory gates to enmesh a whole community of workers in a social matrix welded together by a mixture of material and ideological supports which were both obvious and, at the same time, discrete and subtle. Even those workers in Paisley not directly dependent on the thread firms for employment and wages felt able to identify with their commercial success and civic benevolence, as did the town's smaller enterprises. The procession to mark the inauguration of the George A. Clark Town Hall in 1882 symbolised the social power of the threadocracy. Every trade in Paisley was represented, from blacksmiths to joiners, from bricklayers to engineers, as well as the friendly societies, public authorities and officials. The banners of the various trade societies included inscriptions such as 'Wher'er the Town Hall chimes do ring, the Donors to our minds they bring' (Anchor thread workers), 'Long live the Brothers one and all, the Donors of the new Town Hall' (joiners), 'Combine to support, but not to injure' (bakers).[33] The celebrations were symbolic of the social relations of production, which in Paisley at this time were interpreted by the working class in terms of mutual dependency. It was also shown in their acceptance of Liberalism. Robert Balderstone, manager of Clarks, was a member of Paisley Town Council in the 1880s, and Sir Thomas Glen-Coats was MP for West Renfrewshire. The Liberals received 57.3 per cent of the votes cast in the 1885 general election and this increased to 64.3 per cent in 1910.[34] It was not until 1924 that Labour won the seat.

Among the more obvious elements in the paternalist strategy of the thread employers were welfare schemes and enhanced working conditions within the workplace. As we have seen in another chapter, Margaret Irwin, as part of her report to the Royal Commission on Labour, singled out the firms of Coats and Clarks as model employers in respect of the attention paid to the health and safety of their workers.[35] However, employee welfare also extended

---

[33] *Inauguration of the G. A. Clark Town Hall* (Paisley, 1882), pp. 49–52.
[34] F. W. S. Craig, *British Parliamentary Election Results, 1885–1918* (1976), p. 517.
[35] M. H. Irwin, 'The Employment of Women', *Royal Commission on Labour*, pt. 1, PP, 1893–4, XXVII, pp. 191–2.

to other areas of working life and included the provision of dining halls from 1884; a girls' hostel opened in 1901; a convalescent home in 1911; and bathing facilities in 1913.[36] This form of employee welfare was replicated by many other firms in the textile trades. Lown's study of Courtaulds details similar provisions for a mainly female workforce, as does Bradley's more comprehensive study of the hosiery trade of Nottingham.[37]

However, Coats also rewarded long and loyal service by granting old age company pensions. Although the company pension registers seemed to have disappeared from Coats' Minute Books, it would appear that the minimum qualification for a pension was twenty years. The lowest period of recorded service was Alexander Kennedy, a hoistman, twenty-two years, and the highest was Janet Downie, a hand spooler, at forty-six years.[38] The number of long-serving workers is uncertifiable, but in 1882 Stewart Clark, of Clark and Co., claimed that 'at least one-third of those in our employ can say they have served us for over twenty years'.[39] This was borne out by Margaret Irwin's report in which she estimated that about one-quarter of the firm's labour force had been in continuous employment for fifty to sixty years.[40] The pensions were purely discretionary, however; there was an agreed rate for foremen, male and women workers which reinforced the hierarchical structure of employment in the thread mill. Women were paid eight shillings per week, while men received ten shillings and foremen twenty, although this was reduced after the introduction of state non-contributory pensions in 1908 by the amount they received from the government.[41] It was also paid to victims of industrial accidents and to employees suffering illness or distress. The deaths of thirty-three year old Robina Townsend and fifteen year old Mary Crawford

---

[36] Historical information supplied to J. Currie, Inspector of Factories by United Thread Mills Ltd, 1952 (Paisley Museum and Art Gallery [PMAG], File 4/1/1).
[37] Lown, 'Not so much a factory', p. 39; Bradley, 'Technological change', p. 65.
[38] Coats' Works Committee, Minute Books (1897–1903) (PMAG, file 4/1/1).
[39] *Paisley Daily Express*, 14 Feb. 1882.
[40] Cited in Keir, *Coats' Story*, vol. 11, p. 58.
[41] Coats' Works Committee, Minute Books, 29 Oct. 1908 (Kinning Park Collection, Box A1/3).

resulted in the former's mother being paid a pension of six shillings a week since the daughter was the sole provider, and in the latter being given a donation of £25. The company bore the funeral expenses in both cases.[42] Another young girl of twelve seriously injured in the spooling department had her wages paid during her period of incapacitation and £100 was invested for her by trustees, which she would receive when reaching a suitable age or on marriage.[43] In spite of their arbitrariness, an important aspect of paternalism was fulfilled by these acts of benevolence: support in times of hardship. In a pre-welfare society the promise of a pension in old age tied workers to the company and increased their dependency on it.

Dependency was also fostered through educational initiatives in the areas of half-time and nursery education. Additional provision for technical education reinforced the sexual division of labour in the mills and increased the subordination of women in a workforce hierarchy dominated by men. The education clauses of the Factory Acts had forced employers of child labour to provide some form of schooling for their young workers.

From about mid-century to the late 1880s the leading thread manufacturers had relied on local schools to provide teaching, but disturbingly high levels of truancy among their half-timers,[44] and time lost in travelling between school and mill, encouraged Coats to open their own school in 1887. This initiative allowed the company to control more closely the timetable and syllabus of the school in relation to the requirements of production and socialise the young female workers into the culture of factory life. This was a view adopted by American mill owners, who were of the opinion that the 'best training for future mill work was mill work itself'.[45] As the American Cotton Manufacturers' Association put it in a statement in 1910: 'if you can get them young enough . . . you can train them to work, to acquire industrious habits, and become

---

[42] Coats' Works Committee, Minute Books (1890–97) (PMAG, file 1/10/1).
[43] Coats' Works Committee, Minute Books (1897–1903) (PMAG, file 4/1/1).
[44] Letter Book, 3 Feb.1882 (Kinning Park Collection Box HH3).
[45] G. Saxonhouse and G. Wright, 'Two forms of cheap labor in textile history', *Research in Economic History*, Supplement 3 (1984), p. 16.

excellent workers and good citizens'.[46] With their extensive American interests Coats were in a position to draw on such influential arguments and organise their young workers accordingly. New timetabling arrangements produced an alternating system of school and work similar to that used in the United States, and training was also provided in cooking and sewing. The girls were being educated not only as future workers, but also as wives and mothers too.[47] As Lown has recognised, it was as if the employers were trying to construct a femininity and masculinity in their own image, a particularly important social project since these essentially Christian employers were relying on a workforce whose primary role they saw as being in the home looking after husbands and children.[48]

The half-time school ceased to exist after 1904 when it was handed over to the Paisley School Board. Improved state educational provisions had decreed that all education for those under twelve years of age should be full-time, something which the threadocracy had always opposed.[49] The provision of nursery education from 1880 onwards for the children of 'deserving' workers tied the unmarried and married mothers to the firm. Acceptance was conditional on a woman proving she was 'widowed', or who had 'no income apart from what she herself can earn'.[50] Nursery provision also ensured that older children of working mothers were released from child-minding duties and so were free to enter the mills.[51] Technical education was made available on a voluntary basis. The firms of Coats and Clarks paid the fees of 'all young male workers who wished to attend the local Technical College'.[52] This policy was paralleled in the mills where, after 1910, young male workers of recognised potential were given a varied training in the labour process of each department in the hope that this would lead in time

---

[46] Saxonhouse and Wright, 'Cheap labor', p. 16.
[47] 'Reminiscences of former workers', *Ferguslie News*, April 1954.
[48] Lown, 'Not so much a factory', p. 40.
[49] Coats' Works Committee, Minute Books, 3 Mar. 1895 (PMAG, File 1/10/1); Keir, *Coats' Story*, vol. 1, p. 183.
[50] *Paisley and Renfrewshire Gazette*, 16 Oct. 1880.
[51] *Paisley and Renfrewshire Gazette*, 31 July 1880.
[52] Keir, *Coats' Story*, vol. 11, pp. 111–12.

to them 'taking up responsible positions in the company mills'.[53] Clearly through their educational policies the thread employers furthered the sexual division of labour and authority in the workplace: low-cost basic educational provision for young girls, and wider and more expensive training and experience for young male workers. Meanwhile, employee dependency was increased by the provision of creche and nursery facilities.

Initiatives in the areas of education and pensions were complemented by recreational strategies designed to foster group and company identities. In a meadow near the Ferguslie works Coats built tennis courts, cricket and football pitches, and this led to the formation of works and departmental sides.[54] In addition, bowling greens were established from the 1890s.[55] At away-day excursions races were held by individual departments for their workers only. There were separate races for spoolers, copwinders, re-winders, hankwinders, bleachfield workers, and half-timers.[56]

The excursion itself was, of course, a time to re-affirm company identity. All began with an assembly at the works, followed by a parade accompanied by assorted bands through the main thoroughfares of Paisley to the railway station. On reaching the destination company banners would be unfurled and paraded through the streets.[57] During one excursion to Edinburgh, the workers of Coats 'marched through the streets accompanied by a huge model of thread bobbins'.[58] Although the firms of Coats and Clarks merged in 1896, specific firm loyalties were encouraged and social intercourse with workers from other mills was discouraged. This was enshrined in employment policy as well as in recreation. Coats complained to Clarks about hiring workers from Ferguslie without their permission. In reply Clarks agreed that the practice was 'undesirable' and stated that 'three of our Departments were given definite instructions that they were not to engage workers who

---

[53] Keir, *Coats' Story*, vol. 11, pp. 111–12.
[54] Blair, *Paisley Thread*, p. 81.
[55] Ibid, p. 81.
[56] *Paisley Herald and Renfrewshire Gazette*, 1 July 1878.
[57] Ibid, 1 July 1878.
[58] Keir, *Coats' Story*, vol. 1, pp. 183–4.

have previously been at Ferguslie'.[59] Interestingly, Japanese cotton masters used a similar strategy and from 1888 onwards, before hiring labour, members of the Japan Cotton Spinners' Federation had to receive the consent of the previous employer.[60] Cotton employers worried over labour supply and potential militancy among their workforce seem to have adopted a policy of close control regardless of their nationality. However, in Paisley social separation also extended to recreation. Members of Coats' bowling club had to receive company permission to play at Clarks' Seedhill green.[61] Such a strategy was designed to inhibit the growth of inter-workplace solidarity and maximise rivalry between groups of workers both in and between firms. The advantages of such a strategy were demonstrated in the 1907 strike at the Anchor works. Efforts by the Anchor workers to extend the dispute to the Ferguslie mill failed until intimidation of those still at work forced management to close it, with the workers put on full wages for the duration of the strike.[62]

Like the excursions, soirées were also occasions to re-affirm the hierarchical nature of production and to promote the idea of mutuality between capital and labour. The first annual soirée of the employees of Coats took place in 1871 and was repeated in subsequent years up to the First World War. The platform party contained the leading members of the firm as well as ministers of religion. As they ascended the platform they were normally greeted 'with ringing cheers from the large assembly, many rising to their feet'.[63] The themes of the addresses of the various speakers were similar regardless of the firm involved. Common elements were the 'cordial relations which existed betwixt them and their employees'.[64] Bradley has argued that the family imagery used in the speeches by

---

[59] Letter Books, 1905–11 (Kinning Park Collection Box A2/1).
[60] J. Hunter, 'Recruitment in the Japanese Silk Reeling and Cotton Spinning Industries, 1870s–1930s', *Proceedings of the British Association for Japanese Studies*, 9 (1984), pp. 78–9.
[61] Minutes of Directors of J. & P. Coats, 24 May 1898 (Kinning Park Collection Box A1/2).
[62] *Glasgow Herald*, 3 Oct. 1907.
[63] *Paisley Daily Express*, 7 Feb. 1880, 14 Feb. 1882.
[64] *Paisley Daily Express*, 17 Feb. 1882.

paternalist employers appealed to largely female workforces as 'it resonated with women's own life experiences and interests'.[65] As we shall see, on the whole, the benevolence which underscored this was much praised and welcomed by the female workers as it made them feel part of an industrial family. Other features of the speeches were the success of their company in establishing themselves in highly competitive world markets,[66] as well as exhortions to domestic economy, sobriety and thrift.[67] To the latter end Coats established a Friendly Benefit Society and encouraged their workers to deposit part of their earnings in the local Savings Bank.[68] However, the major thrust of the speeches emphasised the mutuality of capital and labour and, almost contradictorily, to stress the dependency of the workers on their employers. Thus Robert Balderstone, manager of the Anchor works, at a conversazione of Clarks workers claimed it was 'a great source of pleasure . . . to see so many bonny lasses here in response to your [John Clark] kind invitation, and I can assure you . . . that every one in your employment has fully appreciated the honour you have done them in asking them to meet you here on this grand occasion.' (Applause).[69]

While the provision of educational, recreational and welfare amenities demonstrated the beneficient, if somewhat subtle, face of paternalism, this was complemented at suitable times by displays of abrasiveness designed to reinforce power relationships within the workplace. Expressions of dissent in the mills were rarely tolerated, as such 'strikes were treated as breaches of contract' by an employing class deeply attached to the Christian values of discipline and obedience. This ethos was summed up succinctly by Thomas Coats in a dispute with his dyers in 1883 when he remarked that 'he wouldn't be dictated to by the trade, and if they fought against him he would fight too'.[70] The belligerence of the employers in the face of

---

[65] Bradley, 'Technological change', p. 65.
[66] *Paisley Daily Express*, 17 Feb. 1882.
[67] *Paisley Daily Express*, 17 Feb. 1882; *Paisley Herald and Renfrewshire Gazette*, 8 Jan. 1876; *Paisley Daily Express*, 3 Mar. 1883.
[68] *Textile Recorder* (May, 1887), p. 14.
[69] *Paisley Daily Express*, 14 Feb. 1882.
[70] *Paisley Daily Express*, 22 June 1883.

potential challenges to their authority was underscored by the introduction of an elaborate code of industrial discipline. This involved a high degree of bureaucratic surveillance of employee performance. At the end of every working fortnight the foreman was instructed to 'write a report on the workers under his charge', stating whether they had performed satisfactorily, or otherwise, and sent to the sub-manager. Workers found to be guilty of bad timekeeping, inattentiveness, 'behaving badly', or whatever, were summoned before the manager. To assist the manager in coming to a decision on sanctions the complete record of the girl's behaviour and performance at the mill was obtained from record books held in the counting house.[71]

The detailed knowledge Coats had on their employees was also demonstrated by a trivial incident in which an anonymous letter was sent to the company complaining that a female worker in the cop-winding department, who, it was claimed, did not need to work as her husband was making thirty shillings a week in the packing department, and her children were also earning, was denying work to women with small families. Coats made extensive enquiries on the strength of this letter and were able to ascertain the complete family circumstances of the accused, and that of her married children; one of whom was found to be separated from her 'lazy and drunken' husband.[72] It seems that wherever textile employers have adopted the strategy of paternalism it has led to a more defined shaping and regulation of the family and household structure of the workers.[73] Checks, as we have seen elsewhere, were also kept on the movement of workers between firms and mills. Workers found guilty of recalcitrant behaviour found it difficult to evade hostile employers and find work in other mills. The close cooperation of the thread mills on these matters, as well as on pay, increased the dependency of the worker as employers could not be

---

[71] Clark & Co. Ltd, Rules for the Management of Workers, Sept. 1908 (PMAG File 4/1/2).
[72] Letter Book, 1 Mar. 1910 (Kinning Park Collection, Box A/21).
[73] Bradley, 'Technological change'; Lown, 'Not so much a factory'; Bursfield, 'Skill', B14, p. 98.

played off against each other. Managerial strategies could not be challenged with reference to other practices and pay rates.

Although the object of paternalism was, in the words of Sir Peter Coats to a gathering of his workers, to demonstrate that 'Their interests and his were the same . . . namely, the prosperity and success of the Ferguslie Thread Works,[74] the crucial question remains as to how the workers responded to these paternalistic initiatives and policies. On the whole, it has to be said that they reacted positively to paternalism, and for most of the period under investigation were incorporated into the firm's notion of an organic industrial community in which inequality in the distribution of power and wealth was legitimised both in the workplace and the wider society. Evidence for this can be found by examining a series of interconnected aspects of mill life in Paisley, including values, conduct and the language of social relationships, and the way they were derived, or not, from the dominant ideology of the threadocracy.

Thrift, provident living and good works were stressed by the Coats and Clarks in annual speeches to their workforce. The internalisation of these values by the workers was demonstrated in practical ways, among which were the setting up of the Ferguslie Thread Workers' Relief Committee and several company-inspired savings initiatives. The Relief Committee dispensed financial assistance to Paisley households experiencing distress and hardship. During the 1878/9 depression the Ferguslie workers in association with their employers raised enough money to assist 396 households, mainly handloom weavers and labourers, but also skilled workers, in distress. Workers from Clarks' Anchor Mill contributed in the same year £281 towards the upkeep of convalescent homes and the Paisley Infirmary.[75]

Good works were buttressed by the self-improving effects of thrift, something which the mill workers were socialised into from an early age. Half-timers were encouraged to deposit five shillings every month from their earnings in the local savings bank, a sum which was matched by their employers. At the end of three years

---

[74] *Paisley Daily Express*, 7 Feb. 1880.
[75] *Paisley Daily Express*, 1 Mar. 1879.

they had a lump sum of around twenty pounds.[76] The savings habit was fostered by Coats, who in 1884 established a Friendly Benefit Society to cover workers for sickness and death. There was also talk among the workers of forming a works' savings bank but management convinced them of the benefits of continuing their association with the Paisley Savings Bank, whose assets had increased from £60,000 in 1854 to upwards of £96,000 in 1871.[77] Such initiatives encouraged ideas of self-help and individualism, and increased the dependency of the workers, particularly the half-timers, on the firm. However, the provision of friendly society benefits also had an additional advantage for the employers in the sense that they undermined the attractiveness of trade union membership.

Although the acceptance of thrift by the mill workers can be interpreted as functional in a pre-welfare society and, therefore, inconclusive evidence of the internalisation of what might be deemed bourgeois values on the part of the workers,[78] when one relates this to other forms of behaviour the ambiguity seems less obvious. Primary indentification with the threadocracy, particularly at important life cycle events such as marriage and death, was very strong among the mill workers of Paisley.

The celebration of vital family events seemed to unite employers and workers in a shared notion of an organic industrial community. When in 1857 James Coats returned from America with his bride, Ann Auchinloss, Paisley was brought to a 'standstill', as 'hundreds of people . . . waiting late of night' welcomed the newly weds home. *The Paisley Herald* described the scene:

> The deafening shout of the multitude when the first carriage came in sight, the music of instrumental bands . . . there was also artillery to fire midnight salvoes, after which the carriage horses were

---

[76] *Ferguslie News*, Feb./Mar. 1954.
[77] *Paisley Herald and Renfrewshire Gazette*, 21 Jan. 1871; *Textile Recorder* (May, 1887), p. 14.
[78] T. C. Smout, *A Century of the Scottish People, 1832–1850* (1986); R. Q. Gray, 'Thrift and working-class mobility in Victorian Edinburgh', in *Social Class in Scotland: past and present* (Edinburgh, 1976), pp. 128–42.

unyoked, a great army of Ferguslie workers pulled the first carriage up to Woodside House where his father lived.[79]

The scenes were repeated in less spectacular form, but no less enthusiastically, in 1876 on the occasion of the marriage of Thomas Glen-Coats. The Ferguslie mill workers erected an archway at the entrance to the grounds of Ferguslie House, bearing a motto made of roses, saying 'Welcome Home'. Another was erected at the western entrance of the grounds, this time wishing the couple 'Health and Happiness'.[80] Three years later another marriage in the Coats family saw 'crowds of people' thronging the surrounding streets of the Ferguslie Mill and 'cheering' the 'coaches containing the guests'.[81] Death in the family brought communal mourning and expressions of sympathy. The passing of Thomas Coats in 1883 saw most of the public buildings and many of the shops of Paisley closed.[82]

Specific firm identification on the part of labour also demonstrated itself in more trivial, but perhaps no less interesting or profound, ways. A yacht race in 1901 between James Coats and Kenneth Clark for a purse of £500 (approximately ten to twenty times the annual average mill wage) had the town of 'Paisley talking for weeks'; the employees of Coats were said to have 'exulted in their employer's victory', while the Clarks' workers claimed victory was only had at the expense of damage to the latter's vessel.[83] The incident not only reveals the close identification of the workers with the respective mill-owning families, but also shows how inter-firm rivalry divided the workers in the mills into distinct sub-groupings based on specific company cultures. This kind of socialisation of workers in Coats began at an early working age as a few lines from a half-timers' song sung at the expense of their counterparts in the firm of Clarks clearly demonstrates:

> For in Clarks they gang braw
> with their aprons An'a,

---

[79] Keir, *Coats' Story*, vol. 1, p. 73.
[80] *Paisley Daily Express*, 22 April 1876.
[81] *Paisley Daily Express*, 18 Sept. 1879.
[82] Hunter, 'Thomas Coats', p. 334.
[83] Keir, *Coats' Story*, vol. 1, pp. 188-9.

but the Coats' half-timers take
the bray o'them a'.[84]

The language of social relationships provides additional evidence of worker identification with employer structured notions of community and can be gathered from the numerous addresses presented by the mill workers to their bosses at social functions. At the celebrations to mark the inauguration of the George A. Clark Town Hall in 1882, the Anchor Mill workers expressed, in an address to their 'much esteemed and respected employers', feelings of 'respect and admiration'. The address went on to compliment the latter for caring for 'the sick and aged . . . [as well as] the widowed and the fatherless'.[85] Some twenty-six years earlier the workers of the same firm drew up an address thanking their employers for providing a pleasure excursion down the Clyde, and claiming they 'felt privilege[d]' to be employed by 'a firm who are individually distinguished by their Christian character'. Their 'Moral and Religious rule' had, the workers claimed, kept the mill 'free from strife'.[86] More discrete examples of the language of indentification were found in the company banners and other icons of a symbolic nature. Company excursions, as we have seen, were occasions to reaffirm specific attachments to firm and locality. Naturally, locality was personified in the person of the employer. By these means the solidarities of class were transcended by the solidarities of work group culture.

However, after 1900 the paternalism of the threadocracy began to show signs of wear and tear. As changes in the labour process and the geography of recruitment began to affect the relationship between employer and worker, there emerged a more oppositional mill culture, a phenomenon furthered by the growth of trade unionism and the Independent Labour Party (ILP) in Paisley. In these changing circumstances alternative visions and explanations were forwarded to rival those of the employers. Although this will be taken up more fully in the chapter dealing with industrial

---

[84] *Ferguslie News*, April 1954.
[85] 'Inauguration of the G. A. Clark Town Hall', p. 100.
[86] 'Address of Welcome and Congratulation to Matthew Clark Esq.', 17 May 1856 (Kinning Park Collection Box HH3).

relations, one sign of the growing disillusionment of the workers with paternalist initiatives was the failure of J. & P. Coats' Girls' Club. Established in 1901, the Club offered classes in dressmaking, physical culture, millinery and health. There was also a library attached to it with lending rights to members, and also a hall for concerts and dances. The aim of the Club was to 'promote self-knowledge and self-development' among the members.[87] But it failed to attract sufficient interest from the female workers and the Coats family referred to it as a 'non success'.[88] The increasing disenchantment with paternalism and the emergence of an oppositional culture in the mills placed greater stress on the coherence of organisation and cooperation among employers. This also applied to the other branches of the cotton trade. The question is, was their enough common interest among cotton employers to reap the benefit of federation?

Employers and Organisation

Organised cooperation among cotton masters has a somewhat obscure and shadowy history. There appears to be clear evidence that an employers' association existed in cotton spinning in Glasgow in the 1830s, and included such prominent spinners as Henry Dunlop, chairman, William Houldsworth and others.[89] Meetings were held in the Exchange Sale Rooms, Glasgow, but there seems to have been no written rules, or regular subscriptions, except for a charge levied on each member for every thousand spindles in his mill for the upkeep of a secretary.[90] Although the Webbs were of the opinion that there were no fixed times or places for meetings, according to John Houldsworth's evidence to the Select Committee

---

[87] J. & P. Coats, 'Notes on Welfare' (PMAG, File 1/5/72).
[88] J. & P. Coats, Letter Book, 1905–11 (Kinning Park Collection, Box A2/1).
[89] First Report of the Select Committee on Combinations of Workmen, Evidence of J. Houldsworth, PP, VIII, 1837–8, VIII, q. 430, p. 19.
[90] D. Bremner, *The Industries of Scotland: their rise, progress and present condition* (1969 edn), p. 285.

the Glasgow cotton masters' association met on 5 and 29 April 1837. From this we might assume that meetings were held on a fortnightly basis, or more frequently as needs dictated, for example during the spinners' strike of 1837. However, there are no recorded meetings of the employers' association after this date until 1851. The imminence of a strike by the Operative Cotton Spinners of Glasgow led to the convening of a meeting of the Master Cotton Spinners' Association in the Religious Institution Rooms in October, with Henry Dunlop in the chair.[91] Since Dunlop was involved in the 1837 strike it showed that the organisation had a good deal of continuity in terms of its leadership. However, one suspects that the masters' association was an anti-strike body, rather than one concerned with coordinating employers' interests on a wider range of economic concerns.

The nearest thing we have to something resembling the organised interests of the employers was the Glasgow Cotton Supply Association. Although the Association was primarily responsible for the import of raw cotton into Glasgow, it might also have acted as a forum for discussing matters of common interest among employers.[92] But given the cut-throat competition of the spinning trade co-operation on a sustained basis was difficult. This also applied to the weaving sector of the industry. To undermine the smaller and unscrupulous cost-cutting firms, the larger and more respectable firms formed in the 1880s the Power Loom Cloth Manufacturers Association of Glasgow. The main objects of the Association were to establish a uniform rate of wages and to prevent undercutting of prices by unfair employers. The initiative, however, soon collapsed 'owing to mutual distrust and jealousy on the part of the manufacturers'.[93]

It was in the more successful sewing thread sector that employer cooperation went furthest, leading in time to the construction of a cartel. The earliest written mention of a Thread Trade Association

---

[91] *Glasgow Sentinel*, 18 Oct. 1851.
[92] *Cotton Supply Reporter*, 15 Oct. 1851.
[93] M. H. Irwin, 'On the conditions of work in the textile industries of Glasgow and in the calico printing and turkey red dyeing of the Vale of Leven', Royal Commission on Labour, pt. 1, PP, 1893–4, XXXVII, p. 174.

(TTA) occurs in the letter books of J. & P. Coats, and included, in addition to Coats, the firms of Clark & Co., J. Clark, Glasgow, Edmund Asworth and Sons, Bolton, Kerr & Co. and J. Carlisle, both of Paisley. The secretary of the Association was William Borland, a Glasgow lawyer. Brook and Chadwick were also informed of price changes, although they were not members of the Association. The agreement on prices was only applicable in specified markets and 'if any firm belonging to the Association undersells in the countries named, the others are at liberty to ignore any or all of the Continental agreements.' Firms outside the TTA were kept in line with agreed pricing policy by threats of increased competition and undercutting in their most profitable markets.[94]

The institutionalisation of cooperation reached its apotheosis in the establishment of the Sewing Central Agency, which controlled ouput, markets and prices for thread throughout the world. It also acted as a pressure group designed to influence state policy regarding the operation of the Factory Acts. A letter from Messrs Finlayson and Bousfield & Co. referring to the need to resist the introduction of a shorter working week for factory workers was considered by the directors of J. & P. Coats. They suggested that the best strategy was to petition Sir William Arrol MP to lobby the Home Secretary and other MPs to reject the intended changes in the working conditions of factory workers.[95]

The close cooperation of the thread interests was part of the alchemy of successful business operations. The spinning and weaving ends of the industry were too divided and involved in such intense competition that cooperation, even when it was to their advantage, was unsustainable. Their policy was one of confrontation with their employees and their business rivals. Continued downward pressure on wages was their only answer to shrinking markets and foreign competition. Saving on capital rather than labour undermined any

---

[94] Letter from Coats to J. Clark jnr, 9 Aug. 1880 (Kinning Park Collection, Box HH3).
[95] Minute Book of Directors of J. & P. Coats, 1 Aug. 1901 (Kinning Park Collection Box A1/2).

attempts to regulate wages and prices. The thread manufacturers saw the benefits of cooperation on issues of common concern at an early stage in the development of the industry and, as we shall see, were better able to win their workers over to the goals of the enterprise and to exercise control over domestic and world markets.

CHAPTER FIVE

Worker Organisation and Industrial Conflict

THE history of trade unionism in the Scottish cotton industry after 1838 is somewhat obscure. It is generally presumed that prior to the 1837 spinners' strike, cotton workers in the Glasgow and surrounding area were the best organised and most militant cotton workers in Scotland. With the defeat of the spinners by the cotton masters in 1837, however, it is argued that trade unionism failed to recover, and under the impact of increasing feminisation of all sectors of the cotton industry in Scotland, but particularly spinning, it collapsed altogether.[1]

While it is true that the defeat inflicted on the spinners in 1837 was damaging to the cotton spinners' union, and it could be argued to the whole Scottish labour movement, trade unionism continued among male spinners, although with less effectiveness. Craft unionism remained the mode of organisation among key male workers in the weaving sector, where, through kinship networks, effective controls on the supply of labour were established. Only in the thread sector was unionisation very slow to develop as paternalistic authoritarianism and the ages of the largely female workforce made organisation problematic. But, even in such a tightly controlled industrial setting as thread, there were signs of growing organisation towards the end of our period as the workforce expanded and became more ethnically diverse. The role of ethnicity, in particular

---

[1] W. H. Fraser, 'The Glasgow Cotton Spinners 1837', in *Scottish Themes*, eds J. Butt and J. T. Ward (Edinburgh, 1976), pp. 80–97; J. Butt, 'Labour and Industrial Relations in the Scottish Cotton Industry during the Industrial Revolution', in *Scottish Textile History*, ed. J. Butt and K. Ponting (Aberdeen, 1987), pp. 139–60.

that of the Irish, in shaping the contours of industrial relations is important as it provides some insight into the contrasting experiences of conflict in the different sectors of the Scottish cotton industry.

Of course, as Gordon has shown for the Dundee jute industry,[2] and Price for British industry as a whole,[3] the absence of formal membership of a permanent association of labour should not lead to the conclusion that organisation itself was non-existent. Informal workgroup organisation was for much of the nineteenth century a more common form of organisation among workers than membership of a trade union branch. Women especially found *ad hoc* organisation more in keeping with their dual workplace and domestic roles than formal associations.[4] Their low wages also generally militated against the establishment of permanent organisations. Thus much of the organisation of female cotton workers was done on an improvised, 'off the cuff' basis, which has to be taken into account when examining the organisation of workers in the Scottish cotton industry and the way industrial struggles were conducted after 1838.

1. *Trade Unionism in Spinning*

For the first half of the nineteenth century, cotton spinners' unions in Scotland had the reputation of being well organised, militant and, when the occasion demanded, violent. In his seminal study of the cotton spinners' strike of 1837, Fraser has documented the growth, organisation and industrial tactics of the Glasgow Association of Operative Cotton Spinners. The Association combined pre-industrial forms of behaviour with a more recognisably modern administrative structure. The latter might include a visible leadership,

---

[2] E. Gordon, 'Women, Work and Collective Action: Dundee jute workers, 1870–1906', *Journal of Social History*, 21 (1987), pp. 27–47.
[3] R. Price, *Labour in British Society* (1986).
[4] E. Gordon, 'Women, trade unions and industrial militancy, 1850–1890', in *Uncharted Lives: extracts from Scottish women's experiences, 1850–1982*, ed. Glasgow Women's Studies Group (Glasgow, 1983), pp. 52–73.

subscriptions, branch organisation and delegate meetings. The spinners also adopted the primary craft principle of limiting the supply of labour by refusing to teach persons who were not the 'sons or brothers of a spinner'.[5] By doing so they virtually established a closed shop. It was estimated by one working spinner that out of a total of 1,000 spinners in Glasgow in 1837, 850 to 900 were members of the Association.[6] The pre-industrial dimension of their mode of organisation lay in their willingness to use violent tactics to enforce the rules of the Association. Attempts to introduce female spinners almost always ended in violence, such as at Broomward Mill in 1819–20 when the factory was burned down and a woman shot dead. Shootings of blacklegs occurred with alarming frequency, such as in 1824 when a worker was shot and several others were wounded. Three years later workers of the Adelphi Mill were shot in their beds.[7]

Fraser has argued that these tactics were the result of the influx of the Fenian Irish with their history of violence in rural struggles. Indeed, many of the executives of the Association were Irish born.[8] By the second decade of the nineteenth century the Irish had an established presence in spinning and other less skilled preparatory tasks, as well as piecing. The capture of the best paid occupations in Scotland contrasted with the failure of the Irish to occupy much more than positions in the cardrooms and blowing rooms in the Lancashire cotton industry. Henry Houldsworth, cotton master, said of Glasgow in 1833 that 'our mills are almost full of Irish'.[9] An examination of census enumerator books for Bridgeton points to a disproportionate number of Irish heads of households in this important cotton district of Glasgow. In a sample of 153 cotton working households in Bridgeton in 1851 forty-three, or 28 per cent, were of Irish origin. Of those households in which the head was a cotton spinner, out of a total of forty-three, eight, or 18.6

---

[5] Fraser, 'Cotton Spinners', p. 82; First Report of the Select Committee on Combinations of Workmen, PP, 1837–8, VIII, Appendix 3, pp. 299–301.
[6] Combinations of Workmen, qs. 833–4, p. 44.
[7] Fraser, 'Cotton Spinners', p. 86.
[8] Fraser, 'Cotton Spinners', p. 87.
[9] PP, 1833, VI, p. 311.

per cent, were of Irish origin, with only fourteen, or 32.5 per cent, being Glasgow born, and the rest coming from other parts of Scotland.[10] Considering that in 1841 the percentage of Irish born in Glasgow amounted to 16 per cent of the total population,[11] the cotton industry employed a disproportionate number of Irish migrants with the volatile results described above.

In terms of wages and conditions the ends appeared to the spinners to justify the means. As early as the 1820s average wage rates in Glasgow were higher than elsewhere in Britain.[12] The first factory inspector for Scotland, James Stuart, was so impressed by the organisation of the spinners that he was moved to remark: 'the operatives have so completely organised their association, as not only to prescribe the wages to be paid to the members of the association, but to all other persons, from whatever quarter they may come'.[13]

The strike of 1837 was a disaster for the cotton spinners. Not only were the men defeated, but the association of the strike with the worst excesses of violence, including murder and intimidation, led to the trial and deportation of the leaders.[14] After this the Association was but a pale shadow of its former self as the employers established their right to manage their enterprises as they saw fit.

Did defeat, however, render the spinners incapable of mass collective action in the future? Most historians, drawing on the work of the Webbs, have taken a highly pessimistic view on this issue. The Webbs' information came from a Glasgow correspondent, James Robertson, who claimed that since 1838 strikes had occurred only in 'individual concerns', implying that the unit organisation had become the immediate workgroup rather than the union.[15] More recently, Fraser has argued that 'the spinners' union was

---

[10] Census Enumerator Books: Bridgeton 1851, 1871, 1891.
[11] A. Slaven, *The Development of the West of Scotland: 1750–1960* (1976), pp. 141–5.
[12] Fraser, 'Cotton Spinners', p. 82.
[13] A. Ure, *The Cotton Manufacture of Great Britain* (1836), p. 286.
[14] Fraser, 'Cotton Spinners', pp. 95–6. The men were pardoned in August 1840 and were never transported to Australia, spending their time in the hulks on the Thames.
[15] Webb Collection on Trade Unions (BLPES), xxxiv, ff. 425–6.

effectively broken',[16] and this view was underscored by Butt, who claimed the masters had 'virtually destroyed a previously effective trade union and in its mauling reduced its leadership and divided its membership'.[17] The historical orthodoxy was accepted by Bolin-Hort, who, in the most recent statement on the period, claimed that 'attempts to re-establish the [spinners'] union were counteracted'.[18] Although one cannot contest the view that the Glasgow Association lost much of its power in the workplace and its ability to control the labour supply, the capacity for collective organisation, if measured by the means to wage industrial warfare, remained intact.

One of the first reactions of the hand mule spinners to defeat in the 1837 strike was to strengthen their organisation through the inclusion of male self-actor minders.[19] Although they later parted company, this infusion of new members did much to restore the fortunes of the Glasgow Association. By 1844 the Association was able to mount a strike in pursuit of a wage claim for an increase in wages of 10 per cent in eighteen separate establishments in Glasgow.[20] Later published accounts of the strike show that the masters were forced 'to establish a list of prices which was acted upon until 1846'.[21] Another strike followed in the 'big wheel' and 'improved machinery' factories and the employers agreed to the continuance of the price list.[22] These were not individual acts of industrial unrest, indeed, the cotton spinners were still imbued with a collective consciousness. The *Glasgow Saturday Post* reported in late 1849 a meeting 'of all the cotton spinners of the West of Scotland' in Paisley to discuss a demand for an increase in wages.[23] Moreover, there was still active cooperation between the spinners

---

[16] Fraser, 'Cotton Spinners', p. 97.
[17] Butt, 'Labour and Industrial Relations', p. 159.
[18] P. Bolin-Hort, *Work, Family and the State: child labour and the organisation of production in the British cotton industry* (1989), pp. 56–7.
[19] Webb Collection, ff. 381–6.
[20] *Glasgow Saturday Post*, 2 Feb. 1844.
[21] *Glasgow Sentinel*, 17 Dec. 1853.
[22] *Glasgow Sentinel*, 17 Dec. 1853.
[23] 15 Sept. 1849.

and other trades in industrial disputes. A strike in 1850 at Simpsons of Bridgeton, Glasgow, in opposition to longer working hours saw the spinners supported by other trades, including dyers, cloth-wrappers, potters, and so on.[24] One year later mass action in mid-October by mule spinners in support of a wage increase closed all but a 'dozen or so' cotton factories in Glasgow.[25] The all-out strike had resulted from the failure of the spinners' union to pressurise targeted employers – McNaught and Co., Glasgow, and Stevenson and Co., Crosslie – into acceding to its demands and thus breaking the united front of the masters. Interestingly, the Association was able to levy its members at the rate of a shilling a week in support of those members on strike.[26]

Although the outcome of the 1851 strike is unknown, the spinners struck intermittently throughout the 1850s and early 1860s. The Society's organisation was coherent enough to present an address to the famous Scottish explorer, David Livingstone, himself a former cotton spinner, in mid-September 1857.[27] However, the former's effectiveness was constantly being eroded by changes in the labour process.

The process of coupling wheels which had begun in the aftermath of the 1837 strike saw the number of hand mule spinners decrease. From a peak of around a thousand in 1837, the number had fallen to 400 in 1862.[28] While this would not have been too disastrous if the male spinners had been able to continue to occupy a strategic position in the production process, increasing feminisation and the widespread use of the self-actor made this unlikely. The cotton famine of the early 1860s accelerated the process of decline and forced the Association profoundly to alter its position on a number of vital issues. Like other craft unions, the Association opted in favour of emigration as a means of dealing with the question of surplus labour,[29] and supported the introduction of arbitration boards

---

[24] *Glasgow Sentinel*, 19 Oct. 1850.
[25] *Glasgow Sentinel*, 18 Oct. 1851.
[26] *Glasgow Sentinel*, 11 Oct. 1851.
[27] *Commonwealth*, 19 Sept. 1857.
[28] *Commonwealth*, 16 Aug. 1862.
[29] *Glasgow Sentinel*, 16 Aug. 1862.

to settle industrial disputes.[30] The battle to maintain list prices was given up as an impractical chimera and paved the way for a more productivity consciousness among the spinners, as well as an increasingly individualised attitude to earnings. As their delegate, John Wilson, put it at a soirée of hand and mule spinners in April 1863:

> They had battled long with their employers to maintain the same price for spinning a pound of yarn, irrespective of any improved means to increase the quantity in a given time, and hundreds of thousands of pounds had been spent by the operatives in that struggle, but now the idea is exploded, and the question now is, what amount of wages can I make to take home to my family, without reference to increased quantity of yarn by improved machinery.[31]

As part of the new realism of the Association the links with the wider labour movement were severed in September 1867 with its withdrawal from the United Trades Council of Glasgow for being 'too political'.[32] Just prior to the announcement of its deradicalisation, the Association had welcomed the formation of its first female branch, whose object 'was to progress cautiously until they had received the same wages as men for the same quantity of work, and thus promote each other's welfare, or fall together'.[33]

The gender divide in spinning was at last bridged, but unfortunately it was too little too late. The last concerted action by the operative spinners came in the years 1870 and 1871 over wages and employment practices. By 1875 the Webbs could record that 'there was now no organisation among men in the spinning mills' of Glasgow.[34] The once all-powerful spinners' union had ceased to exist and the possibility of reforming the union on the basis of a largely female workforce was nullified by further changes in the labour process. The introduction of the previously referred-to

---

[30] Webb Collection on Trade Unions, f. 423.
[31] *Glasgow Sentinel*, 11 April 1863.
[32] *Glasgow Sentinel*, 30 Sept. 1867.
[33] *Glasgow Sentinel*, 6 Apr. 1867.
[34] Webb Collection on Trade Unions, ff. 381–6.

multi-part system so effectively subordinated the female minders that organisation was to prove impossible.

2. *Trade Unionism in Weaving*

In spite of being overshadow by the impressive cohesion of the cotton spinners in the years before 1837, the power loom factory workers established powerful sectional societies based on craft principles after 1850. These societies were small and exclusively male. Made up of occupations such as tenters, beamers and warpers, they were able to exert controls on entry to the trade and to determine the sex of the power loom weavers through kinship networks and their strategic positioning in the process of production. The organisation of the female power loom weavers generally failed, in spite of a number of attempts during the nineteenth century. Indeed, when reviewing the evidence it is hard to avoid the conclusion that the lack of organisation among women was the result of collusion between employers and the craft unions. It was only in the late nineteenth century that the former achieved organisational cohesion and much of this was due to outside middle-class assistance. Until then what instances we find of industrial action among power loom weavers tend to have been *ad hoc* and mostly firm-specific.

The most powerful trade society in the weaving trade was the Glasgow and West of Scotland Power Loom Tenters' Society (GWSPLTS). As we have seen in a previous chapter, the time-served tenters were responsible for the day-to-day organisation of production: putting in and taking out the web, as well as disciplining and overseeing the work of the female weavers. According to the Report on Trade Unions (1905–7), the Society was officially founded in 1850; contemporary accounts, however, point to an earlier date. It would appear that the tenters' society was inaugurated at a meeting on 2 March 1848 in the Lyceum Rooms, Glasgow. The impetus behind the formation of the new organisation came from the depression of the previous two years, which had forced the tenters on to short time. The solution was recognised as one of controlling the supply of labour, particularly that flowing in from the rural areas of Scotland, in order 'to get back to full table prices whenever a revival of trade takes place'.[35] From the outset the establishment of fundamental craft controls over entry was the main policy of the union. In spite of the paucity of its membership, with only 350 at its peak in 1907,[36] the society was able to maintain an exclusion policy achieved through its power to determine the ratio of tenters to looms and by refusing to accept the employment of male power loom weavers.

The power of the new union was recognised as early as the late 1850s, and the Glasgow press was flooded with complaints regarding the 'tyranny' of the tenters' society.[37] By keeping weaving exclusively female; the Society was able to preserve the idea of the tenter as a master craftsman with, of course, the wages to complement this status. The introduction of male weavers would have involved greater competition for the more highly paid work, and also would have undermined the use made by the tenters' society of gender as a means of establishing pay differentials.

Given the importance of the tenter in the production process, employers appeared willing to accept the constraints imposed on recruitment by the rules of the union. Indeed, the discipline the tenters exercised over the female weavers was an acceptable trade-off to the employers. As a former leader of the GWSPLTS observed before a strike in 1883: 'There had been no trouble, while negotiations and conciliation efforts between masters and men prevented anything in the way of industrial disturbances'.[38] This cosy relationship between the employers and their overseers was finally broken in 1907/8 when a dispute broke out over the employment of learners or apprentices. To preserve their right to regulate the ratio of learners to tenters, the GWSPLTS engaged in a strike lasting around four months. The Society was defeated by the hiring of blacklegs from the ranks of the unemployed male textile workers,

---

[35] *Glasgow Saturday Post*, 4 Mar. 1848.
[36] Report on Trade Unions, PP, 1909, xxxix, p. 26.
[37] *Commonwealth*, 20 Mar. 1858.
[38] W. Freer, *My Life and Memories* (Glasgow, 1929), pp. 66–7.

of which there were large numbers, given the depression in the Lancashire cotton industry in that period.[39]

Below the rank of tenter was another tier of workers claiming craft status, including beamers and warpers, organised in a variety of small, but powerful unions. In strict chronology the first to be formed was the Glasgow Power Loom Beamers' Society (GLBS) in 1855, followed by the Glasgow Handmill and Horizontal Warpers' Society (GHHWS) in 1886, and, finally, the Scottish Ball Warp Brush Beamers' Society (SBWBBS) in 1896. Although membership figures are unavailable for most of our period, the data for the first decade of the twentieth century demonstrates quite vividly the numerical insignificance of these organisations. The GLBS reached a peak of 160 in 1903, falling to 100 in 1907. The respective figures for the GHHWS were 180 and 167, while the SBWBBS had the almost laughable total of 46 in both years.[40] Unfortunately the census does not provide the kind of occupational data which would allow for comparison between union membership and the total number employed in a trade, but it would appear that a virtual closed shop was established. The warpers' society had a membership of 180 in 1903, while the total number of male warpers for Lanarkshire was put at 233 in the 1901 census.[41]

The object of the unions was similar to that of the tenters' society and all had rules governing the recruitment and training of apprentice labour. The SBWBBS' rule on this issue was typical, stating that 'members must get the sanction of the committee before proceeding to learn any apprentice or apprentices'.[42] The other issue of primary importance to these unions was the exclusion of female labour. As the skill involved in beaming or warping was socially rather than technically constructed, there was no reason why female workers could not develop the skills or assume the responsibilities involved in these occupations. Employers, in the

---

[39] *Glasgow Herald*, 7 Oct. 1907; Board of Trade, Reports on Strikes and Lockouts (PRO, LAB 34/25).
[40] Report on Trade Unions (1909), pp. 26–34.
[41] Eleventh Decennial Census of Scotland, PP, 1904, CVIII.
[42] Rules of the Scottish Ball Warp and Brush Beamers' Society (Scottish Record Office [SRO]: FS.7/55).

early 1900s, recognised this and a strike was fought out between the warpers and the firm of Hollins and Co., Bridgeton, over precisely this issue. However, failure by the management to recruit blackleg labour saw the former maintain gender exclusiveness in warping.[43]

Facing hostile opposition from both management and unions, as well as the difficulties deriving from their subordination both in the workplace and the wider society, to say that the organisation of female power loom weavers was problematical would be something of an understatement. In spite of this, there was a society of West of Scotland Power Loom Female Weavers dating back to 1833. However, little is known of the history of the organisation and it would appear it was a short-lived affair. During the 1849 power loom weavers' strike in Glasgow over an increase in wages, the workers claimed that they had 'no union and no organisation', and that they were in 'each factory . . . left to [do] in their own case as they think best'.[44] Ironically, it was the combination of the large manufacturers to defeat the strike that led to the call for district meetings, strike levies, and proper organisation.[45] Until the extent of employer cohesion was evident, it was claimed by the strikers that 'workers of one end of the town did not know the position . . . with those at the other'.[46] The determination of the former to defeat the strike, as well as the opposition of the male workers to 'the refractory workers',[47] led to the collapse of the strike in early June with the female workers returning 'on the old terms'.[48] The possibilities which opened up during the strike for the establishment of a permanent association of female power loom workers were negated in the wake of its defeat. And although the Webbs mention the existence of a female organisation in the weaving sector in 1863 for the 'protection of their industry',[49] nothing is known

---

[43] Annual Report of the Glasgow Trades Council (1902–3), p. 11.
[44] *Glasgow Saturday Post*, 21 April 1849.
[45] *Glasgow Courier*, 24 May 1849.
[46] *Glasgow Saturday Post*, 12 May 1849.
[47] *Glasgow Courier*, 28 April 1849.
[48] *Glasgow Courier*, 5 June 1849.
[49] Webb Collection on Trade Unions, XLVII.

of its activities or membership. If evidence of industrial action is indicative of worker organisation, apart from a strike in February 1863, then it was moribund until the late 1870s and 1880s. These strikes were generally small, unsuccessful affairs of short duration affecting individual enterprises rather than the industry as a whole. Like cotton spinning, the mode of organisation among the female workers continued to be informal and *ad hoc*. It was not until the 1890s that a fresh initiative was launched to organise female workers.

That move was initiated by middle-class women within the Women's Protective and Provident League (WPPL), with the assistance of the Glasgow Trades Council (GTC) following a successful strike in 1890. A meeting held in Bridgeton in the summer of that year and presided over by such local dignitaries as Professor Edward Caird and 'other traders and gentlemen', led to the formation of a branch in the district with a membership of around 200 female power loom weavers.[50] The membership was said to be spread over seventeen leading factories and organised by a 'fully equipped staff of office bearers'. There were also two delegates to represent the female weavers on the GTC.[51]

By 1893 membership of the WPPL had grown to 450. However, the new organisation had a short and uncertain lifespan. During the years 1895–7 it was unable to send delegates to the GTC, and in spite of a modest revival in 1897, by 1900 the organisation had collapsed. The Annual Report of the GTC for 1904–5 stated that 'The organisation of women workers of the city engaged the attention of the Council some years ago, and quite a number of women's unions . . . were formed . . . These have all ceased to exist some time ago'.[52] By that time the WPPL had transformed itself from a body concerned with the industrial organisation of women into a pressure group for securing legislation for improving working conditions for women in general.[53]

In spite of the failure of the WPPL's initiative, another attempt

---

[50] Annual Report of the Glasgow Trades Council (1890–1), p. 18.
[51] *The Trade Unionist*, 4 July 1891.
[52] Annual Report of the Glasgow Trades Council (1904–5), p. 17; E. Gordon, *Women and the Labour Movement in Scotland, 1850–1914* (Oxford, 1991), p. 215.
[53] Gordon, *Women and the Labour Movement*, p. 214.

was made to organise female weavers in 1907 largely through the work of Agnes Pettigrew.[54] In that year the West of Scotland Weaving Factories Female Workers Industrial Union (WSWFFWIU) was formed with an initial membership of 300, which was less than one-tenth of the total number of female weavers counted in the 1901 census.[55] The membership was open to all female workers employed in cotton factories, as well as those in carpet factories and other textile establishments, but the overwhelming number came from the weaving sector. The objects of the new union included the improvement of working conditions, the establishment of a 'fair rate of wages for all classes of work', whether paid by piece or fixed rates, and the provision of assistance for victimisation, strikes, lockouts, and so on. Unlike its predecessors, the new union was essentially proletarian and run by working-class women, with the exception of the president who was a man.[56]

The more working-class composition of the union's executive was reflected in its desire to combine with other textile occupations. Two years after its formation the WSWFFWIU affiliated to the Scottish Textile Trades Association (STTA), and four years after this merged its identity within the new Association. The defeat of the craft unions in the weaving sector following the 1907 tenters' strike allowed the GTC to galvanise the remnants of the organised workers into the STTA.[57] The weaving industry was finally organised on industrial lines, but in terms of effectiveness it was too much too late. By this time the cotton weaving industry was a pale shadow of its former self and the STTA had little power to challenge the strength of the employers. The weakness of the STTA was apparent from the start when the delegate of the beamers stated that its formation would 'prove a powerful factor in the prevention of those disastrous strikes which crippled trade and did so much harm to all concerned'.[58]

---

[54] Annual Report of the Glasgow Trades Council (1907–8), p. 24.
[55] Report on Trade Unions (1909), p. 34; Eleventh Decennial Census of Scotland.
[56] The rules, reports and balance sheets of the West of Scotland Female Textile Workers Industrial Union (SRO: FS.7/107).
[57] *Glasgow Herald*, 21 Oct. 1909.
[58] *Glasgow Herald*, 21 Oct. 1909.

3. Trade Unionism in Thread

In the authoritarian, paternalist factory regime of the thread combines trade unionism faced one of its sternest challenges. The power of the manufacturers was in stark contrast to the weakness of the workers, who had little to bargain with in terms of skill or in the scarcity of their labour. Moreover, since the majority of workers in the thread industry were single, young females their amenability to authority made challenges to the fiat of the employers unlikely. Beyond the skilled male dyers, trade unionism was unknown in the thread trade of Paisley, as were strikes, for almost the whole of the period under examination. There were no powerful trade unions, such as the cotton spinners' association, or small societies made up of strategic work groups, whose control of the labour process and entry was directly inverse to the size of their membership. Moreover, worker subordination to worker as, for example, in the case of the weaver/tenter system, did not exist in the thread industry. The workers were subordinated to capital and its functionaries in the workplace, thus denying key workers, such as tenters, control of the labour process. This was of enormous benefit to the thread manufacturers since voluntary disruption of production by the workforce was rare and new technology could be installed with little resistance. There is no doubt that the absence of organisation among the thread workers gave their employers an important commercial advantage over their counterparts in the spinning and weaving sectors of the Scottish cotton industry.

However, the stability of industrial relations in the Paisley thread industry was threatened in the first decade of the twentieth century by the interference of outside forces – the National Federation of Women Workers (NFWW) and the Independent Labour Party (ILP). Preceding, and laying the foundations for, institutional intervention was the partial disintegration of the paternalist regime of the threadocracy. The amalgamation of Clarks and Coats in 1896 established the new firm as one of the largest in the world. The ever increasing scale and scope of operations led to greater stress on bureaucratic methods of control. It also forced the company to look for supplies of labour from outside Paisley. An examination of thread workers' birthplaces from census enumerator books covering the years 1851, 1871 and 1891 shows how the organic industrial community of Paisley was becoming more fragmented and less stable. In 1851 it was noted that the Irish failed to establish themselves in Paisley since they had little connection with the shawl trade, which employed half the adult male labour force of the town.[59] Unmarried girls and women also failed to establish a presence in the emerging thread industry, preferring to find work in the jute industry of Dundee.[60] An examination of heads of households working in the textile industry underscores the insular structure of Paisley's population in 1851. Out of a sample of 178 heads of households, 137, or 77 per cent, were born in Paisley. However, there were signs that the closeknit textile community was breaking up, with 59.2 per cent (122 heads of households out of a total of 206) in 1871 being born in Paisley. By 1891 the number dramatically fell to 44.9 per cent (88 heads of households out of a total of 196). If this picture is broken down to include only heads of households employed in the thread industry then the fragmentation is even more acute, as the following table shows:

Table 25. *Place of birth of thread mill worker heads of households*

Date	Paisley No	%	Scotland No	%	Ireland No	%	England No	%
1871	63	51.6	50	40.9	6	5.7	3	2.5
1891	63	38.9	65	41.1	17	10.5	16	9.9

[Source: Census Enumerator Books: Paisley, 1871 and 1891]

Matthew Blair, in *The Paisley Thread Industry* (1907), highlighted the role of immigrants not only in boosting the native population,

---

[59] B. E. A. Collins, 'Aspects of Irish Immigration into two Scottish Towns (Dundee and Paisley) during the first half of the Nineteenth Century' (M. Phil, University of Edinburgh, 1978), p. 160.

[60] B. Collins, 'Irish Emigration to Dundee and Paisley during the first half of the nineteenth century', in *Irish Population, Economy and Society*, ed. J. M. Goldstrom and L. A. Clarkson (Oxford, 1981), p. 201.

but also the way in which 'The incomers brought many new ideas and practices, which have materially changed the homely style of life that previously existed'.[61] Their experience of a different process of socialisation made them amenable to alternative definitions of their social position. Moreover, the demand for labour saw an influx of daily workers from the more cosmopolitan culture of Glasgow. Coming mainly from skilled working-class households, these female workers saw labour organisation as both legitimate and natural expressions of working-class interests. The female workforce itself was becoming less stable and this resulted in relatively high rates of labour turnover in the key age cohorts, as the following table shows:

Table 26. *Labour turnover in specific age cohorts at the Ferguslie Mill (1902)*

	14–20	%	20–25	%	25–30	%
Working	1060	77	586	61	370	67
Left	296	21	283	30	143	26
Married	16	1	78	8	35	6
Dead	5	1	5	1	1>	
Pensioned	0		0		1>	1
Total	1377	100	952	100	550	100

[Source: Letter Books 1905–1911 (Kinning Park Collection, Box A2/1)]

What is interesting is that very few of the females who left the employment of Coats did so because of marriage. In the age cohort 20 to 25 the ratio of marriage to other causes of leaving work was almost 1:4; and in the cohort 25 to 30 it was just over 1:4. Greater opportunities in the labour market as a consequence of the growth of the service sector, as well as an increasing willingness of women to play by market rules, threatened to undermine the effectiveness of company culturalism. The end of the half-time system furthered this process and denied Coats a hand in the socialisation of its future workforce. Thus, the threadocracy's view of the personal relationship

---

[61] pp. 182–3.

it supposedly had with its workers was becoming increasingly anachronistic and unreal, a point reinforced by the intensification of industrial strife in the Paisley mills after 1897 and the move towards the setting up a trade union for female mill workers.

Although there had been a bobbin turners' strike in 1868 at Clarks' mill and a strike by tenters at Ferguslie in 1882, the first major blow to the paternalism of the thread combine came in 1897 with a strike of 800 female spoolers over the introduction of new reeling machinery.[62] Another two strikes took place in 1900, with the copwinders walking out in March and the ring spinners in November.[63] The company resorted to dismissing the ringleaders and posting notices saying that 'workers interfering with others who wish to continue at their occupations would be dismissed'.[64] Four years later a strike of 200 hankwinders over wages led to the walk out of a further 2,800 workers in sympathy.[65]

The policy of the company to divide the workers by occupation was breaking down as the former were realising the advantages of collective action. A further stike by eighty hankwinders at the Anchor Mills in 1905 led to mass demonstrations in the streets of Paisley and the barracking and harrying of managers.[66] The growing tempo of industrial conflict led to the intervention by Keir Hardie and the ILP and a meeting before a packed audience was held in the Clark Town Hall at the end of June 1906.[67] The chairman, Bailie Baird, spoke of how, in spite of threats from the company, the girls 'had gone on quietly forming their union, which was increasing in membership at every meeting'.[68] The threat from the company was its refusal to build a new mill at Paisley and instead

---

[62] *Glasgow Evening Times*, 1 Nov. 1897.
[63] Minute Book of the Works Committee of J. & P. Coats, 2 March 1900 (Kinning Park Collection Box HH3); Accounts and Papers on Labour Statistics, PP, 1900, LXXXIII, p. 56.
[64] Minutes of Directors of J. & P. Coats, 29 Mar. 1900 (Kinning Park Coll, Box A1/2).
[65] Board of Trade, Reports on Strikes and Lockouts (1904) (PRO, LAB 34/22).
[66] *Paisley and Renfrewshire Gazette*, 11 Mar. 1905.
[67] *Glasgow Herald*, 30 June 1906.
[68] *Glasgow Herald*, 30 June 1906.

locate in a foreign country if the workers continued to press for trade union recognition.[69] The minutes of the board of directors noted that the threat 'had an excellent effect on the workers'.[70]

After this the policy of the thread combine was to publicly declare non-opposition to their workers 'forming themselves into a trade union for the protection and promotion of their interests', while in private resolving 'that it would be against the interests of the company to permit outside interference or recognise outsiders as representatives of the workers'.[71]

The intransigence of the employers on the issue of union recognition made it impossible to resolve the growing discontent on the mill floor within an institutional framework. Sectional grievances became workplace issues and easily escalated into all-out stoppages. In September 1907, for example, a strike by mill boys in the turning shop of the Anchor Mills over a reduction in piece rate payments led to a walk out of 500 female hankwinders and block polishers in sympathy, though not before they had smashed every window in the mills with spoolwood sticks. Intimidation of the Ferguslie workers led to the closure of all the firm's mills in Paisley with 5000 workers made idle.[72] The strike was marred by violence and there were clashes between the girls and the police, who were liberally 'spattered with pease meal and flour'.[73] During the course of the seventeen-day strike extra police were drafted in to Paisley.[74] Around 85,000 working days were lost during the strike, which ended with a commitment by the employers to consider the grievances of the mill boys 'fully and carefully'.[75]

The events of the autumn of 1907 in Paisley saw the Coats' management take an even tougher line on industrial protest and worker organisation. A strike of fifty-three cone-winders against a

---

[69] Letter Book, 16 May 1906 (Kinning Park Collection, Box A1/2).
[70] Minutes of Directors of J. & P. Coats, 14 June 1906 (Kinning Park Collection, Box A1/3).
[71] Minutes of Directors of J. & P. Coats, 14 June 1906.
[72] *Glasgow Hearld*, 24 Sept. 1907.
[73] *Glasgow Herald*, 2 Oct. 1907.
[74] *Glasgow Herald*, 3 Oct. 1907.
[75] *Glasgow Herald*, 5 Oct. 1907.

reduction in wages in May 1908 led to the dismissal of 'every woman who had shown a spark of resistance to unfair treatment',[76] and the threat to dismiss any workers striking in sympathy to the extent of closing the mills if necessary.[77] As the journal of the NFWW – *The Woman Worker* – remarked: 'Surely now the women workers of Paisley must realise that the only alternative to absolute serfdom is to join the ranks of organised labour'.[78] However, the major breakthrough for the NFWW came not at Coats' mills, but at the rival ESCC mill in Neilston, where a strike by copwinders in May 1910 over parity with wage rates in the Anchor mills was taken up by the union and the GTC. The recruitment of the strikers by the NFWW was rapid, and by early June the GTC was able to report that 'practically all' of the women (around 1,000) now locked out from a total of 1,700 were members of the NFWW.[79] Under the auspices of the Board of Trade both parties agreed to new working arrangements designed to increase wages and output.[80] The strike established the NFWW in the Neilston mills in such strength that its members in the spooling department were able to pressurise management to remove four non-unionists.[81] The refusal of management to interfere on this issue led to a strike in August in the spooling room.[82] After another strike in the copwinding department in October that year over wage rates,[83] the four non-unionists were removed.[84] Later in December the copwinders were able to force a member in arrears of dues to pay up after demanding that she be dismissed.[85]

Although progress was clearly being made on the question of

---

[76] *Woman Worker*, 5 June 1908.
[77] Minutes of Directors of J. & P. Coats, 7 May 1908 (Kinning Park Collection, Box A1/3).
[78] 5 June 1908.
[79] Annual Report of the Glasgow Trades Council (1909–10), p. 14.
[80] *Glasgow Herald*, 18 June 1910.
[81] Minutes of the Executive Committee of the English Sewing Cotton Company [ESCC], 8 Aug. 1910 (Manchester Central Library, M127/1/1–6).
[82] Minutes of the Executive Committee of the ESCC, 11 Aug. 1910.
[83] *Daily Record and Mail*, 4–5 Oct. 1910.
[84] Minutes of the Executive Committee of the ESCC, 14 Nov. 1910.
[85] Minutes of the Executive Committee of the ESCC, 5 Dec. 1910.

organisation, most female thread workers remained outside the ranks of trade unionism. While paternalism in the Coats' combine had begun to show signs of fracturing, the resolution of the management on the question of representation never faltered. Coats remained set against the idea of trade unionism for females. It was only in the less powerful mills of the ESCC at Neilston that the union was able to overcome employer hostility. Thus, for most of the period between 1850 and 1914, the Scottish cotton industry was characterised by weak trade unionism and strong and determined employer organisation. It was only in weaving where strategically placed workers, such as tenters, exercised relative autonomy in the labour process, that there existed organised resistance to the power of capital, and that was only achieved at the expense of other workers. The question which emerges from the contrasting organisation of labour and capital is how did that effect the intensity and nature of industrial conflict?

4. *Industrial Conflict*

The Scottish cotton industry in the second half of the nineteenth century was characterised by weak labour organisation and powerful employers. As we have seen, only in the weaving sector did there exist specialist groups of workers able to exercise control over recruitment and the labour process. This situation did not inhibit the outbreak of industrial conflict, with a number of major strikes taking place in the period 1840 to 1914. However, their occurrence tells us very little about the frequency of disputes, the number of workers involved, their duration, or their outcome, and nothing at all regarding the varied experiences of the main sectors of the industry. Was one sector more prone to strikes than the others and, if so, why? What were the special characteristics of the sectors which shaped the pattern of the disputes? Did they occur in clusters in response to shifting trading conditions, or were they isolated and sporadic events exhibiting no particular chronology or pattern?

To answer these questions the data regarding industrial disputes in the Scottish cotton industry has to be analysed in two ways;

firstly, for the industry as a whole; and, secondly, comparatively, in order to assess the relative experience and performance of each sector. Most of the data has been drawn from newspaper reports and company records, although from 1888 onwards use has been made of the Board of Trade's reports on strikes and lockouts in British industry. The data gathered refers only to workers actively involved in the production of cotton products and does not include workers in ancillary occupations, such as bleaching and dyeing.

Obviously any attempt to analyse the history of industrial relations in the second half of the nineteenth century can, at best, be only partial in its coverage. Until the introduction of a systematic method of collecting information on industrial disputes by the Board of Trade in the late 1880s, most of our detail is culled from reports in the local and national press. Because of this there are often large gaps in the recording of such important issues as the numbers of workers involved, the number of working days lost, and, even more important, the outcome of the conflict. Strikes are often initially reported in the press to have occurred, but on too many occasions the labour correspondent or the newspaper has failed to follow them up. Thus, while we are able to record between 1840 and 1914 a total of fifty-seven strikes in the Scottish cotton industry, we have information regarding the numbers involved in them in only thirty cases, and only in twenty-eight disputes do we know the length of the dispute, and, finally, in only twenty of them do we have any indication of the number of working days lost. This applies with more force to the early decades of our period, and because of this there is a large lacuna relating to the activities of the cotton spinners after 1840. In spite of being involved in twelve strikes between 1840 and 1871, we have almost no data on the important questions mentioned above. As the century draws to a close the position is improved enormously through official publication of reports on strikes and lockouts. From these reports we are able to gain a very full impression of all the most salient points regarding the nature of industrial conflict in the industry.

However, leaving aside the problems concerned with the discontinuities in our knowledge, the raw data in our possession would suggest that, at 0.8 strikes per year between 1840 and 1914, the level of industrial conflict was low in the Scottish cotton industry.

When they did occur disputes tended to be concerned with wages, involved a fairly large number of workers, both directly and indirectly, were of fairly short duration, and, on the whole, were more likely to fail than to succeed, as the following table shows:

Table 27. *Industrial disputes in the Scottish cotton industry, 1840–1914*

Strikes	No.	%	Causes	No.	%	Outcome	No.	%
Weaving	27	47	Wages	35	61	Failure	13	23
Thread	17	30	Other	17	30	Success	7	12
Spinning	13	23	Unknown	5	9	Compromise	11	19
						Unknown	26	46
Total	57	100		57	100		57	100

As the weavers were at the forefront of wage reductions in the second half of the nineteenth century, it is not surprising that the weaving trade should experience the greater number of stoppages. However, there is a chronological dimension to the pattern of industrial conflict. From the 1840s through to the early 1870s it was the spinning industry which experienced a higher number of disputes than either weaving or thread, with twelve, or 75 per cent, of a total number of sixteen recorded strikes taking place within it. The last spinners' strike occurred in 1871 over the length of the working week.[86] From the 1870s until the late 1890s the weaving trade became the focus of industrial conflict, with eighteen, or two-thirds, of the twenty-seven recorded stoppages occurring in this period. The intensification in the weaving trade, both at home and abroad, saw employers press down hard on labour costs in order to maintain a competitive advantage in the market, provoking sporadic outbursts of opposition from the weavers. From 1897 onwards the main site of industrial conflict was the Paisley thread industry, where changes in the labour process and the threat they posed to earnings combined to produce a marked increase in the number of disputes.

---

[86] *Glasgow Sentinel*, 29 Apr. 1871.

From Table 27 it can be seen that wages was the most likely factor in bringing about a dispute. However, disputes over wages tended to be reactive rather than proactive. Almost all were concerned with resistance to wage cuts rather than for increases. Among the causes listed in the 'other' category, the most prominent were those connected with poor-quality materials and industrial discipline, particularly in weaving, and the labour process, particularly in thread. Strikes took place in 1889 and again in 1898 in the weaving sector over these issues, the first involving 250 workers, and the second 300; none, however, was successful.[87] Disputes concerned with the labour process first occurred in the thread industry in 1897, when 637 female spoolers struck over the mechanisation of bobbin distribution, which created delays and led to a loss of earnings.[88]

However, many of the disputes over wages were also connected with changes in the labour process and work routines, and vice versa. Although a strike might take place over the introduction of a new machine, or the quality of working materials, it was ultimately the effect that these innovations might have on wages which was uppermost in the minds of the workers. A strike at the ESCC's Neilston mill in 1913 by twisters regarding the number of spindles to be operated was in essence a wage dispute, since the workers were less concerned with the number of spindles, and more with the fact that they received lower wages than those paid to twisters in the Paisley mills for minding fewer spindles.[89]

As Table 27 shows, the success rate of strikes was not particularly good at only 12 per cent, although the fact that a further 19 per cent ended in some form of compromise between employers and workers suggests a greater measure of success for the latter than one could have expected, given the poor organisation of the cotton workers. Refining the statistical success/failure rate further, it would appear that the likelihood of some form of gain to the strikers was

---

[87] Board of Trade, Reports on Strikes and Lockouts, PP (1890), LXVIII, pp. 71, 89; PP, 1899, XCII, p. 58.
[88] *Glasgow Herald*, 2 Nov. 1897.
[89] Minutes of the Executive Committee of the ESCC, 14 Jan. 1913.

greater in the thread sector than in either spinning or weaving. Of the seventeen strikes which took place in the thread industry, successes, including compromises, numbered eight, with only three outright failures, and a further six whose outcome is unknown. Thus, strikers in the thread industry had a better than two to one chance of achieving some form of success in pursuit of their demands. The comparable figures for weaving were eight successes, though only two outright victories, eight failures and a further eleven unknown.

The difference between thread and weaving was more than likely to do with chronology, since most of the industrial stoppages occurred in the former after 1897 at a time of improving labour organisation and workers seemed to be genuinely more class conscious. However, it might also have been connected with the fact that the production process in thread was far more integrated and, therefore, a sectional strike involved a general closure. Such prospects pressurised management into resolving outstanding grievances quickly to minimise the effect they might have on output. Workers in the weaving sector had less power to disrupt production in a meaningful sense as the employers, given the seasonality of the industry, could use stoppages simply to run down existing, unsold stocks.

Although strikes in the Scottish cotton industry occurred at the rate of less than one a year in the period 1840 to 1914, they were not always the short, sharp affairs that some historians have depicted.[90] Indeed, the data leads to a somewhat different interpretation, as the following table shows:

Table 28. *Statistics relating to industrial stoppages in the Scottish cotton industry, 1840–1914*

★ No. of Strikers		† Duration of Strikes		‡ No. of Days Lost	
Mean	Median	Mean	Median	Mean	Median
861	250	22 days	7.5 days	14,417	5000

[★ Based on 31 strikes; † based on 28; ‡ based on 20]

[90] Gordon, *Women and the Labour Movement*, p. 98.

The mean figures are, of course, easily distorted by strikes which were untypical, either because of the excessive numbers involved, or the extreme opposite. Thus, if we take the mean number of strikers directly involved in a dispute, we find it was as few as sixty in the 1908 dispute at Clarks' mill, Paisley, and as many as 5,000 in the mill boys' strike a year earlier. Similarly, if we were to probe deeper into the figures for the other two categories, we would find that the length of a strike could vary from an extreme of only two days in a weaving strike in 1898, to 147 in the tenters' strike of 1907/8; and that the number of days lost in a dispute could range from as few as 180 in the 1908 thread strike to 85,000 in the 1907 mill boys' dispute. Therefore, the introduction of the median value provides a more realistic figure for the above categories.

The general data, of course, tells us nothing regarding the different experiences and performances of the various sectors of the Scottish cotton industry in respect of the categories listed above. Thus, a comparative dimension to these issues must be added if we wish to understand fully the implications of industrial conflict on sectoral performance in the wider economic sense. Unfortunately, the data for spinning is so sparse that it is practically meaningless in statistical terms and, therefore, can only be used when it throws an interesting comparative light on a particular phenomenon. For the purposes of this section of the chapter we will concentrate on the thread and weaving industries, and look firstly at the number of workers involved, both directly and indirectly, in industrial stoppages:

Table 29. *Workers and strikes in the thread and weaving sectors, 1840–1914*

	Strikes (1)	Strikes (2)	Strikers (1)	Strikers (2)	Mean (1)	Mean (2)	Median (1)	Median (2)
Weaving	14	5	8364	18892	597	3778	230	400
Thread	15	6	17525	2187	1168	364	483	343

[(1) directly involved; (2) indirectly involved]

The table shows clearly the damaging effect of an industrial dispute between the two sectors if judged by the number of workers, with almost twice as many in thread as in weaving. However, each data set suffers from a wide dispersion of observations as witnessed by the high figures for the standard deviation in Table 30. Strikes in the thread industry could involve as few as thirty workers as in 1882, or as many as 5,000, as in the 1907 strike, whereas weaving could involve as few as 52 workers, as in a strike in 1897, or as many as 4,500, as in the 1849 strike. As the nineteenth century drew to a close large-scale strikes were located exclusively in the highly integrated thread industry. From 1893 through to 1914 the largest number of strikers involved in an industrial dispute in the weaving industry was 300, in 1898,[91] while the thread industry experienced strikes directly involving 1,900 workers in 1900, 3,000 in 1904, and the same number in 1905, culminating in the 1907 strike involving 5,000 workers. Because of this strikes in the thread industry were rarely likely to involve other workers not directly in dispute with management. This is in sharp contrast to the weaving trade, where strikes by small craft societies had the effect of shutting down the mill and putting large numbers of workers out of work. However, the number of observations, at five and six respectively, is so small that we should perhaps not place too much stress on these figures.

The duration of strikes also shows a tendency to deviation between thread and weaving:

Table 30. *Duration of strikes (days) in the weaving and thread sectors, 1840–1914*

	Strikes	Mean	Median	SD
Weaving	13	31	10	49
Thread	12	8	5	10

Strikes in the thread industry were on the whole of much shorter duration than in weaving, whatever basis of calculation is used. They were also less likely to show a tendency to a wide dispersal of observations. Weaving experienced long disputes, with strikes lasting for eighty-one days in 1883, ninety-eight days in 1892, culminating in the tenters' strike of 1907/8 which lasted for 147

---

[91] Reports on Strikes and Lockouts, 1899, p. 58.

days. The differences between the sectors can be traced to the style of management and, perhaps, the consciousness of the workers and their attitude to authority. The power loom mills were managed by lesser capitalists locked into a cut-throat cycle of competition, and conscious of the need to keep costs down. Given the labour-intensive nature of production, the largest savings were to be made on the wages bill. Reductions in wages, as we have seen, were the most common cause of strikes as workers fought to defend their standard of living. These actions could often be protracted as the weaving millowner, faced with a volatile and seasonal market, sometimes used the strikes as an opportunity to run down accumulated stocks of cloth.

The greater stability of the thread market through the establishment of cartel-like arrangements demanded a constant flow of production, which enhanced the disruptive effect of industrial disputes to management. Thus, managers had to develop more proactive policies geared to winning the adherence of the workforce and ensuring the smooth flow of output. Paternalist strategies, as we have seen, were used to a far higher degree than in the Glasgow weaving trade to socialise workers into management-defined goals of enterprise. Thus, workers in thread industry, until the first decade of the twentieth century, were more tractable and amenable to appeals to common sense preached by their bosses. For example, the 1897 strike over the introduction of a machine to mechanise the distribution of spools ended when management stated that they 'were quite willing to adjust in every way in their power the differences between the firm and their employees'.[92] Given this assurance the female strikers returned to work willing to give the new machine a 'fair trial'. This means of settling a dispute was by no means untypical of the thread industry, where the personal intervention of a member of one of the leading families was normally enough to bring about a settlement.

However, it is also the case that when they did occur strikes in the thread sector involved a far larger number of days lost than in weaving, as the following table shows:

---

[92] *Glasgow Evening Times*, 2 Nov. 1897.

Table 31. *Days lost in strikes in the weaving and thread sectors, 1889–1914*

	No. of Strikes	No. of days lost	Mean	Median
★ Weaving	8	90,961	11,370	560
† Thread	12	197,380	16,448	5,580

[★ First observation 1889; † 1897]

The size of the huge thread mills and their integrated ownership and production methods inevitably meant that strikes in the industry would have a more damaging effect on output than in the smaller scale firms which made up the west of Scotland weaving trade. It is hardly surprising that the strategy of social control in the thread industry was more sophisticated than that in weaving, or that management was more creative and proactive in dealing with their workers.

If we compare the management styles between the two sectors, it is clear that if the Coats' combine clung to paternalism and bore the social overheads involved in such a strategy, then it is perhaps because they had little choice. A strategy of conflict as used by the weaving manufacturers would have brought disaster to the thread industry as markets were lost through constant disruption of production. A stable market needed a stable set of industrial relations.

Conclusion

At the beginning of this study a typology of fortune was constructed which split the Scottish cotton industry into three distinct groups: losers, hangers-on and winners. The outstanding success was thread manufacture, and the most prominent failures, in chronological order, were the combined spinning and weaving firms and the spinning sector. Among the hangers-on were the specialist weaving houses in Glasgow's east end. However, discounting the experience of the thread trade, it is fair to say that the nineteenth century was a period of dynamic cyclical decline, and the early years of the twentieth century marked the virtual disappearance of the spinning and weaving sectors, the engines of Scotland's industrial revolution.

Why firms, or indeed whole industries, fail is, of course, the subject of continuous analysis and debate within the academic disciplines of economics and management sciences. All would agree that the answer is far from being monocausal; the result of a combination of factors ranging from the quality of entrepreneurship, to foreign competition, to labour difficulties, and so on. However, the mix of factors is always unique and what we have to decide is: firstly, how far did the experience of the Scottish cotton industry resonate with general explanations of industrial decline and, in particular, those concerning the decline of the English cotton industry, in the twentieth century; and, secondly, why did the experiences of the various sectors of the trade in Scotland vary so markedly from one another? For it would appear that given the favourable factor endowment enjoyed by the cotton industry in the west of Scotland decline was far from inevitable. Unlike coal or iron, for instance, there were no finite geological limits to growth; thus decay was not a predictable and natural outcome of its development. Therefore, as the first major casualty in the historical process of de-industrialisation, the case of the Scottish cotton industry becomes of general importance to the whole experience of industrial decline in Britain. In saying that, can we apportion blame? Was decline the result of poor management, unproductive workers, or alternatively was it the result of external factors beyond the control of even the most aggressive and innovative management talent? And why should thread succeed and the other major sectors of the Scottish cotton industry fail?

In answering these vital questions we must recognise, firstly, that decline was a dynamic cyclical process. Rejecting R. H. Campbell's early decline thesis,[1] it would appear, if we use employment statistics as a guide, that the cotton industry's troubles really set in after 1880. The decline was uneven, with the integrated spinning and weaving firms suffering first, and the specialised spinning and weaving mills following in the former's wake. When it set in, however, decline was absolute, with only the weaving firms in the fancy end of the market retaining a share of total British output. The integrated firms collapsed first since they lacked the flexibility to buy yarn in the cheapest markets, mainly Lancashire, which increased the cost of the finished product. Spinning soon followed. The main problems lay in the technical sphere and the organisation of the labour process. To break the power of the male spinners' union the Glasgow employers opted for a policy of increasing feminisation of spinning through the use of self-actors, a process which was furthered by the haemorrhaging of male labour after the Cotton Famine, and reached its peak with the introduction of the multi-pair system in the 1880s. The problem was that, compared to men, women were only physically capable of operating a limited number of spindles. This in itself did not constitute a major handicap. The Japanese cotton industry was almost totally feminised and it was able to overtake Lancashire, even in the Indian markets, during the inter-war period. However, the difference between the Scottish producers and their Japanese rivals was that the latter provided their workers with the appropriate technology. With exceptionally high rates of labour turnover the Japanese producers introduced a high-throughput

---

[1] R. H. Campbell, *Scotland since 1707* (1985 edn)

and low level skill technology in ring spinning. Scottish producers were in advance of Lancashire in this respect but operated under greater constraints than the Japanese. Factory legislation prevented the use of child labour on an extensive scale and regulated the length of the working day. It also minimised the running time of the spinning machinery.

Labour costs, although lower than in Lancashire, were higher too, not simply because the age structure was more advanced, but also because Scottish cotton producers had to compete with other trades for labour, which bid up its price. Technically, the emphasis placed by cotton masters in Scotland on spinning higher counts favoured the mule over the ring spindle as the strain on the latter led to far too many breakages. Transport costs were also a factor as the mule cop held more yarn than the ring bobbin and weighed less. Given these constraints, Scottish spinners fell back on the cheap labour of women organised in a labour process after 1880 which reinforced their subordination to men, but did little to increase their productiveness.

Weaving was able to hang on after the decline of spinning was diagnosed as terminal. It did this because it was able to exploit opportunities in the product and labour markets, as well as benefiting from flexible production strategies. However, like shipbuilding in the twentieth century, it was a strategy based on survival rather than growth – one which was influenced by the fragmentation of output in a host of enterprises each competing for a share of a shrinking market and a system of craft regulation which it gave rise to. The abandonment of coarse or plain weaving after 1860 saw Scottish weavers specialise in the fancier end of the market. As the production runs were small, the market unpredictable and, in many respects, seasonal, weaving masters rationally opted for a mode of production which was capital- rather than labour-saving. However, this had a number of drawbacks for the employers, not the least being that relying on a system of production which was labour intensive meant effectively placing control over the labour process in the hands of key work groups. In weaving, the tenters were able to control both recruitment and the labour process.

Expansion of the industry was tied to the ratio of tenters to learners permitted by the latter's trade society. Craft controls also structured the distribution of employment along strict gender defined lines. Unlike Lancashire, where both men and women worked the looms, the tenters were able to confine this work to women only. By labelling the women's work as unskilled they were able to appropriate the 'skilled' work and to be paid craft rates, as much as four times as those earned by the female weavers. This inevitably led to output constraints. The low wages and status of the power loom weavers made it difficult to recruit and retain good quality workers. The Scottish power loom weaver had, at nine years on average, a much shorter working life than her English counterpart. This meant that the majority of the best workers left the industry before the age of twenty-five and employers continually complained of the lack of trained labour.

Another feature of the Lancashire trade was the four-loom system as opposed to the two-loom system in Scotland. As we have seen, much has been made of the loom differential question as the key to understanding the decline of the Scottish weaving trade. This appears to have been much exaggerated. The complexity of fancy weaving and the greater strain placed on the weaver to mend broken threads made the operation of more than two looms humanly and technically difficult. Moreover, the higher the number of looms to be tended, the greater the number of stoppages to be attended to, making for a loss of valuable labour time.

As Lazonick has noted, by reducing the number of looms to be tended the machines could be run at a faster rate with less interruption, leading to higher output per loom, and a lower total unit factor cost.[2] Rather than concentrating on the loom question, more consideration ought to be given to the fragmentation of output and the level of competition in the Scottish weaving trade, as well as the particular system of labour relations which this industrial structure created.

In Lancashire damaging internecine competition among weaving firms was minimised by the use of wage lists. These lists were designed to adjust as far as possible the pay of weavers to the amount and difficulty of the work they performed. By adhering to them

---

[2] W. Lazonick and W. Mass, 'The Performance of the British Cotton Industry, 1870–1913', *Research in Economic History*, 9 (1984), pp. 25–6.

employers, in what was a highly competitive and labour-intensive industry, were able to prevent wage cutting competition.[3] For the workers, wage lists guaranteed that hard work would be adequately rewarded as greater output would not lead to a cutting of piece rates. This level of cooperation did not exist among Scottish weaving masters. As we have seen, distrust and fear undermined attempts to form a west of Scotland power loom employers' association in the 1880s to regulate wages and prevent undercutting. The failure to minimise competition saw the masters continue to take advantage of the low level of worker organisation to ensure that the female weavers shouldered the burden of recession and tougher competition through wage reductions. Individualised bargaining and the highly competitive nature of weaving manufacture in Scotland meant that wage rates varied from firm to firm, and that in most cases they were fixed on an arbitrary basis. An alteration in customary workloads brought no guarantees that the weaver would be any better off. Thus, the Scottish weaving trade gradually contracted, unable for the reasons stated above to break out of the mentality of survival and opting for a policy of integration and growth.

If the failure of the weaving and spinning sectors is to be viewed in terms of their inability significantly to alter the constraints under which they operated, why was the thread trade of Paisley able to succeed in doing just that? The simple answer to that question is that the Paisley threadocracy operated under far fewer constraints than the spinning and weaving masters. From the outset they enjoyed fewer labour difficulties, were free to adopt relevant technologies, and appreciated the benefits to be reaped from a strategy of firm and market integration. The labour process in thread-making ensured that there existed no system of worker subordination to worker as, for example, in the case of the weaver/tenter relationship, which meant that the workforce was subordinated to capital and its functionaries in the mill. This denied key workers, such as tenters, control of recruitment and the labour process. As the industry was feminised from the beginning, with the women employed as

---

[3] W. Lazonick, 'The Cotton Industry', in *The Decline of the British Economy*, ed. B. Elbaum and W. Lazonick (Oxford, 1986), pp. 25–6.

winders, and the spinning until the late 1880s done elsewhere, there were no craft, male traditions to defend, and, consequently, there were no powerful trade unions, such as the cotton spinners' association, or small craft societies whose influence in the weaving mill was directly inverse to the size of their membership. The system of paternalism practised by the leading thread firms was able to harness the allegiance of the workers to a vision of the enterprise and its goals which was structured by management. The advantage such a strategy conferred on the leading firms was enormous since it meant that voluntary disruption of production was rare and new technologies could be introduced without the resistance of the labour force.

Until the end of the nineteenth century, when paternalism came under increasing stress from external social and political forces, it played a key part in the successful development of the large thread companies. While the spinning and weaving employers of the west of Scotland, faced with the problem of increased competition in a period of relative decline, adopted a regressive wage policy and laid out little in meeting the social costs of production, the threadmakers, in a situation of decreasing competition and expanding output, stressed the importance of nurturing human capital. This was important in securing and retaining an adequate supply of labour. Conditions in the thread factories owned by Clarks and Coats were among the best in Britain. One factory inspector described them as 'representing the highest standard I have met as regards the sanitation and general internal appointments'.[4] The workplace amenities were not provided at the expense of wages. Data on wage rates in the thread industry for copwinders show that they were comparable to spinning, far superior to power loom weaving, and much better than in service sector occupations such as shopwork. Working conditions in spinning and weaving could not have been more different and were a highly important factor in explaining the degree of labour drift in these sectors. Spinning was not considered a desirable occupation for young women; indeed it was seen as

---

[4] M. Irwin, 'The Employment of Women', Royal Commision on Labour, PP, pt 1, 1893–4, XXXVII, p. 191.

'somewhat rough' and, because of the heat, 'exhausting'.[5] The greater the heat in the spinning mills the scantier the dress of the women, which raised issues regarding respectability. Given the slow growth in wage rates and the undersirable aspects of much of the female spinner's working conditions, employers found it increasingly difficult to recruit sufficient supplies of intelligent and hard working women workers. Similarly, the weaving trade was found to be uncongenial, except that here the problem was not heat, but poor ventilation and bad sanitation in the mills. Also the fact that they worked without shoes or stockings [6] made the occupation seem less feminine and, hence, less respectable than, say, shopwork, which constituted a major difficulty in attracting young women into the trade. But the main grievances lay in the seasonal nature of the fancy weaving trade and the system of 'driving', which caused all sorts of infringements of the Factory Acts, particularly in respect of working hours. Denied the services of child assistants which their counterparts in Lancashire enjoyed, female power loom weavers in Scotland were forced to work additional unpaid hours to carry out preparatory tasks to keep up their wages.[7] While the thread manufacturers found little difficulty in recruiting and retaining labour, the other sectors faced serious and continuing problems in this area. Expansion of output was thus severely impeded in times of boom for want of workers.

Stabilisation of the market may have afforded opportunities for the spinning and weaving enterprises to adopt a more progressive attitude to their workers as it offered the hope of better social guarantees. However, they were locked in to a highly fragmented and fiercely competitive industrial structure which they seemed mentally unable to break away from. On the other hand, the thread industry from a comparatively early date was actively engaged in the business of minimising competition both horizontally, through amalgamations and take overs, and vertically, through the integration

---

[5] Scottish Council for Women's Trades, Occupations for Girls: a guide to girls in selecting an employment (Glasgow, c.1900), p. 6.
[6] *Forward*, 29 Oct. 1912.
[7] Irwin, 'The Employment of Women', p. 175.

of the whole process of production. The thread manufacturers realised that the mass market which had opened up in the wake of the invention of the sewing machine needed to be policed and regulated. As Lazonick put it, 'the development of the firm's ability to mass distribute is a necessary condition for the development of its incentive to mass produce. Firms' control over markets must precede, or at least emerge simultaneously with, the development of large scale, standardized production'.[8] By 1880 the threadocracy had established the TTA to control the selling price of thread in specified markets, and this process culminated in the setting up of the SCA. The latter agency controlled output, markets and prices throughout the world. It was assisted by the growing domination of the firms of Coats and Clarks in the domestic and international markets. By a ruthless takeover drive Coats and Clarks swallowed up their rivals in Paisley, reducing the number of thread firms from nine in 1880 to one by 1896, the year of their amalgamation. By establishing the SCA the remaining British thread firms were drawn into their orbit, with the only serious rival being the much weaker ESCC. By establishing subsidiaries in countries as diverse as the USA and Russia, Coats and Clarks not only limited world competition, but also found ways round international tariff barriers erected at various times in the nineteenth century.

Control of the market made the possibility of integrating the production process a feasible prospect. In the course of the second half of the nineteenth century Coats controlled the production of thread from the spinning of the yarn all the way through to the dyeing, and, finally, the packing of the end product for distribution. This gave the thread manufacturers several important advantages over their rivals in the other sectors of the cotton industry. Firstly, by establishing spinning facilities from the 1880s onwards at Ferguslie, Coats were able to negate the short-run incentive spinning producers had of passing on inferior yarn and breakage costs to the thread-makers. They also were able to exercise quality control over raw cotton supplies which did so much to influence the quality of the yarn. Secondly, the vertical integration of production lowered

---

[8] Lazonick, 'Cotton Industry', pp. 42–3.

transport costs between the various stages of production, something which the specialised spinning and weaving firms could not economise on. Finally, the closer cooperation between firms in the thread industry established by the setting up of the SCA led to a greater willingness of the member firms to share ideas and knowledge. Companies were able to pass on to others in the agency the costs and benefits of experimentation with different machinery and processes. Expansion into the American market was also beneficial in this respect. Technology transfers put the firms of Coats and Clarks at the frontier of technical change in Britain. Without the experience gained in the USA it is doubtful if Coats would have invested so heavily, for example, in ring spinning at Ferguslie. Moreover, with the American clothing market taking 85 per cent of the thread output of Coats by 1855, the company was able to move towards specialised forms of production at a relatively early stage in its development. As a result production runs were longer, economies were made in both machines and skills, as well as in the make-up of materials like labels and wrappers.

By using large supplies of relatively cheap and unorganised labour on the most up-to-date technology, the large thread manufacturers were able to maintain a cost competitiveness over their rivals in a manner unavailable to Scottish spinning and weaving producers. Much of this was made possible by the determination of the large companies to grow rather than simply to survive. To this end fragmentation of output and internecine competition were eliminated by them. Stabilisation of the market also stabilised the system of industrial relations, and the economic and technical benefits which flowed from this were enormous, enabling the Coats thread combine to dominate world output of sewing thread.

The experience of the thread trade shows that the decline of the Scottish cotton industry was neither inevitable or predictable. However, it does highlight that only by superior planning of markets and the elimination of wasteful competition, combined with greater freedom in the use of labour and capital can industrial decline be halted and, perhaps, reversed. Manufacturing consent for the flexible use of labour and capital, however, can only be achieved within an industrial culture which invests management with a moral leadership. Through the sophisticated application of paternalism, the great thread manufacturing firms were able for almost the whole of the nineteenth century to assume such a moral authority within the walls of their mills, as well as in the wider society of Paisley. Unfortunately, the dim awareness of this on the part of spinning and weaving producers in Scotland, as well as their failure to resolve the labour and technical constraints imposed on them, won for them the title of the first major casualties in the long historical process of de-industrialisation in Britain.

Bibliography

* Place of publication London unless otherwise stated.

1. MANUSCRIPT SOURCES

Board of Trade, Reports on Strikes and Lockouts (PRO: LAB34/21-32)
Census Enumerator Books: Bridgeton and Paisley, 1851, 1871 and 1891 (Scottish Record Office [SRO], Register House, Edinburgh)
J. & P. Coats Collection (the archives were held in three different sites: a) Kinning Park Works, Glasgow [these have since been transferred to the University of Glasgow's Business Archives]; b) Paisley Museum and Art Gallery; c) Paisley Public Library
Brown, Malloch & Company, Cotton Spinners, Johnstone: Sequestration c.1887 (SRO: CS. 333/7 and CS. 318/35/No. 21)
Cotton Trade Employers, Copy of Circular (27 April 1905) and list of firms sent to with a view to increasing the number of monthly employers returns (PRO: LAB 2/1478/CL&SL/545/1909)
Duntocher & Faifley Cotton Spinners Friendly Society (SRO: FS. 1/7/11)
Export Book of George Robinson and Company, showing the amount of cotton goods shipped from Clydeside to India and China, 1839-1880 (Manchester Central Library Archives, ms. f. 382. 2R1)
Archives of James Finlay and Company (University of Glasgow Business Archives)
Glasgow Warpers Friendly Society, articles of (SRO: FS. 3/57)
Glasgow and the West of Scotland Power-Loom Tenters, articles of (SRO: FS. 1/16130)
Archives of the Lanark Spinning Company (University of Glasgow Business Archives)
Mill Wages Book, Cotton Works, Kirkintilloch, 1789-1790 (SRO: CS96/No. 1370)
Mill Wage Book, Newton Stewart, 1809-1810 (SRO: CS96/1960)
Minute Books of Anderson and Robertson (Glasgow University Business Archives, [GUA/D29 10/1])
Minutes of Glasgow Trades Council (Mitchell Library, Glasgow)
Minutes of the Executive Committee of the English Sewing Cotton Company (Manchester Central Library, M127/1/1-6)
Paisley Female Friendly Society, List of members, 1846-50 (SRO: FS. 1/21/29)

Paisley Seedhill Friendly Society (SRO: FS. 1/21/42)
Paisley United Trades Council Minutes 1904–1914 (Paisley Public Library)
Rules of the Crofthead Thread Works Male Workers' Friendly Society (Manchester Central Library, Misc. 867)
Scottish Ball Warp and Brush Beamers Society, 1906–9 (SRO: FS. 7/55)
Scottish General Workers Union (SRO: FS. 14/34)
Scottish Textile Workers Union, Rules, 1917 (SRO: FS. 14/36/1)
Trade Union Membership and Years of Formation: Female Membership, 1910–1919 (PRO: LAB 69/114)
Underwood Friendly Society (SRO: FS. 1/21/42)
Valuation Rolls: Paisley 1871, 1881 and 1891 (SRO)
Webb Collection on Trade Unions (British Library of Political and Economic Science)
West Arthurlie Cotton Mill Funeral Society (SRO: FS. 1/21/57)
West of Scotland Female Textile Workers Industrial Union, Rules, report and balance sheet, 1907–13 (SRO: FS. 7/107)
George Wilson & Company, Muslin Manufacturer (SRO: AD. 14. 81/34)
John Yuill Junior, Power-Loom Cloth Manufacturer, Bridgeton: Sequestration (SRO: CS96/68 & CS318/9 No. 340)

2. GOVERNMENT REPORTS

1833 PPXXI: Second Report of the Factories Inquiry Commission
1834 PPXIX: Supplementary Reports of the Commissioners on Childrens Employment in Factories
1836 PPXLV: Factory Report
1837–8 PPVII: First Report from the Select Committee on Combinations of Workmen
1840 PPX: Second Report from the Select Committee on Mills and Factories
1840 PPX: Fourth Report from the Select Committee on Mills and Factories
1844 PPXXVII:Decennial Census (Scotland) 1841
1847 PPXLVI: Factory Returns
1848 PPXXVI: Half Yearly Report of Inspector of Factories
1850 PPXXIII: Factory Report
1850 PPXLII: Factory Returns
1852–3 PPLXXXVIII: Decennial Census (Scotland) 1851
1852–3 PPXL: Factory Reportxxxx
1854 PPXIX: Factory Report
1854–5 PPXV: Factory Report
1857 PPIII: Factory Report
1857 PPXIV: Factory Returns
1857–8 Vol. XXIV: Factory Report
1860 PPXXXIV: Factory Report
1860 PPXXII: Report of the Select Committee on Masters and Operatives
1861 PPXXII: Factory Report

1862 PPLV: Factory Returns
1864 PPLI: Decennial Census (Scotland) 1861
1863 PPXVIII: Factory Report
1867–8 PPLXIV: Factory Returns
1871 PPLXII: Factory Returns
1871 PPXIV: Factory Report
1872 PPLIV: Factory Returns
1873 PPLV: Report on Proposed Wages, Hours and Ages of Employment in Textile Factories
1873 PPLXIII: Decennial Census (Scotland) 1871
1875 PPLXXI: Factory Returns
1876 PPXXIX: Report from the Commissioners on the Factory and Workshops Acts
1876 PPXXX: Select Committee on the Factory and Workshops Act, pt II
1878–9 PPLXV: Factory Returns
1883 PPLXXXI: Decennial Census (Scotland) 1881
1884 PPXXXI (11): Royal Commission on Technical Instruction
1884 PPXVIII: Factory Report
1884–5 PPLXXI: Factory Returns
1886 PPXXI: First Report of the Royal Commission on the Depression in Trade and Industry
1886 PPXXII: Second Report of the Royal Commission on Depression in Trade and Industry
1886 PPXXIII: Final Report of the Royal Commission on Depression of Trade and Industry
1887 PPLXXXIX: Returns of Wages, 1830–1886
1889 PPLXX: Returns of Wages in the Textile Trades
1890 PPLXVIII: Returns of Wages in the Minor Textile Trades
1890 PPLXXIII: Report on Strikes and Lockouts
1890 PPLXVII: Factory Returns
1890–1 PPXIX: Factory Report
1892 PPXX: Factory Report
1893–4 PPXVII: Factory Report
1893–4 PPXXXVII: Royal Commission on Labour, pt 1
1893–4 PPCVIII: Decennial Census (Scotland) 1891
1893–4 PPLXXXIII: Report on the Wages of the Manual Labouring Classes in the UK, pt 11
1897 PPXVII: Factory Report
1898 PPXIV: Factory Report
1898 PPLXXXVIII: Board of Trade Report on Strikes and Lockouts
1899 PPXII: Commissioner's Report on Accidents (Cotton)
1900 PPLXXXIII: Accounts and Papers, Strikes and Lockouts
1903 PPLXIV: Factory Returns
1903 PPLXXXVI: Decennial Census (Scotland) 1901
1908 PPXCIII: Report on the Housing Condition of the Population of Scotland

1909 PPCII Census of Production, 1907,
1909 PPLXXIX: Factory Returns
1909 PPLXXXIX: Returns of Employment in Textile Workshops
1909 PPLXXX: Report on Earnings and Hours of Labour: 1. Textiles Trades
1910 PPXXVIII: Factory Report
1912–3 PPCXX: Decennial Census (Scotland) 1911
1913 PPXXIII: Factory Report
1914 PPXXIX: Factory Report
1914–6 PPXXI: Report of the Board of Trade on the State of Employment in the United Kingdom

3. OTHER REPORTS

Connal & Co., *Clyde Market Reports* (1840–1888)
Glasgow Trades Council, *Annual Reports* (1890–1914)
Report of the Cotton Mission (London, 1931)
M. H. Irwin, 'The Employment of Women', *Royal Commission on Labour*, PP, pt 1, 1893–4, xxxvii
E. Orme, 'Conditions of Work in Scotland', *Royal Commission on Labour*, PP, pt 1, 1893–4, xxxviii
A. Slaven, 'Management and Shipbuilding on the Clyde, 1919–1976: a study in industrial decline' (Social Science Research Council end of project report, 1981)
J. Strang, *Report on the Mortality Bills of the City of Glasgow and Suburbs* (Glasgow, 1851)
J. Strang, *Report on the Returns of the Registrars of the City of Glasgow, 1855* (Glasgow, 1856)
J. Strang, *Report on the Vital and Economic Statistics of Glasgow for 1857* (Glasgow, 1858)
J. Strang, *Report on the Vital and Economic Statistics of Glasgow for 1861* (Glasgow, 1862)
Scottish Council for Women's Trades, *Annual Reports* (1901–2, 1905–6)

4. NEWSPAPERS

Ayr Advertiser
Commonwealth
Cotton Factory Times
Cotton: It's Growth, Manufacture and Commerce
Cotton Supply Reporter
Daily Record and Mail
The Economist
Ferguslie News
Forward
Glasgow Argus
Glasgow Courier

Glasgow Evening Times
Glasgow Herald
Glasgow Saturday Post and Paisley and Renfrewshire Reformer
Glasgow Sentinel
North British Daily Mail
Paisley Daily Express
Paisley Herald and Renfrewshire Advertiser
Paisley and Renfrew Gazette
Sentry Times
The Textile Manufacturer
Textile Trade Review
The Textile Recorder
The Times
The Trade Unionist
The Woman Worker

5. PAMPHLETS

T. Bazley, *Cotton as an Element of Industry* (1852), 70 pp
Bonami, *The Doom of the Cotton Trade and the Fall of the Factory System* (Manchester, 1895) 15 pp
J. & P. Coats, *Coats the threadmakers, 1830–1980* (Paisley, 1980), n.p.
J. Rawlinson, *The Silver Question as it Affects the Cotton Trade* (Manchester, 1889), 26 pp
J. Stephenson, *"Five Bob a Week": Stirling Women's Work, 1900–1950* (Stirling, 1988), 32 pp

6. BOOKS

A) *Contemporary*

J. Baynes, *The Origin, Rise, Progress and Present Extent of the Cotton Trade* (London, 1857)
M. Blair, *The Paisley Thread* (Paisley, 1907)
M. Blair, *The Paisley Shawl and the Men Who Produced It* (Paisley, 1904)
M. Blair, *A Short History of the Glasgow Technical College (Weaving Branch)* (Paisley, 1908)
R. Burn, *Statistics of the Cotton Trade* (1847)
M. Byington, *Homestead. The Households of a Mill Town* (Pittsburg, 1975 edn)
Clarke's Barrhead and Neilston Directory, 1896–7 (Glasgow, 1897)
J. Campbell, *History of the Rise and Progress of Power-Loom Weaving* (Rutherglen, 1878)
J. Cleland, *The Former and Present State of Glasgow* (Glasgow, 1840)

The Cotton Year Book (Manchester, 1911)
T. Ellison, *The Cotton Trade of Great Britain* (1886)
T. Ellison, *Hand Book of the Cotton Trade* (1858)
D. M. Evans, *The Commercial Crisis 1847–1848* (1848)
W. Fairbairn, *Mills and Millwork, Pt 11* (1865)
Fowler's Paisley and Johnstone Commercial Directory, 1851–2 (Paisley, 1852)
W. Freer, *My Life and Memories* (Glasgow, 1929)
Glasgow and Greenock Commercial List, 1870–71 (Glasgow, 1870)
Glasgow Post Office Directories (1860–61, 1869–70, 1880–81, 1890–91, 1900–1901)
A. Graham, *The Impolicy of the Tax on Cotton Wool* (Glasgow, 1836)
Griffin's Book of Trades (Glasgow, 1854)
F. H. Groome, *Ordnance Gazetteer of Scotland: a survey of Scottish topography*, vol. 3 (1883)
S. Harada, *Labour Conditions in Japan* (New York, 1928)
E. Johnston, *Autobiography, Poems and Songs* (Glasgow, 1867)
Kelly's Textile Directories (1880, 1885, 1889, 1893, 1897, 1906, 1922, 1928)
G. MacGregor, *The History of Glasgow: from the earliest period to the present time* (Glasgow, 1881)
R. MacIntyre, 'Textile Industries', in *Local Industries of Glasgow and the West of Scotland*, ed. A. McLean (Glasgow, 1901), pp. 133–57
Memoirs and Portraits of One Hundred Glasgow Men, 2 vols (Glasgow, 1886)
J. Montgomery, *The Theory and Practice of Cotton Spinning* (Glasgow, 1836)
J. Montgomery, *The Cotton Manufacturing of the USA compared with that of Great Britain* (Glasgow, 1840)
J. Mortimer, *Cotton Spinning: the Story of the Spindle* (Manchester, 1895)
J. Myles, *Chapters in the Life of a Dundee Factory Boy* (Edinburgh, 1850)
J. Nasmith, *Modern Cotton Machinery – Its Principles and Construction* (1890)
J. Nasmith, *Student's Cotton Spinning* (Manchester, 1896)
J. Nasmith, and F. Nasmith, *Recent Cotton Mill Construction and Engineering* (1909, 3rd edn)
The New Statistical Account of Scotland, Vol. VI, Lanark (Edinburgh, 1845)
J. Nicol, *Vital Social, Economic Statistics of the City of Glasgow, 1881–1885* (Glasgow, 1885)
The Paisley Directory, 1901–2 (Paisley, 1902)
J. Parkhill, *The History of Paisley* (Paisley, 1857)
A. S. Pearse, *The Cotton Industry of Japan and China* (Manchester, 1929)
A. S. Pearse, *The Cotton Industry of India* (Manchester, 1930)
J. Pilkington, *Cotton: its mission politically . . . socially morally and religiously* (Blackburn, 1857)
Rev W. D. D. Scoresby, *American factories and their female operatives* (1845)
Rev W. D. D. Scoresby, *The Condition and Prospects of Female Operatives* (1846)
Scottish Council for Women's Trades, *Occupations for Girls: A Guide to Girls in Selecting an Employment* (Glasgow, 1900)
J. Strang, *Statistics of Glasgow* (Glasgow, 1855)
J. Strang, *Statistics of Glasgow and the West of Scotland* (Glasgow, 1862)

J. B. Sturrock, *Looking Back* (Paisley, 1910)
A. Ure, *The Cotton Manufacturers of Great Britain*, 2 vols (1836)
J. Watson, *The Theory and Practice of the Art of Weaving by Hand and Power* (Glasgow, 1863)
J. Watson, *The Art of Spinning and Thread Making* (Glasgow, 1878)
A. Watt, *The Vital Statistics of Glasgow, 1843–1844* (Glasgow, 1846)
Worrall's Textile Directory: Ireland, Scotland and Wales (Oldham, 1897/8–1913)

B) *Modern*

M. Anderson, *Family Structure in Nineteenth-Century Lancashire* (Cambridge, 1971)
T. Bell, *Pioneering Days* (1941)
H. E. Blyth, *Through the Eye of a Needle: The Story of the English Sewing Cotton Company* (1947)
P. Bolin-Hort, *Work, Family and the State: Child Labour and the Organisation of Production in the British Cotton Industry, 1780–1920* (Lund, 1989)
H. Braverman, *Labour and Monopoly Capital* (1974)
D. Bremner, *The Industries of Scotland: their rise, progress and present condition* (1969 edn)
M. Burawoy, *The Politics of Production: factory regimes under capitalism and socialism* (1985)
R. H. Campbell, *Scotland since 1707* (1985 edn)
R. H. Campbell, *The Rise and Fall of Scottish Industry, 1707–1939* (Edinburgh, 1980)
S. G. Checkland, *The Upas Tree: Glasgow 1875–1975* (Glasgow, 1976)
S. and O. Checkland, *Industry and Ethos: Scotland 1832–1914* (1984)
W. G. Cochran, *Sampling Techniques* (New York, 1977 edn)
S. Cooper, *The Scottish Education Act of 1872 in Lanarkshire* (Hamilton College of Education Publications, no. 3, *c*.1973)
R. Dalziel and T. Harrison, *Two Hundred Years of Catrine and Sorn Parish: A Cotton Tale* (Catrine, Sorn and District Local History Group, 1987)
P. Duus (ed.), *Cambridge History of Japan: 20th Century, Vol. 6* (New York, 1988)
James Finlay and Company Limited, Manufacturers and East India Merchants, 1750–1950 (Glasgow 1951)
D. A. Farnie, *The English Cotton Industry and the World Market, 1815–1896* (Oxford, 1979)
E. Gordon, *Women and the Labour Movement in Scotland, 1850–1914* (Oxford, 1991)
E. Gordon and E. Breitenbach, *The World is Ill-Divided: women's work in Scotland in the nineteenth and early twentieth centuries* (1992)
I. I. Hughson, *Neilston Mill. The Survivor* (Barrhead and Neilston Historical Association, *c*.1984)
J. R. Hume, *The Industrial Archaealogy of Glasgow* (Glasgow, 1974)
E. H. Hunt, *Regional Wage Variations in Britain, 1850–1914* (Oxford, 1973)
B. L. Hutchins and A. Harrison, *A History of Factory Legislation* (1966 edn)
G. T. Jones, *Increasing Return* (1933)
P. Joyce, *Work, Society and Politics: The Culture of the Factory in Later Victorian England* (1980)

D. Keir, *The Coats Story*, 4 vols (unpublished history, Coats Vyella, 155 St Vincent Street, Glasgow [Glasgow, 1964])
J. L. Kerr, *The Eager Years: an autobiography* (1940)
H. M. Knox, *250 Years of Scottish Education* (Edinburgh, 1973)
W. H. Marwick, *Economic Developments in Victorian Scotland* (1936)
J. Mavor, *My Windows on the Street of the World* (1923)
B Mitchell and P. Deane, *Abstract of British Historical Statistics* (1962)
B. Mitchell, *British Historical Statistics* (Cambridge, 1988)
C. More, *Skill and the English Working Class, 1870–1914* (1980)
N. Murray, *The Scottish Handloom Weavers, 1790–1850: a social history* (Edinburgh, 1978)
H. Newby, et al., *Property, Paternalism and Power: class and control in rural England* (Wisconsin, 1978)
K. Otsuka, et al., *Comparative Technology Choice in Development: the Indian and Japanese Cotton Textile Industries* (1988)
Open University, *Technology and Change 1750–1914, Textile Machinery* (Milton Keynes, 1983)
Renfrew County Council, *The Industries of Renfrewshire* (Glasgow, 1958)
A. Slaven, *The Development of the West of Scotland, 1750–1960* (1975)
T. C. Smout, *A Century of the Scottish People, 1830–1950* (1986)
H. A. Turner, *Trade Union Growth, Structure and Policy* (1962)
US Department of Labor, Bureau of Labor Statistics, *Industry Wage Survey, Textile Mills, 1985* (Washington, 1987)
W. M. Walker, *Jutepolis: Dundee and its Textile Workers, 1885–1923* (Edinburgh, 1979)

7. ARTICLES

A) *Contemporary*

G. Anderson, 'The Factory Half-time System and the Education Test', *Transactions of the National Association for the Promotion of Social Science* (1860), pp. 379–84
D. M. Barton, 'The Course of Women's Wages', *Journal of the Royal Statistical Society*, xxxii (1919), pp. 508–44
H. Campion, 'Pre-war fluctuations of profits in the Cotton Spinning Industry', *Journal of the Royal Statistical Society*, xcvii (1934), pp. 626–32
S. J. Chapman, 'The Regulation of Wages by Lists in the Spinning Industry', *Economic Journal*, ix (1899), pp. 592–9
S. J. Chapman and T. S. Ashton, 'The size of businesses, mainly in the textile industries', *Journal of the Royal Statistical Society*, xxvii (1914), pp. 469–549
M. T. Copeland, 'Technical Development in Cotton Manufacturing since 1860', *Quarterly Journal of Economics*, xxiv (1910), pp. 109–59
'The Ferguslie Thread Works of Messrs J. & P. Coats', *Illustrated Weekly Telegraph*, 31 October 1885
'Industries of Lanarkshire: New Lanark and its Mills', *Hamilton Advertiser Pictorial Review* (1932)

'The Industries of England: The Manufacture of Sewing Cotton – The "Anchor" Thread Works of Messrs Clark & Company, Paisley', *The British Mercantile Gazette*, 15 October 1876

I. W., 'Cotton', *Encyclopedia Britannica*, Vol. VI (Edinburgh, 1877), pp. 482–502

J. Ingram, 'Notes on the early textile industries of Glasgow', in *A Short History of the Glasgow Technical College*, ed. M. Blair (Paisley, 1908), pp. 61–75

M. H. Irwin, 'Women's Industries in Scotland', *Proceedings of the Philosophical Society of Glasgow*, xxvii (1885–6), pp. 70–91

T. Johnes, 'Notes on the Social and Economic Transition in Japan', *Economic Journal*, 31 (1921), pp. 50–60

G. M. Mitchell, 'The English and Scottish Cotton Industries', *Scottish Historical Review*, 22 (1925), pp. 101–14

M. M. Paterson, 'Memories of a Woman Inspector', *Scots Magazine*, 13 (1930), pp. 365–71

J. Strang, 'Comparative View of the Money Rate of Wages in Glasgow and the West of Scotland in 1851, 1856 and 1858', *Journal of the Royal Statistical Society*, xxi (1858), pp. 421–6

J. Strang, 'On the Money-Rate of Wages of Labour in Glasgow and the West of Scotland', *Journal of the Statistical Society*, xx (1857), pp. 308–12

'The Thread Works of Paisley', *The Mining Journal*, 20 November 1871

G. H. Wood, 'Statistics and wages in the nineteenth century, pt xix: Cotton Industry', *Journal of the Royal Statistical Society*, 73 (1910), pp. 584–633

B) *Modern*

M. Anderson, 'The study of family structure', in *Nineteenth-Century Society: essays in the use of quantitative methods for the study of social data*, ed. E. A. Wrigley (1972) pp. 47–81

M. Anderson, 'Standard tabulation procedures for the census enumertors' books 1851–1891' in *Nineteenth-Century Society: essays in the use of quantative methods for the study of social data*, ed. E. A. Wrigley (1972), pp. 135–45

M. Anderson, *et al.*, 'The National Sample from the 1851 Census', *Urban History Yearbook* (1977), pp. 55–9

W. A. Armstrong, 'The Census enumerators' books: a commentary', in *The Census and Social Structure*, ed. R. Lawton (1978), pp. 28–81

E. Asher, 'Industrial Efficiency and Biased Technical Change in American & British Manufacturing: the case of textiles in the nineteenth century', *Journal of Economic History*, 32 (1972), pp. 431–42

M. Barratt and M. Mackintosh, 'The Family Wage: some problems for socialists and feminists', *Capital and Class*, 11 (1980), pp. 51–72

V. Beechey, 'On Patriarchy', *Feminist Review*, iii (1979), pp. 66–82

V. Beechey, 'The Sexual Division of Labour and the Labour Process: a critical assessment of Braverman', in *The Degradation of Work?*, ed. S. Wood (1982), pp. 54–73

J. M. Bellamy, 'Occupation Statistics in the Nineteenth-Century Censuses', in *The Census and Social Structure*, ed. Richard Lawton (1978), pp. 165–84

L. Billington, 'British Humanitarians and American Cotton, 1840–1860', *Journal of American Studies*, II (1977), pp. 313–34

M. Blaug, 'The Productivity of Capital in the Lancashire Cotton Industry During the Nineteenth Century', *Economic History Review*, 13 (1960–1), pp. 358–81

H. Bradley, 'Technological change, managerial strategies and the development of gender-based job segregation in the labour process', in *Gender and the Labour Process*, ed. D. Knights and H. Wilmott (Aldershot, 1986), pp. 54–73.

I. Bruegel, 'Women's Employment, Legislation & the Labour Market', *Women's Welfare, Women's Rights*, ed. J. Lewis (Beckenham, Kent, 1983), pp. 130–69

A. Bullen, 'Pragmatism vs Principle: cotton employers and the origins of an industrial relations system', in *Employers and Labour in the English Textile Industries, 1850–1939*, eds. J. A. Jowitt and A. J. McIvor (1988) pp. 27–43

D. Bursfield, 'Skill and the Sexual Division of Labour in the West Riding Textile Industry, 1850–1914', in *Employers and Labour in the English Textile Industries, 1850–1939*, eds. J. A. Jowitt and A. J. McIvor (1988), pp. 153–70

J. Butt, 'The Scottish Cotton Industry During the Industrial Revolution 1780–1840', in *Comparative Aspects of Scottish and Irish Economic and Social History*, eds. L. M. Cullen and T. C. Smout (Edinburgh 1977), pp. 116–28

J. Butt, 'Labour and Industrial Relations in the Scottish Cotton Industry during the Industrial Revolution', in *Scottish Textile History*, eds. J. Butt and K. Ponting (Aberdeen, 1987), pp. 139–60

A. K. Cairncross and J. B. K. Hunter, 'The Early Growth of Messrs J. & P. Coats, 1830–1883', *Business History*, 29 (1987), pp. 157–77

H. Catling, 'The Development of the Spinning Mule', *Textile History*, 9 (1978), pp. 35–57

S. D. Chapman, 'Workers' Housing in the Cotton Factory Colonies, 1770–1850', *Textile History*, 7 (1976), pp. 112–39

S. D. Chapman, 'The Transition to the Factory System in the Midlands Cotton Spinning Industry', *Economic History Review*, xviii (1965), pp. 526–43

G. Clark, 'Why Isn't the Whole World Developed? lessons from the cotton mills', *Journal of Economic History*, 47 (1987), pp. 141–73

T. Clark and T. Dickson, 'Class and Class Consciousness in Early Industrial Capitalism: Paisley 1770–1850', in *Capital and Class in Scotland*, ed. T Dickson (Edinburgh, 1982), pp. 8–60

M. Clough, 'James Clark', *Dictionary of Scottish Business Biography, 1860–1960, Vol. 1, The Staple Industries*, eds. A. Slaven, and S. Checkland ((Aberdeen, 1986), pp. 223–5

I. Cohen, 'Worker's Control in the Cotton Industry: a comparative study of British and American Mule Spinning', *Labor History*, 26 (1985), pp. 53–85

B. Collins, 'Irish Emigration to Dundee and Paisley during the First Half of the Nineteenth Century', in *Irish Population, Economy and Society*, eds. J. M. Goldstrom and L. A. Clarkson (Oxford, 1981), pp. 195–212

A. J. Cooke, 'Richard Arkwright and the Scottish Cotton Industry', *Textile History*, 10 (1979), pp. 196–202

D. Creamer, 'Recruiting Contract Laborers for the Amoskeag Mills', *Journal of Economic History*, 1 (1941), pp. 42–56

B. Dick and G. Morgan, 'Family Networks and Employment in Textiles', *Work, Employment and Society*, 1 (1987), pp. 225–46

T. Dublin, 'Women, Work and Protest in the Early Lowell Mills: "The Oppressing Hand of Avarice Would Enslave Us"', in *American Working Class Culture: Explorations in American Labour and Social History*, ed. M. Cantor (Westport, 1979), pp. 167–87

H. I. Dutton and J. E. King, 'The Limits of Paternalism: the cotton tyrants of northern Lancashire', *Social History*, vii (1982), pp. 59–74

Z. Eisenstein, 'Developing a Theory of Capitalist Patriarchy and Socialist Feminism', in *Capitalist Patriarchy and the Case for Socialist Feminism*, ed. Z. Eisenstein (New York, 1979) pp. 5–40

T. Elger, 'Braverman, Capital Accumulation and Deskilling', in *The Degradation of Work*, ed. S. Wood (1982), pp. 25–53

A. Frances, 'Markets and Hierarchies: efficiency or domination?', in *Power, Efficiency and Institutions: a critical appraisal of the 'markets and hierarchies' paradigm*, eds. A. Frances, et al. (1983), pp. 105–16

W. H. Fraser, 'The Glasgow Cotton Spinners 1837', in *Scottish Themes*, eds. J. Butt and J. T. Ward (Edinburgh, 1976), pp. 80–97

A. L. Friedman, 'Management Strategies, Market Conditions and the Labour Process', in *Firms, Organisation and Labour*, ed. F. H. Stephen (1984), pp. 176–200

M. Friefield, 'Technological Change and the "Self Acting" Mule: a study of skill and the sexual division of labour', *Social History*, ii (1986), pp. 319–43

V. A. C. Gatrell, 'Labour, power and the size of firms in Lancashire cotton in the second quarter of the nineteenth century', *Economic History Review*, xxx (1977), pp. 95–139

J. B. S. Gilfillan and H. A. Moisley, 'Industrial and Commercial Developments to 1914', in *The Glasgow Region: a general survey*, eds. R. Miller and J. Tivy (Glasgow, 1958), pp. 150–89

E. Gordon, 'Women, trade unions and industrial militancy 1850–1890', in *Uncharted Lives: extracts From Scottish Women's Experiences 1850–1982*, ed. Glasgow Women's Studies Group (Glasgow, 1983), pp. 52–73

E. Gordon, 'Women, Work and Collective Action: Dundee Jute Workers 1870–1906', *Journal of Social History*, 21 (1987), pp. 27–47

M. Grieco and R. Whipp, 'Women and the Workplace: Gender and Control in the Labour Process', in *Gender and the Labour Process*, eds. D. Knights and H. Wilmott (Aldershot, 1986), pp. 117–39

Z. Grosicki, 'Textiles and Clothing', in *Third Statistical Account of Scotland: Glasgow*, eds. J. Cammeron and J. B. S. Gilfillan (Glasgow, 1958), pp. 240–51

J. D. Hall, *et al.*, 'Cotton Mill People: work, community and protest in the textile South, 1880–1914', *American Historical Review*, 91 (1986), pp. 245–86

C. Harris and L. Morris, 'Households, Labour Markets and the Position of

Women', in *Gender and Stratification*, eds. R. Crompton and M. Mann (Cambridge, 1986), pp. 87–96

B. Harrison and H. Mackett, 'Women in the Factory: the state and factory legislation in nineteenth century Britain', in *State, Private Life and Political Change*, eds. L. Jamieson and H. Corr (1990), pp. 137–62

H. Hartmann, 'Capitalism, Patriarchy and Job Segregation by Sex' in, *Capitalist Patiarchy and the Case for Socialist Feminism*, ed. Z. Eisenstein (New York, 1979), pp. 206–47

W. O. Henderson, 'The Cotton Famine In Scotland and the Relief of Distress, 1862–1864', *Scottish Historical Review*, 30 (1951), pp. 154–64

P. Hilden, 'Class and Gender: conflicting components of women's behaviour in the textile mills of Lille, Roubaix and Tourcoing, 1880–1914', *Historical Journal*, 27 (1984), pp. 361–85

M. Huberman, 'The economic origins of paternalism: Lancashire cotton spinning in the first half of the nineteenth century', *Social History*, 12 (1987), pp. 177–92

J. R. Hume, 'The Industrial Archaealogy of New Lanark', in *Robert Owen: Prince of Cotton Spinners*, ed J. Butt (Newton Abbott, 1971), pp. 215–53

J. Humphries, 'Mines Regulation Act 1842', *Feminist Review*, 7 (1981), pp. 1–31

J. B. K. Hunter, 'Otto Ernst Philippi', in *Dictionary of Scottish Business Biography, Vol. 1, The Staple Industries*, eds. S. Checkland and A. Slaven (Aberdeen, 1986), pp. 389–92

J. B. K. Hunter, 'Thomas Coats', in *Dictionary of Scottish Business Biography, Vol. 1, The Staple Industries*, eds. S. Checkland and A. Slaven (Aberdeen, 1986), pp. 332–4

J. B. K. Hunter, 'Archibald Coats', in *Dictionary of Scottish Business Biography, Vol. 1, The Staple Industries*, eds. S. Checkland and A. Slaven (Aberdeen, 1986), pp. 329–32

J. Hunter, 'Recruitment in the Japanese Silk Reeling and Cotton Spinning Industries, 1870s–1930s', *Proceedings of the British Association for Japanese Studies*, 9 (1984), pp. 63–85

'James Coats . . . a life well spent' (a *Life and Work* Supplement, March 1987)

D. T. Jenkins, 'The Cotton Industry in Yorkshire, 1780–1900, *Textile History*, 10 (1979), pp. 75–95

A. Kilpatrick and T. Lawson, 'The Strength of the Working Class' in *The Economic Decline of Modern Britain: the debate between left and right*, eds. D. Coates and J. Holland (1986), pp. 250–8

M. W. Kirby, 'Institutional Rigidities and Economic Decline: reflections on the British experience', *Economic History Review*, xlv (1992), pp. 637–60

G. B. Kulik, 'Patterns of Resistance to Industrial Capitalism, Pawtucket Village and the Strike of 1824', in *American Working Class Cullture: Explorations in American Labor and Social History*, ed. M. Cantor (Westport, 1979), pp. 209–39

H. Land, 'The Family Wage', *Feminist Review*, 6 (1980), pp. 55–78

W. Lazonick, 'Industrial relations and technical change: the case of the self-acting mule', *Cambridge Journal of Economics*, 3 (1979), pp. 231–62

W. Lazonick, 'The Cotton Industry', in *The Decline of the British Economy*, eds. B. Elbaum and W. Lazonick (Oxford, 1986), pp. 18–50

W. Lazonick and W. Mass, 'The Performance of the British Cotton Industry, 1870–1913', *Research in Economic History*, 9 (1984), pp. 1–44

C. H. Lee, 'The Cotton Textile Industry', in *The Dynamics of Victorian Business: problems and perspectives to the 1870s*, ed. R. A. Church (1980), pp. 161–80

J. Lewis, 'The Debate on Sex and Class', *New Left Review*, 149 (1985), pp. 108–20

E. Lorenz and F. Wilkinson, 'The Shipbuilding Industry, 1880–1965', in *The Decline of the British Economy*, eds. B. Elbaum and W. Lazonick (Oxford, 1986), pp. 109–34

J. Lown, ' "Not so much a factory, more a form of patriarchy": gender and class during industrialisation', in *Gender, Class and Work*, eds. E. Gamarnikov, et al. (Aldershot 1985, 2nd edn), pp. 28–45

J. Mark-Lawson and A. Witz, 'From "family labour" to "family wage"? the case of women's labour in nineteenth century coalming', *Social History*, 13 (1988), pp. 51–74

S. A. Marglin, 'Knowledge and Power', *Firms, Organisation and Labour*, ed. F. H. Stephen (1984), pp. 146–64

J. Mason, 'Spinners and Masters', in *The Barefoot Aristocrats: a history of the Amalgamated Association of Operative Cotton Spinners*, eds. A. Fowler and T. Wyke (Littleborough, 1987), pp. 36–58

J. Mason, 'Cotton spinning in the Industrial Revolution', in *The Barefoot Aristocrats: a history of the Amalgamated Association of Operative Cotton Spinners*, eds. A. Fowler and T. Wyke (Littleborough, 1987), pp. 1–13

S. A. Matthies, 'Families at work: an analysis by sex of child workers in the cotton textile industry', *Journal of Economic History*, 42 (1982), pp. 173–80

D. Mazumdar, 'Labour Supply in Early Industrialization: the case of the Bombay Texile Industry', *Economic History Review*, xxvi (1973), pp. 477–96

R. McDonough and R. Harrison, 'Patriarchy and relations of production', in *Feminism and Materialism: Women and Modes of Production*, eds. A. Kuhn and A. Wofe (1978), pp. 11–41

A. MacIvor, 'Cotton Employers' Organisations and Labour Relations Strategy, 1890–1939', Research Working Paper, Polytechnic of South London, 19 (1982)

J. Melling, 'Scottish Industrialists and the Changing Character of Class Relations in the Clyde Region, c1880–1918', in *Capital and Class in Scotland*, ed. T. Dickson (Edinburgh, 1982), pp. 61–142

N. J. Morgan, 'James Paterson', in *Dictionary of Scottish Business Biography, Vol. 1, The Staple Industries*, eds. S. Checkland and A. Slaven (Aberdeen, 1986), pp. 383–5

N. J. Morgan, 'John Colville', in *Dictionary of Scottish Business Biography, Vol. 1, The Staple Industries*, eds. S. Checkland and A. Slaven (Aberdeen, 1986), pp. 337–9

N. J. Morgan, 'John Clark', in *Dictionary of Scottish Business Biography, Vol. 1, The Staple Industries*, eds. S. Checkland and A. Slaven (Aberdeen, 1986), pp. 326–8

S. Nenadic, 'The Life Cycle of Firms in Late 19th Century Britain', in *The Birth and Death of Companies*, eds. P. Jobert and M. Moss (Lancashire, 1990), pp. 181–95

S. Nenadic, 'Record linkage and the exploration of nineteenth century social groups: a methodological perspective on the Glasgow middle class in 1861', *Urban History Yearbook* (1987), pp. 32–42

H. Newby, 'Paternalism and Capitalism', in *Industrial Society: class, cleavage and control*, ed. R. Scase (1977), pp. 59–73

D. J. Oddy, 'Urban Famine in 19th Century Britain: the effect of the Lancashire Cotton Famine on Working Class Diet and Health', *Economic History Review*, xxxvi (1983), pp. 68–86

R. Penn, 'Skilled Manual Workers and the Labour Process', in *The Degradation of Work?*, ed. S. Wood (1982)

R. Penn, 'The course of wage differentials between skilled and non-skilled manual workers in Britain between 1856–1964', *British Journal of Industrial Relations*, 21 (1983), pp. 69–90

A. Phillips and B. Taylor, 'Sex and Skill: notes towards a Feminist Economics', *Feminist Review*, 6 (1980), pp. 79–88

L. Putterman, 'On some recent explanations of why capital hires labor', *Economic Inquiry*, 22 (1984), pp. 171–87

A. J. Robertson, 'David Blyth Anderson', in *Dictionary of Scottish Business Biography 1860–1960, Vol. 1: the staple industries*, eds A. Slaven and S. Checkland (Aberdeen, 1986), pp. 305–7

A. J. Robertson, 'The Decline of the Scottish Cotton Industry 1860–1914', *Business History*, 12 (1970), pp. 116–28

A. J. Robertson, 'Textiles', in *Dictionary of Scottish Business Biography 1860–1960, Vol. 1: the staple industries*, eds A. Slaven and S. Checkland (Aberdeen, 1986), pp. 297–304

R. Rodger, 'Concentration and Fragmentation: capital, labor and the structure of Mid-Victorian Scottish industry', *Journal of Urban History*, 14 (1988), pp. 178–213

R. Rodger, 'Employment, Wages and Poverty in the Scottish Cities, 1841–1911', in *Perspectives of the Scottish Cities*, ed. G. Gordon (Aberdeen, 1985), pp. 25–63

P. H. Sadler, 'Sociological Aspects of Skill', *British Journal of Industrial Relations*, viii (1970), pp. 22–31

M. Savage, 'Capitalist and patriarchal relations at work: Preston cotton weaving, 1890–1940', in *Localities, Class and Gender* (Lancaster Regionalism Group, 1985), pp. 77–94

M. Savage, 'Women and work in the Lancashire Cotton Industry, 1890–1939', in *Employers and Labour in Textiles*, eds. J. A. Jowitt and A. J. McIvor (1988),

G. A. Saxonhouse, 'A Tale of Japanese Technological Diffusion in the Meiji Period', *Journal of Economic History*, xxxiv (1974), pp. 149–65

G. Saxonhouse and G. Wright, 'New Evidence on the stubborn English mule and the cotton industry, 1878–1920', *Economic History Review*, xxxvii (1984), pp. 507–19

G. Saxonhouse and G. Wright, 'Rings and mules around the world: a comparative study in technological choice', *Research in Economic History*, 3 (1984), pp. 271–300

G. Saxonhouse and G. Wright, 'Two forms of cheap labor in textile history', *Research in Economic History*, 3 (1984), pp. 3–32

W. Secombe, 'Patriarchy Stabilised: the construction of the male bread winner wage norm in nineteenth century Britain', *Social History*, 2 (1986), pp. 53–69
P. T. Silvia, 'The Position of Workers in a Textile Community: Fall River in the early 1880s', in *American Working-Class Culture: Explorations in American Labor and Social History*, ed. M. Cantor (Westport, 1979), pp. 189–208
P. M. Tillot, 'Sources of inaccuracy in the 1851 and 1861 censuses', in *Nineteenth-Century Society: essays in the use of quantative methods for the study of social data*, ed. E. A. Wrigley (1972), pp. 82–128
J. D. Tomlinson, 'The First World War and British Cotton Piece Exports to India', *Economic History Review*, xxxvi (1983), pp. 494–506
J. H. Treble, 'The characteristics of the female unskilled market and the formation of the female casual labour market in Glasgow, 1891–1914', *Scottish Economic and Social History*, 6 (1986), pp. 33–46
P. Tsurumi, 'Female Textile Workers and the Failure of Early Trade Unionism in Japan', *History Workshop Journal*, 18 (1984), pp. 3–27
M. J. Twomey, 'Employment in Nineteenth Century Indian Textiles', *Explorations in Economic History*, 20 (1983), pp. 35–57
J. T. Ward, 'The Factory Reform Movement in Scotland', *Scottish Historical Review*, xli (1962), pp. 100–23
A. Warde, 'Industrial Discipline: Factory Regime and Politics in Lancaster', *Work, Employment and Society*, 3 (1989), pp. 49–63
M. I. Watson, 'The Cotton Trade Unions and Labour Representation in the late Nineteenth Century', *Northern History*, 20 (1984), pp. 207–16
J. West, 'Women, Sex and Class', in *Feminism and Materialism*, eds. A. Kuhn and A. Wolpe (1978), pp. 220–53
R. Whipp, 'Labour Markets and Commodities: an historical view', *Sociological Review*, 33 (1985), pp. 768–91
O. E. Williamson, 'The Organisation of Work: a comparative institutional assessment', in *The Economic Nature of the Firm*, ed. L. Patterson (Cambridge, 1980), pp. 292–311
O. E. Williamson, 'Efficient Labour Organization', in *Firms, Organisation and Labour*, ed. F. H. Stephen (1984), pp. 87–118
H. Wright, 'The Uncommon Mill Girls of Lowell, *History Today*, 23 (January 1973), pp. 10–9
K. Yamamura, 'The Role of Meiji Militarism in Japan's Technological Progress', *Journal of Economic History*, 37 (1977), pp. 113–35
S. Yoshisaka, 'Labour Recruiting in Japan and its Control', *International Labour Review*, 12 (1925), pp. 484–99
J. Zeitlin, 'Craft Control and the Division of Labour: engineers and compositors', *Cambridge Journal of Economics*, iii (1979), pp. 263–74.

8. THESES

A. J. M. Albert, 'Patterns of Employment of Working Class Women in Glasgow, 1980–1914' (unpublished M.A. thesis, University of Victoria, 1985)

B. E. A. Collins, 'Aspects of Immigration into two Scottish Towns (Dundee and Paisley) during the mid-nineteenth century' (unpublished M.Phil., University of Edinburgh, 1978)

J. C. Holley, 'The Redivision of Labour: two firms in nineteenth century South East Scotland' (unpublished Ph.D., University of Edinburgh, 1978)

W. Sloan, 'The Supply of Labour for Cotton Spinning in Scotland, $c.1780$–1836' (undergraduate dissertation, Department of History, University of Strathclyde, 1980)

W. Sloan, 'Aspects of the Assimilation of Highland and Irish Migrants in Glasgow, 1830–1870' (unpublished M.Phil., University of Strathclyde, 1987)

Index

ADAM, William 127
American Cotton Manufacturers' Association 130-1
Anchor Mill 108, 125, 133-4, 136, 139, 161-2
Anderson, David Blyth 117
Anderson, D. J. 117
Anderson, John 117
Arkwright's water frame 43-4
Atlantic Mill 111
Arrol, Thomas 122
Arrol, Sir William MP 142
Ashley, Lord 115
Auchinloss, Ann 137

BATTENING (spinning) 48
beamers 63, 152
Balderstone, Robert 118-19, 128
Birkmyre, Henry 117-18
Birkmyre, William 117
Blackburn 88, 91
Blair, Matthew 110-11, 159-60
Board of Trade, 163, 165
Bolin-Hort, Per—
  and child labour 46
  and industrial relations 10-11
  and price lists 73
  and spinners' union 149
  and subcontracting 55-6
Borland, William 142
Bradley, Hariet 123, 129, 133-4
Braverman, Harry 39-40
Bremner, David 36-8
Bridgeton, 31, 55, 66, 96-7, 103, 123-5, 147, 150, 155-6
Burnley 66, 89
Bursfield, D. 123

CAIRD, Edward 156
Cairncross, A. K.—
  and investment statistics 4
  and wage costs 85, 106
Campbell, R. H.—
  and early start thesis 5, 27, 174
  and investment 27-8
  and consumption of raw cotton 35-6, 38
Carlisle, J. 142
Carlyle, Thomas 115
Catrine 53, 123, 125
census—
  and problems with 18, 23, 25
child labour 21, 42-3, 46, 50, 54-6, 59, 65-6, 78, 82-4, 136-8, 160
Clark & Company 78-9, 80, 82, 105, 111, 115, 117, 128, 131, 161
  and cartelisation 142, 180
  and employment policy 132
  and housing 125
  and pensions 129
  and worker recreation 132
  and wages
Clark, G.—
  and Japanese cotton industry 59
  and world loom ratios 71
Clark, Kenneth 138
Clark, James 78, 117
Clark, John 117-18, 134
Clark, Peter 77
Clark, Stewart 129
Clark, William 109
Coats, J. & P., Company Ltd. 78-9, 80, 84, 105, 111, 115, 124, 128, 131
  and cartelisation 4, 142, 180
  and Board of Trade 106

and business records 3–4
and employment policy 132
and Factory Acts 142
and housing 125–6
and immigrant labour 159–60
and industrial discipline 135–6
and investment 81
and labour turnover 160
and paternalism 13, 142, 180
and pensions 129–30
and worker recreation 132, 140
and trade unionism 161–2
and US market 81, 180–1
and wages, 96, 108, 113
Coats, James 117, 122, 137–8
Coats, Peter 117, 119, 136
Coats, Thomas 117–19, 134, 138
Cohen, I.—
and pieceing system 45–7
and apprenticeship 52
Colville, John 117
Combing 41
Copeland, M. T. 75–6
copwinders—
and strikes 163
and wages 108, 112, 178
Cotton Famine 20, 35, 54–5, 95
cotton industry and industrialisation 1–2
cotton industry: Japan—
and employment policy 133
and female labour 58, 60, 174
and looms 71
and operating costs 59
and output 58
and ring spinning
cotton industry: Lancashire 1–2, 17, 174–5
and child labour 65, 179
and loom question 35, 62, 65, 70–3
and married women 66–7
and paternalism 120
and relation with thread industry 82
and spindleage 30–1
and subcontracting 56
and wages 88–9, 176–7

and weaving productivity 69
cotton industry: Scotland, *passim*
and cotton mills 28–30
and cyclical development 17, 25–6
employment 17–27
  age structure of 21–3
  sexual structure of 19–21
and exports 36–7
and female labour 22–5
and households 124
and investment 28–35
and raw cotton imports 4
cotton industry: USA—
and Northrop Loom 68, 70–1
and ring spinning 61
Cotton spinners' strike (1837) 2, 11, 13, 19, 51, 53, 93–4, 145, 148–9
Courtaulds 129
Crompton's power mule 42, 44–5, 49–50, 51–2, 60
Crouzet, F. 28

DICKENS, Charles 115
Dictionary of Scottish Business Biography 116
doffers (spinning) 56
domestic service 24–5
dressmaking 24–5, 112
Dundee jute industry
  and child labour 59—
  and female labour 159
  and wages 112
Dunlop, Henry 141

EDINBURGH 132
Edmund Ashworth & Sons, 142
Education [Scotland] Act (1872) 59
Elbaum, B.—
  and industrial decline 11–12
Ellison, Thomas—
  and economics of weaving 34
English Sewing Cotton Company—
  and productivity
  and strikes 163–4, 167
  and wages 105, 107–8

INDEX

entrepreneurship 7–9, 58–9, 115–18, 171

FACTORY Acts 84, 102, 175, 179
Ferguslie Mill 78, 82–4, 107, 113, 133, 136, 180–1
Ferguslie Thread Workers' Relief Committee 136
Finlay, James 53–4, 118
Fleming, Alexander M. 118
Fleming, James 118
France 71, 77, 110
Fraser, W. H.—
  and cotton spinners' strike (1837) 146–9
Free Church 118
Friedfeld, M.—
  and female spinners 53–4
  and male exclusionsim 45
  and spinning skills 52–4

GLASGOW 3, 18, 28, 43, 47, 50–1, 55–6, 68, 70, 72, 74, 87, 93, 96, 102, 105, 113, 122–4, 140, 145, 147–8, 152–3, 160, 173
Glasgow Association of Operative Cotton Spinners
  and arbitration 150–1
  and collapse of 151–2
  and emigration 150–1
  and organisation 146–7, 149–50
  and price lists 151
  and violence 147
Glasgow Cotton Masters' Association 141
Glasgow Cotton Spinning Company 31, 58
Glasgow Handmill and Horizontal Warpers' Society 154
Glasgow Herald 55, 71, 73, 76, 102
Glasgow Power Loom Beamers' Society 63, 154
Glasgow Saturday Post 149
Glasgow Sentinel 55, 95
Glasgow Trades Council 70, 151, 156, 163

Glasgow and West of Scotland Power Loom Tenters' Society—
  and foundation 152
  and labour supply
  and membership 153
Glen-Coats, Sir Thomas MP 128, 138
Gordon, Eleanor 146
Gourock Rope Works 117–18

HALIFAX, 89
hankwinders (thread) 161–2
Hardie, Keir 161
Hobsbawm, E. J. 1
Houldsworth, Henry 147
Houldsworth, John 28, 48, 51, 140–1
Houldsworth, William 140
Hunter, J. B. K, see Cairncross, A. K.

INDIA 77
Independent Labour Party 139, 158, 161
intermediate spinning 42
Ireland 124
Irish 145–8, 159–60
Irwin, Margaret—
  and child labour 59
  and entrepreneurship 115–16
  and female spinners
  and health and safety 128
  and wages 74, 96–7, 100, 107–8
  and ages of weavers 66
  and appearance and education of weavers 103
  and weaving skills 64

JOYCE, Patrick—
  and paternalism 120–2, 127

KERR and Company, 80
Kilpatrick, A.—
  and industrial decline 9–10
Kirby, Maurice—
  and Elbaum/Lazonick thesis 12–13

LABOUR and Monopoly Capital 39
Labour Party 128

Lanarkshire 18, 22, 23–5, 32, 57–8, 60, 66, 154
Lawson, T. see Kilpatrick
Lazonick, W.—
  and entrepreneurship 8
  and industrial decline 11
  and loom question 72, 176
  and male authority 52
  and markets 180
  and skill 48
  and subcontracting 48
Liverpool 93, 122
Livingstone, David 150
Liberal Party 128
Looking Back 110
Lorenz, E.—
  and shipbuilding 7–8
Lowell, Massachutes, 110
Lown, J. 129

MacIntyre, R. 31
McNaught, Peter 45
McNish, James 94
Manchester 88, 91, 110, 122
Mason, J. 50
Mexico 71
mill boys (thread) 162
millinery 24–5
Montgomery, J.—
  and economics of spinning 51–2
Muir, James 118
Muir, John 118
Mule Spinning Process, The 52

National Federation of Women Workers 158, 163
Neilston 79, 163–4, 167
Neste, Kurte 52
Newark, New Jersey, 80, 109
Newby, H.—
  and paternalism 121, 127–8
New Lanark 50, 53, 123, 125
Northrop Loom 68, 70, 74–5
nurses—
  and social origin 113

and wages 112–13

Oldham 88, 91

Pacific Mill 111
Paisley, 18, 32, 77–8, 80, 84, 87, 105, 110, 117, 118–19, 123–6, 132, 137–8, 149, 158–9, 161–2, 177, 180, 182
Paisley Grammar School 117
Paisley Herald 137–8
Paisley Savings Bank 137
Paisley School Board 131
Paisley Thread Industry, The 159
Paisley Town Council 128
paternalism, 13, 119–40
Paterson, James 117
Paterson, Mary—
  and weavers' grievances 72
  and weavers' intelligence 103
  and weaving skills 65
Pawtucket, Rhode Island, 80
Pettigrew, Agnes 157
philanthropy 118–19
piecers 43, 46, 47–8, 50, 54–6, 93
Porter, R. P. 110
Power Loom Cloth Manufacturers' Association of Glasgow 141
Preston 50, 88, 91
Price, Richard 146
productivity 89–93
Putterman, L. 127

Renfrewshire 18, 22, 25, 32, 58–60
ring spinning 31, 57–60, 75, 81, 174
Roberts, Richard 49
Robertson, A. J.—
  and cyclical decline 5–6
  and entrepreneurial failure 6–7, 10, 115
  and weaving skills 64
Robertson, James 148
Russia 70, 180

Savage, Michael 66–7
Scottish Ball Warp Brush Beamers' Society 154–5

Scottish Field 110
Scottish Textile Trades Association 157
Scottish Council for Women's Trades 64
self-acting mule 2, 20, 48–55, 150
Sewing Central Agency 79–80, 142, 180
shop assistants—
  and hours of work 113
  and wages 112–13, 178
sizing 93, 104
Slaven, Anthony 7
Slubbing (spinning) 41–2
spinners (cotton)—
  and apprenticeship 48, 52
  and employment 91
  and ethnicity of 147–8
  and females 43, 45, 47, 49, 53–6, 97, 178–9
  and health 98–9, 179
  and hours of work 60, 98
  and power mule 42
  and trade unions 53
  and working conditions 97–9, 178–9
  numbers of 51
  productivity of 61, 91–2
spinning (cotton)—
  and apprenticeship 48
  and consumption of raw cotton 35–6, 95
  and employers 57–9, 93, 141
  and employment 26–7, 47
  and industrial failure 13, 32, 173–4, 179–80
  and investment 30–1
  and labour process 40–61
  and male employment 20–1, 147, 150
  and multi-pair system 56, 96
  and output 37–8, 91
  and transport costs 60–1, 93
  production process 41–2
spinning and weaving combines 13, 174
spooling machinery 78
Strang, J. 94
Sturrock, Rev J. B. 110

strikes—
  and spinning sector 149, 150, 166 (see also cotton spinners' strike)
  and thread sector 133–4, 161–3, 166–7, 169–72
  and weaving sector 153, 155–7, 166–7, 169–72
  causes of 166–7
  days lost 172
  duration of 168–9, 170–1
  numbers involved 170
Stuart, James 148

TENTERS (weaving)—
  and employment 19
  and organisation 152, 164
  and supervision 67
  and wages 67, 100
Textile Manufacturer, The 67, 71
Textile Trade Review 115
Thread (cotton)—
  and child labour 21, 78, 82–4, 136–8, 160
  and depression 109
  and education 130–2
  and employment 26–7, 78, 83
  and housing 125–7
  and investment 31–2
  and labour process 77–85, 177
  and labour turnover 83, 106–7, 160
  and paternalism, 125–40, 171–2, 178
  and production process 77–9, 81–2
  and ring spinning 81
  and industrial success 13, 177–8, 180–1
  and tariff question 80, 109–10, 180
  and US operations 80–1
thread workers—
  and grievances 109
  and hours of work 111
  and illegitimacy 110
  and physical appearance 109–11
  and productivity 80
  and skill 82–3, 85
  and working conditions 111, 178

social origins of 127, 159–60
Thread Trade Association 141–2, 180
throstle spinning 44, 50
Todd, Charles 49
trade unionism (cotton)—
   and spinning sector 53, 145–52
   and thread sector 158–64
   and weaving 152–7
   and women 146, 151–2, 155–64
twisters—
   and strikes 167
   and wages 108

UNITED Presbyterian Church 118
University of Glasgow 118
Ure, Andrew—
   and cotton workers 3, 21
   and labour relations 43
   and self-acting mule 49–50
   and women and physical exertion 48

VINES, Ms. 114

WAGES—
   and spinning sector 49, 55, 89, 91, 93–9, 112, 148, 178
   and thread sector 84–5, 105–14, 178
   and weaving sector 63, 67, 73, 99–104, 112, 177–8
   and women 113
   in England 89, 91, 114
   in Scotland 89, 91, 101, 107, 114
   records of 3
warpers 152
warping 62–3, 72
weavers (power loom)—
   and dress 103, 179
   and 'driving' 102, 179
   and education 103
   and grievances 72, 101
   and marital status 66
   and organisation 152, 155–7
   and productivity 69–70, 92
   and seasonal employment 102

   and skill 62–5, 72, 74
   and working conditions 104, 178
   social origins of 103
weaving (cotton)—
   and apprenticeship 65, 68
   and commission weavers 76, 102
   and employment 19, 26–7, 66–7, 92
   and employers 62, 73, 74, 76, 171, 174, 177
   and exports 38
   and investment 32–5
   and labour process 62–77
   and labour supply 67–8
   and loom question 34–5, 62, 69–71, 92–3, 176
   and output 38, 92
   and product lines 60, 62, 64, 68, 72, 75–6
   production process 62–3, 76
Webbs, Beatrice and Sidney—
   and employers 140–1
   and female trade unionists 155–6
   and hand mule spinning 50
   and investment 30–1
   and self-acting mule 54
   and 1837 spinners' strike
   and spinners' union 151
Weild, William 78
Weiner, Martin 8–9
West of Scotland Power Loom Female Weavers' Society 155
West of Scotland Weaving Factories Female Workers' Industrial Union 157
Wilkinson, F, see Lorenz
winders (weaving) 100
Women's Protective and Provident League 156
The Woman Worker 163
Wood, G. H. 87–8
Wright, Col. C. D. 109

YORKSHIRE 89
Young, John 122